At the Feet of a
Himalayan Master

At the Feet of a Himalayan Master

Remembering Swami Rama

volume one

Prakash Keshaviah, Ph.D., Editor

Himalayan Institute Hospital Trust
Swami Ram Nagar, P.O. Doiwala
Distt. Dehradun 248140, Uttarakhand, India

Acknowledgments

Several individuals have helped in the creation of this book. We would like to thank Wesley van Linda for his advice, guidance and encouragement through the many phases of the project. We are truly grateful to Connie Gage for the beautiful cover design. Our heart felt thanks to Swami Veda Bharati, Linda Johnsen and Dr. John Clarke for taking time from their crowded schedules to review the manuscript and provide quotes for the back cover. We thank Dr. V. Rajesh for her foreword to this volume. The painstaking efforts of Vijaya Keshaviah, Mayank Keshaviah and Parvathy Rangappa in proofreading the manuscript are truly appreciated. We are grateful to Swami Rama Society for underwriting the cost of printing this book. We dedicate this book to our beloved Gurudev H.H. Swami Rama, whose compassionate grace continues to guide and inspire us.

Editor: Prakash Keshaviah, Ph.D.
Cover design by Connie Gage
© 2009 Himalayan Institute Hospital Trust. All rights reserved.
Library of Congress Control Number: 2009931484
ISBN 978-81-88157-62-4
All proceeds from the sale of this book go to benefit Swami Rama Society, Inc. and Swami Rama Centre.
Printed at Thomson Press, New Delhi, India

Published by:

Himalayan Institute Hospital Trust
Swami Ram Nagar, P.O. Doiwala
Distt. Dehradun 248140
Uttarakhand, India
tel: 91-135-247-1233, fax: 91-135-247-1122
src@hihtindia.org, www.hihtindia.org

Distributed in USA by Lotus Press, PO Box 325, Twin Lakes, WI 53181, USA, www.lotuspress.com, 800-824-6396. Distributed in India by Swami Rama Centre, HIHT, Swami Ram Nagar, P.O. Doiwala, Distt. Dehradun 248140, Uttarakhand, src@hihtindia.org, 0135-241-2068.

Dedication

To my beloved Gurudeva,
H.H. Swami Rama,
who infused meaning and
purpose into my life and
taught me not to look
for happiness in all the
wrong places.

Himalayan Sages

Gentle sages in Himalayan caves,
Silently radiate their love for all humanity.
Summoning the cool mountain breezes,
They whisper their healing message
To be carried to the sun-scorched plains below,
Where humanity toils seeking pleasures endlessly,
But harvesting only sorrow and strife.
"Seek not happiness in all the wrong places,
All pleasures are accompanied by their twin pains;
Go silently within, to that Source
From which flows peace, bliss and joy."

Prakash Keshaviah

Contents

Foreword   *ix*

Preface   *xi*

PART ONE: Prakash's Narrative   1

1. My First Meeting with Swami Rama   3
2. "Have you thought about getting married?"   8
3. Burning Off Some Karma?   15
4. Freedom from the Bondage of Karma   18
5. Training to be a Mantra Initiator   23
6. The Sannyasi's Complaint   28
7. Time to Start a Family   31
8. Ministering to Mayank   36
9. A Death in the Family   40
10. "I am dealing with your situations one by one."   44
11. Raising the Kids   49
12. Are you an Insider or an Outsider?   60
13. The Guru Knows All   63
14. The Guru's Healing Touch   69
15. The Guru's Protection   73
16. Bio-magnetism, Drug Use and Other Things   77
17. The Ramana Maharshi Book Project   80
18. Visiting Hansda Ashram   86
19. Sadhana   92
20. Other Encounters with Swamiji   105

21. Swamiji Graces Our New Home 115
22. Pulverizing the Ego 119
23. An Inspiring Conversation with Pandit
    Rajmani 137
24. An Inspiring Lecture 143
25. Career Conundrum 146
26. Our Last Meeting with Swamiji 149
27. Returning Home 157

PART TWO: Kamal's Narrative 169
1. My First Encounter with Swami Rama 171
2. New Beginnings 179
3. From Honeymoon to Boot Camp 188
4. An Uncertain Future 215
5. A Remarkable Patient 220
6. Cosmic Flushes 225
7. The Case of the Missing Cashmere 233
8. My First Visit to India 236
9. Relentless Matchmaker 242
10. Kirtan Evenings 248
11. Mastering Sleep 258
12. Brahmacharya Vows 267
13. Fund Raising through the Islands 275
14. Himalayan Mountain Tricks 280
15. A Little Bird 286
16. Moscow Fever 291
17. A Trip to Tarkeshwar 301
18. Mahasamadhi 312

Swami Rama 321
Glossary 323

Foreword

It is a privilege to pen the foreword for this book written by my dear guru brother, Dr. Prakash Keshaviah, and my dear guru sister, Kamal (Patrice Hafford).

Dr. Prakash is an internationally acclaimed scientist in the field of dialysis for kidney failure. He has many scientific publications and patents to his credit. Apart from his scientific achievements, Prakash is a serious sadhaka, well-versed in the scriptures. He has been guided by *Swamiiji* for more than 25 years, and has been trained by him to be a mantra initiator. Prakash is generous in giving of his time to those who approach him for help with spiritual practices. Prakash has also edited many of Swamiji's books. It is a pleasure to read his reminiscences of Swami Rama.

Kamal is the Director of the Swami Rama Centre at the Himalayan Institute Hospital Trust and has been actively involved in preserving and propagating Swamiji's works. Kamal served as Swamiji's personal assistant for over 16 years. It would be pertinent to add here, that Dr. K.S. Duggal, a Padma Bhushan awardee and former member of the Rajya Sabha dedicated his book, *A Multi-Splendoured Sage*, to Kamal. In many of his seminars, Swamiji would declare that Kamal was more than a mother to him, taking care of him and protecting him. However, despite his great regard for her, in his role of spiritual guide, Swamiji was a hard task-master, as you will see from Kamal's narrative.

As Kamal says in the book, students of Swami Rama used to experience three phases with him: They could do no wrong; they could do nothing right; they did not exist! As is to be expected, all students basked in the sunshine of Swamiji's love and attention in the first phase. Many dropped out in the second phase and many more in the third phase. The fortunate few, who successfully persevered through all three phases, were rewarded with Swamiji's spiritual guidance. It is clear that both Prakash and Kamal belong to this group of the fortunate few.

The authors are very frank in narrating their experiences with Swami Rama. Once I started reading the manuscript, I could not put it down. I am sure that readers of the book will find it equally absorbing, will have many questions answered, and will learn many new lessons, through the experiences of Kamal and Prakash.

In the preface to the book, Prakash, using the parable of the nine blind men examining an elephant, has clearly indicated that no one could really know Swamiji in all his various aspects. Each of us who knew him, knew only that small part of him that he allowed us to perceive. However, what we can all agree on is that he taught us the meaning of unconditional love through example. He guided us, and is still guiding us, towards the goal of life, with infinite patience and love. I will leave you to enjoy the book and take from it what you can for making your life meaningful.

Dr. V. Rajesh
HIHT, Dehradun, India
30 May 2009

Preface

It is my privilege to serve as the editor of a new series, *At the Feet of a Himalayan Master: Remembering Swami Rama*. This is the first volume of the series. We hope to launch a new volume every year, at the annual observance of Swami Rama's mahasamadhi. I have taken the editorial privilege of launching the first volume of the series with my reminiscences, along with those of Kamal (Patrice Hafford). Kamal served Swamiji tirelessly for 16 years, and is now the Director of the Swami Rama Centre on the campus of the Himalayan Institute Hospital Trust.

My part-time avocation as an editor of Swami Rama's books began in 1972, when he asked me to edit the second edition of *Lectures on Yoga*. He told me that people had found the first edition very useful, but complained of the numerous typographical and grammatical mistakes in the book. It was a great privilege for me to edit this book and gave me an opportunity to discuss various aspects of yoga with Swamiji in my role as editor. On my visits to Honesdale, I was also blessed to receive from Swamiji many of his manuscripts before they were published, for my review and comments. I particularly remember making some revisions to *Science of Breath* and *Choosing a Path*, which Swamiji approved of, these revisions appearing in the published books. Upon coming to the Himalayan Institute Hospital Trust in 1998, I was again privileged to edit *Conscious Living* and *Om the Eternal Witness*, both books being based on Swamiji's public lectures. I look upon editing Swamiji's books as part of my spiritual sadhana, and look forward to continuing this aspect of my sadhana, with the forthcoming volumes of this series.

There is the amusing story of nine blind men examining an elephant, each one describing the elephant very differently, depending on which part of the elephant they got hold of. The one who got the tail, described the elephant as a thick rope; the one with the trunk, compared the elephant to a mighty serpent; the ones who hugged its legs spoke of mighty columns and the ones who touched the elephant's flanks spoke of the elephant as being like a sheer wall going up to the sky. If they had assembled their impressions into a composite whole, they might have arrived at a better understanding of the elephant.

Swamiji's disciples, bless them all, can know only certain aspects of Swamiji's multi-faceted persona, because, like the blind men examining the elephant, we are blinded by the ignorance of Maya. However, we all did touch the 'elephant' through our minds and hearts. The reminiscences of Swamiji's disciples, taken individually, can no more provide a true picture of Swamiji, than the nine blind men, individually describing the elephant. However, taken together, collectively, the multi-volume series may provide a composite understanding of the spiritual giant, known to us as Swami Rama of the Himalayas.

Though Swamiji had always encouraged me to maintain a spiritual diary, I had not always persevered in this discipline. I have used the diary entries that were available, to describe certain episodes, but have had to rely on my memory in other cases. As a house-holder, I was guided by Swamiji in both my inner and outer life, but my time with him was limited to a few visits a year. Kamal, a *brahmacharini*, living at the Himalayan Institute and serving Swamiji as his personal assistant, has a very different and unique perspective. However, our experiences are complementary, and shed some light on Swamiji, the sage and guru, Swamiji, the man, and Swamiji, the child.

Kamal had compiled the first draft of her reminiscences a few years back and had shown it to me. Before I could do any editing, she changed her mind and asked me to destroy the manuscript, telling me that she did not want to publish her reminiscences. A month back, I happened to drop in to see her at the Swami Rama Centre, and suggested that we consider combining our reminiscences into a single book. She was glad to hear my suggestion, and told me that she had had a dream of Swamiji that morning, in which she and I were collaborating on a project narrating Swami Rama's life. Considering her dream and my suggestion as auspicious omens, we began to work on the manuscript in earnest.

Kamal revised her earlier work, adding new episodes and pruning earlier ones. She decided to do her narration chronologically. I set myself the discipline of a 40-day effort, composing at least 1,000 words each night with a target of around 40,000 words. I finished the task with a few days to spare, in spite of my limited typing skills and some problems with the cursor on my laptop, which had a mind of its own, and jumped to previous lines and paragraphs without any warning, necessitating the frequent use of the 'undo typing' command. I have used a thematic approach, though within a theme, there is some attempt at chronological order. The book appeared to write itself, and only my inept typing seemed to slow the flow.

Sanskrit/Hindi words which are not explained in the text have been explained in the glossary. Only the first appearance of these words is italicized.

Swami Rama was, or more correctly, is a diamond of many facets. It would be well nigh impossible for us to understand him, at all the various levels at which he operated. Ramana Maharshi once advised a disciple to understand himself first, rather than trying to understand the guru. This is sage advice. We hope that this book will help us to understand ourselves, rather than trying to fathom the depths of the phenomenon called Swami Rama.

Much has been written about the *siddhis* exhibited by Swami Rama, and his exquisite control of involuntary states. To me, his greatest siddhi was his enormous capacity for unconditional love. Tens of thousands, maybe millions, who came in contact with Swamiji, felt that they had established a special relationship with him, and occupied a special corner in his heart. One can only imagine the size of his heart, when so many feel this way! Having totally eradicated duality, he saw the One in all, and all in the One. In one of his lectures, which I attended, a questioner asked Swamiji if he had realized the Self. Swamiji replied that if he said, "Yes," he would be considered arrogant and if he replied, "No," he would be lying. So, he concluded, "Let me just say that wherever I look, I see only God."

Prakash Keshaviah
HIHT, Dehradun, India
30 May 2009

Part One:
Prakash's Narrative

Prakash Keshaviah

Dr. Prakash Keshaviah is a biomedical scientist whose expertise is in the field of dialysis for kidney failure. Born in Bangalore, India, he had his schooling in Bangalore, Bombay (Mumbai) and Madras (Chennai). His first professional degree, B.Tech. in Mechanical Engineering, was from the Indian Institute of Technology, Madras. About a year after his graduation, he left the shores of India for the University of Minnesota, U.S.A., getting his M.S. in Mechanical Engineering, his Ph.D. in Biomedical Engineering and later his M.S. in Physiology.

Prakash met Swami Rama for the first time in the fall of 1969. He received his first mantra initiation in the spring of 1971 from Dr. Usharbudh Arya. Soon after this, Swami Rama took over Prakash's spiritual guidance, helping him strive for balance between the external world and the world within. Swami Rama's guidance was then extended to his wife Vijaya and their two children, Mayank and Aparna.

Prakash spent 15 years at the Minneapolis Medical Research Foundation engaged in dialysis research, and then joined Baxter Healthcare as Director of Advanced Product Development. Prakash was directed by Swami Rama in March, 1996, to wind up his affairs in the U.S. and come to the Himalayan Institute Hospital Trust (HIHT) in Jolly Grant, Dehradun, to establish dialysis services at the Himalayan Hospital. At the age of 53, Prakash resigned from his position as Vice President of Research and Development at Baxter, and moved with his wife Vijaya to Jolly Grant. He has been at HIHT for over 11 years, at the time of this writing, and is involved with teaching, administration and technical support.

1.

My First Meeting with Swami Rama

"A genuine spiritual teacher, one who is assigned to teach according to tradition, searches out good students. He looks for certain signs and symptoms; he wants to know who is prepared. No student can fool a master. The master easily perceives how well the student is prepared. If he finds that the student is not yet ready, he will gradually prepare him for the higher teachings. When the wick and oil are properly prepared, the master lights the lamp. That is his role. The resulting light is divine."

Sadhana: The Essence of Spiritual Life

I was a post-graduate student at the University of Minnesota. One fall morning in 1969, I was walking across the campus when I spotted a poster at the corner announcing that a Himalayan monk, Swami Rama, would be giving an afternoon lecture on Thursday, at the student union building, Coffman Union, on the training of monks in the monasteries of the Himalayas. I was intrigued and resolved to attend the lecture. Thursday was Thanksgiving, and I was invited to an American friend's home for Thanksgiving. I was anxious to leave for the lecture, and unmindful of etiquette, I decided to eat and run.

Arriving at Coffman Union, I was dismayed to find the main entrance locked. I tried the side doors and the back door and they were all locked. Being new to the U.S., I did not realize that everything shuts down over the Thanksgiving weekend. I was sorely disappointed at having missed the lecture.

The next week on campus, I saw that the poster was still up, and on taking a closer look, realized that Swami Rama's lecture was that Thursday and not the previous Thursday. Greatly relieved, I made sure that I was in Coffman Union at the appointed time on Thursday. I took a front row seat and waited for the lecture to begin. Dr. Usharbudh Arya, a Professor of Sanskrit at the University, introduced Swami Rama. Swami Rama was an impressive figure, clad in a white *kurta* and *dhoti,* and he spoke with a fairly heavy Indian accent. Instead of talking about the training of monks in Himalayan monasteries, most of his lecture that afternoon was on para-kaya pravesha, the ability of yogis to enter other bodies to do their work. He also narrated stories of his witnessing the conscious act of yogis dropping their bodies at a predetermined time. To me, this was all very bizarre. Swami Rama also talked about the importance of being aware of the currents and cross-currents of life, and for some reason, I found this phrase amusing, and often joked about it afterwards with a roommate who also attended the lecture. In my arrogance, I used to believe that I had great will power and could outstare anyone with a weaker will. Being in the front row, I decided to test my will power on Swami Rama, and tried to catch his eye throughout the lecture. He caught my eye several times during the lecture, refused to get involved, and more or less ignored me. I left the lecture disappointed, speculating that Swami Rama, like other so-called yogis, was in the West just to make a quick buck. Oh, the incredible hubris of youth!

The lecture was soon forgotten. The next summer, I was on my way to Bangalore to attend my sister's wedding, and was stuck at the Bombay airport for several hours because of some flight problems. Sitting across from me in the airport lounge, was a figure clad in white. He was sitting with a middle-aged woman and her young son, and she had placed a marigold garland around his neck. I recognized Swami Rama and was prompted to go up and speak to him, but balked at doing so, as I had not been too impressed with his Minnesota lecture. He sat in the lounge for several hours; many times the inner prompting to go up to him was suppressed consciously. In later years, I would rue the missed opportunity of spending several hours in the company of Swami Rama.

Dr. Usharbudh Arya, Professor of Sanskrit at the University of Minnesota, had an advertisement in the campus newspaper, 'The Minnesota Daily,' about a course in *raja yoga,* which he planned to teach in the fall of 1970 in the attic of his home near the Mississippi river. I called the number given in order to enroll, and found myself talking to Dr. Arya, who was very happy to hear that an Indian student was interested in the course! All of his other students were Americans.

It was very hot that fall and temperatures in the attic were reminiscent of India. The attic was packed with aspiring, perspiring raja yogis. Dr. Arya's lectures were brilliant. I was fascinated by the science of raja yoga, having been nurtured only on Western sciences during my education in India. One day, Dr. Arya announced that his guru would be coming to town, to lecture at the downtown Curtis Hotel. I was thrilled at the prospect of meeting the guru of this inspiring teacher. On the appointed evening, I hurried to the Curtis Hotel. My face fell when Dr. Arya introduced the audience to his guru, Swami Rama! I do not remember much of the evening's lecture, so great was my disappointment.

In baseball, you have the phrase, 'Three strikes and you're out!' I had struck out three times in my encounters with Swami Rama, thanks to my youthful arrogance. But as Swami Rama's kindness and grace are unbounded, he decided to give me one more chance. It was in the fall of the same year, 1970, if memory serves me right. I had started meditating according to the teachings of Dr. Arya. It being a Sunday, feeling sleepy, I had gone back to sleep after my morning meditation. The sun was just beginning to rise, when the phone woke me up. It was Dr. Arya, requesting me to pick up an important package that had arrived from India for Swami Rama, and to hand-deliver it to him at the Holiday Inn in downtown Minneapolis. My first impulse was to politely decline, as I was tired and sleepy and in no mood to drive downtown that early on a Sunday morning. However, the ingrained respect for elders, from my Indian upbringing, prevented me from refusing. I quickly showered, changed and drove to Dr. Arya's residence to pick up the package for Swami Rama.

Arriving at Swamiji's hotel room, I rang the bell and the door was opened by an impressive looking, lithe African American, whom I came to know later as Charles Bates, Yogi Achala. There were one or two others in the room. Swamiji sent them all off and welcomed me into the bedroom of his suite. His hair was tousled and he was looking very relaxed. He had me sit beside him on the bed. I was surprised at his treating me so familiarly with no trace of reserve. He told me that he had been waiting for me for a long time. Being literal-minded, I remonstrated that I had come with the package as soon as I could, without any delay. He shook his head and smiled. It suddenly dawned on me that his time of reference was different from mine, and I was awe-struck! He spoke to me with great kindness and love for about half an hour, and to this day, I cannot recollect the details of our conversation, except his loving selflessness, and my wondering what I had done to deserve so much love from someone I had considered a stranger until then. My arrogance melted away, and I felt that I was in the company of someone who was closer to me than my own father. The yogi had entered my being and stolen my heart and soul. My life was on the threshold of a great change. A new sense of purpose would now fill my life, thanks to the unbounded love and grace of Swami Rama.

2.
"Have you thought about getting married?"

"Although family life is the very basis of society, human beings are still experimenting with the family institution. Human relationships, at peril these days, should not be taken lightly but as something deep and meaningful. Marriage should be seen as a pleasant responsibility and not as a mere game that is played out of biological necessity. Marriage is a process that includes sharing, understanding, and adjusting. Adjustment is a skill that leads to contentment."

Let the Bud of Life Bloom:
A Guide to Raising Happy and Healthy Children

It was the spring of 1971, and Swamiji was visiting Minneapolis. I called upon him at the downtown Holiday Inn. He asked me, point blank, whether I had thought about getting married. On my visit to India the previous summer, I had met a young lady who was related to me, and with her father's permission, we had begun to correspond through letters. I told Swamiji about the young lady and he emphatically declared that he knew her very well, that she was the right girl for me, and that I should go home and write to her that I was prepared to marry her. Unfortunately, my faith in his conviction was not that strong, and I implored him to at least look at a photograph of her that I had at home, to ensure that we were both talking about the same girl. He said that this was not necessary, but I kept insisting, and he agreed to take a look at the photograph the next day. I went back the next day with the photograph. Swamiji barely glanced at it, and again emphatically declared that he knew her, that she was the girl for me and that I should write to her indicating that I was prepared to marry her. Again, my faith was weak, and I decided to wait until I was able to visit India that summer on my way to an international conference in Australia.

Though I was just a post-graduate student working on my Ph.D., my advisor, Dr. Perry Blackshear, was kind enough to sponsor my trip to Australia, once my paper was accepted for presentation at an international biomedical conference in Melbourne, in August, 1971. I decided to go to Australia via India. Soon after I arrived, I requested permission from the young lady's father to go out with her, to discuss our future together.

We went boating near India Gate, New Delhi and to this day, my wife claims that the boat hardly moved, but that there was a lot of water being splashed all round the boat. After my feeble attempt at boating, we sat and talked for many hours, discovering that we had a lot in common and decided to get married. Before the wedding, I decided to visit Sadhana Mandir, Swamiji's *ashram* in Rishikesh, for a few days of retreat, to quietly contemplate the big step I was taking in my life, from brahmacharya to *grihasta*.

The bus from Delhi dropped me off on the outskirts of Rishikesh at Ramnagar, and I got directions to the ashram along a narrow muddy footpath from the main road towards Sadhana Mandir. There were hardly any houses there in 1971, and it was mostly an area with woods and grazing cattle. The ashram was very quiet. There were no ashramites, only a caretaker who was also the cook and gardener. I gave him the letter of introduction from Swamiji, and he took it to the ashram's custodian, *Mahantji*, in Rishikesh. Mahantji came by to welcome me to the ashram, and the caretaker-gardener-cook was given instructions for my stay. In those days, there was only the main building, which is now the reception and lounge. The dining room, meditation hall and new annex were to come much later. Also, there was no barrage at that time, and the Ganga flowed swiftly by the ashram, filling the atmosphere with the reverberations of *Om, Om, Om,* all day long.

I spent my days in introspection, sitting on what was then an open balcony on the first floor, over-looking the flowing Ganga. I also had access to the books in Swamiji's library. I remember, in particular, an inspiring biography of Swami Rama Tirtha. The Mahantji sent me an invitation to lunch through his young son, who also gave me a tour of some of the ashrams in Rishikesh, like the Shivananda Ashram and Gita Ashram. At lunch, I was thrilled to hear from Mahantji that whenever Swamiji was due to arrive in Rishikesh, Mahantji received the 'telegram' in his meditation, and lost no time in getting the ashram cleaned up and ready for Swamiji's arrival!

Though my stay at the ashram had been full of meditative peace, I missed my fiancée Vijaya's company and returned to Delhi, to participate in the wedding arrangements. We got married on the first day of August, 1971. Delhi had never witnessed such heavy rains as on our wedding day. I was assured that this was a good omen, and not a sign of Nature weeping! We had to move our wedding indoors. The roads were flooded and people had to wade through knee deep water. My sister's departure for America the next morning was possible only because we borrowed a jeep with a high clearance that could

Photograph of Vijaya
shown to
Swami Rama

Wedding
photo of Vijaya
and Prakash

navigate safely through the flooded streets of Delhi to the airport.

After a short honeymoon in Kashmir, I left for the conference in Australia. I had had very little public speaking experience until then, and it was 'baptism by fire' to have to make my debut at an international conference. Fortunately, with Swamiji's blessings, the presentation was well received, and I returned to India to complete passport and visa arrangements for Vijaya to accompany me back to the U.S. I also made arrangements for Vijaya to fly with me on the University of Minnesota student charter flight, from Paris to Minneapolis. We left India for London, en route to Paris and Minneapolis, to visit some of Vijaya's cousins as well as my other sister, who had not been able to make it to the wedding. Immigration authorities at Heathrow put us through the 'Spanish Inquisition' as our student charter flight details from Paris to Minneapolis had not been confirmed. The visa stamps on my passport, attesting to my having been to Australia and back, saved the day, and we were allowed into London. Now it was Air India's turn. Some of our luggage had not made it on the flight and would arrive on a flight a couple of days later.

We stayed overnight in London, and then traveled to Stratford on Avon, home of the great bard William Shakespeare. It was a beautiful autumn day, swans glided gracefully down the Avon River, and we found Ann Hathaway's cottage absolutely charming. We journeyed on to Birmingham and then to Durham, before returning to London to claim our lost luggage. As time for our boat-train to Paris was short, Vijaya left for the departure terminal of the boat-train, while I made a detour to pick up our luggage from the cargo terminal. I got stuck in London traffic, Vijaya got lost in a strange new city, and we missed the boat-train.

After a frantic search, we found each other, and made alternate arrangements to Paris, now having to travel first by a steamer and then through France on a train without visas! We were discovered and fined, our meager foreign funds being reduced considerably. We had to stay overnight in Paris, and could find no accommodations to suit our wallet. We thought of spending the night watching a late night movie, but the theaters were closed. We were forced to sit up all night on a cold bench in the Paris North station. We were in danger of being evicted from the station bench as well, but for the train ticket stubs I had held on to. My poor bride finally fell asleep leaning her head against my shoulder.

The next morning, we decided that as fate had not been too kind so far, we should get to the airport as early as possible, to avoid further misadventures. Little did we know what fate still had in store for us. Soon after we left the railway station, Vijaya discovered that her diamond earring was missing and surmised that it had fallen off at night when she slept with her head against my shoulder. We hurried back to the station and found the bench occupied with people who were either drunk or fast asleep. We crawled on our hands and knees, rearranging the legs that got in our way, until we finally found the fallen earring.

At the airport, I was able to check in, but Vijaya's name was not on the student manifesto for the flight, and they refused to let her check in. They were rather rude and informed us that as it was a student charter, they faced heavy penalties if a non-student was allowed on the flight. We were being sorely tested. I had no money left for another night's stay in Paris, and did not look forward to sleeping on an airport bench. I finally realized that it was time to surrender to the Divine will. My sorry plight led me to think of Swamiji, and even though he had taught me that prayer should be God-centered not ego-centered, I, in my desperation, prayed to him with all my heart to deliver me from this horrendous situation. The results were immediate and miraculous.

The rude lady at check-in suddenly became extremely gracious and offered to try to get us on the flight with the pilot's permission. She whisked us through immigration without any checking. The flight ladder was being withdrawn as the plane was getting ready to taxi down the runway. The lady got into a vehicle and rushed to the plane to speak to the pilot. The pilot agreed to let us board and, to our great relief, we made it on the flight to Minneapolis. We had been sorely tested on this journey, but all of the drama had unfolded only to help us discover the guru's grace.

3.

Burning Off Some Karma?

"Such a great man has power to show the path of freedom to others. Whether he is in the world or outside, he can also heal the sickness arising from karmic debts. He can remain untouched and above without being involved or reaping the fruits arising from others' karmic debts. A true master has control over himself and moves freely in the world."

Sadhana: The Essence of Spiritual Life

My wife and I settled into a small studio apartment on University Ave. S.E., about a mile from campus. The first few months in Minneapolis, Vijaya missed her parents and home, her friends, and India, very deeply. I was immersed in my Ph.D. work, and spent many hours away at the University. Compared to India, Minneapolis was incredibly quiet, in spite of the traffic on University Avenue. With the approaching cold weather, one hardly saw people walking around. New Delhi, by contrast was so vibrant and full of life. Vijaya's loneliness would often get the better of her, and I would come home to find her eyes red from weeping. When she realized that this upset me a great deal, because of my guilt at having taken her away from all that was near and dear to her, she would go into the bathroom to cry and wash up, to conceal traces of her sorrow.

Before we got married, Vijaya had been a lecturer in philosophy at one of the colleges of Delhi University. She taught courses in logic and Greek philosophy. She had had an extensive grounding in both Eastern and Western philosophies. I tried to get her to attend Dr. Arya's lectures on yoga and Indian philosophy but she demurred, saying that it reminded her of her courses and exams, and she wanted to get over that phase of her life.

I told Vijaya about Swamiji having been the *Shankaracharya* of Karvirpitham. He had relinquished this high spiritual position to continue his training in Himalayan caves, for his mission of integrating science with spirituality, integrating the beautiful form of Western culture with the heady fragrance of Eastern traditions. I told her about Swamiji's experiments at the Menninger Foundation of Topeka, Kansas, where he demonstrated his exquisite voluntary control over so-called involuntary processes like the regulation of heart rate, generation of brain waves, and control of body temperature. I also told her of my personal experience of his being able to fathom the depths of my mind and respond to unasked doubts and questions. This siddhi of Swamiji scared Vijaya, as she felt that there were many thoughts that passed through one's mind that should remain private and not be read by another.

We learnt that Swamiji was visiting Minneapolis in the fall. I was eager to see him and introduce (or should I say re-introduce?) Vijaya to him. Vijaya was filled with some trepidation at meeting one from whom there were no secrets, one who could penetrate the innermost recesses of her mind. Allaying her fears, and reassuring her that Swamiji would not intrude on her private thoughts, we went to Dr. Arya's home to meet Swamiji. Swamiji greeted us with warm hugs and laid his hand on our heads in blessing. Vijaya was drawn to Swamiji, as a daughter drawn to her father. Gone were her fears of unwarranted mind reading.

Soon after we returned home, Vijaya took ill very suddenly. There had been no sniffles or sore throat to presage this sudden illness. Her temperature rose to a very high level, her pain-wracked body was weak and limp, she had no appetite, and she hardly got out of bed for almost three days. Then the illness passed, almost as suddenly as it had come. Surprisingly, soon after this illness, she became interested in knowing more about meditation and began to practice in a walk-in closet that she converted into a meditation room. Her faith in Swamiji was now becoming even stronger than mine.

This sudden illness, and her sudden change in attitude, made me wonder if Swamiji's placing of his hand over her head had been a blessing that quickly burnt off some of her past *karma*, the burning process manifesting as the high fever that wracked her body. Swamiji always worked quietly behind the scenes and one was always left guessing!

Swamiji bought a new property in one of the western suburbs of Chicago and Mrs. Arya and Vijaya were invited to go over to convert the house into a home with new curtains, decorations and other subtle touches that only a woman knows how. When it was time to come back to Minneapolis, she had the same wrenching feeling that a daughter has when leaving her father's home. However, knowing that Swamiji was around and often visited Minneapolis, gave her a sense of having found a new home. The intensity of her separation from India began to diminish. Swamiji's healing touch was evident.

4.
Freedom from the Bondage of Karma

"We can say that karma is the source of misery. We can focus on karma as suffering from the consequences of action. We can say karma is what shackles us to this world and all its painful imperfections. There is another perspective, a higher view. We can see karma as the curriculum we must take to achieve the clarity of pure consciousness. Nothing more. Follow the rope of karma through the maze we call life and find the absolute Reality. Until Reality is found, we keep moving through the maze, or back to this platform of worldly life."

Sacred Journey:
Living Purposefully and Dying Gracefully

Some of Dr. Arya's students from the Meditation Center in Minneapolis acquired a rural property between Minneapolis and Duluth. It was decided that this would be the site of a week's retreat with Swami Rama, in the summer of 1972. Several weeks before this retreat, groups went up to the site to clear the brush and convert it into a suitable camping ground. Vijaya and I went up one weekend to help with the clearing. The mosquitoes were big and plentiful, and could bite through tough denim. It is no joke that Minnesota's state bird is the mosquito. We wore hats with attached netting to protect our faces from the mosquitoes. It was hot and the hard work soon raised blisters on our hands. The next day I discovered aching muscles I never knew I had. Some of the more handy students built two geodesic domes (à la Buckminster Fuller), a large one for the retreat lectures and a smaller one to house Swami Rama. It was then that we met a slim but strapping blond girl, who was hauling heavy railroad ties on her young shoulders. This strong lady was Samskriti (Linda Blanchard), who would later become an important part of Swamiji's mission in Glenview and at Honesdale.

During the retreat, it was very hot and humid in the lecture dome, and we vied with each other to take turns in fanning Swami Rama. The lectures were profound and inspiring, and helped us ignore the heat. The lecture notes of one of the retreat participants, Dr. Roger Jones, a professor of physics at the University of Minnesota, were typed up and edited into the book, *Freedom from the Bondage of Karma*.

We stayed in tents, and bathed in the stream running through the property. Having no camping gear of our own, we had borrowed a small pup tent from a friend. It barely housed the two of us. Each morning, Vijaya faced the challenge of draping a six yard *sari* around herself, without being able to stand up fully in the small pup tent. Our humble tent, however, conferred one significant advantage on us. When Swamiji walked around the grounds, he would often come and sit on a mat we spread out for him outside our tent. He said that he was drawn by our humble abode. The mosquitoes were fierce that summer. I had heard Swamiji's story about a mantra for honey bees. I naively asked Swamiji if there was a mantra to protect one from mosquitoes. He dismissed my question with a smile, calling attention to my foolishness. I was not in the least offended, feeling like a child in his fatherly presence.

Minnesota retreat, 1972

Open air *kirtan* at Minnesota retreat

Open pit latrines were used for the retreat, and one of the chores assigned to work teams was clearing the latrines of the accumulated wastes. My turn came, and I was nauseated by the task, and was not looking forward to my next turn. Fortunately, Dr. Arya assigned some other duties to me, and I was spared another turn with the latrine clean-up crew.

During this retreat there was an incident that, to me, appeared to be Swamiji testing my attachment to material objects. One day, he handed me an expensive camera, without any explanation. Fortunately, I merely thought that the camera had been entrusted to me for safe keeping. I did not use the camera, and on the last day of the retreat I returned the camera to Swamiji. The look on his face told me that I had passed his test.

During this retreat, Swamiji told us that we were no better than barbarians if we did not offer thanks before every meal. He taught us how to say grace before a meal, with a Sanskrit prayer that invokes the supreme *Brahman*. The One offering the sacrifice is Brahman, the sacrificial offering is Brahman, the digestive fire into which the sacrifice is offered is Brahman, and the ritual act of yagna or sacrifice is verily Brahman. This prayer has stayed with us over the years and we are truly grateful to Providence for every meal that graces our table.

During one of the lectures, I asked Swamiji about God's grace. He explained the concept with a simple analogy. He said that if we were to buy an orchard, the land, the trees and the fruit were part of the purchase price and symbolized our human efforts; but the cool shade provided by the trees had not been paid for. The shade symbolized God's grace, which is added on, when one has made sincere efforts.

Another memorable experience of this retreat was a beautiful lecture that Swamiji delivered about Mother

Kundalini and the flowering of the lotuses of the various *chakras*, as kundalini ascends upwards from the *muladhara* chakra to the *sahasrara* chakra. I had read books on kundalini and the chakras. They all seemed to repeat the same boring information. However, Swamiji's descriptions were full of rich details, and he spoke with a conviction that could only come from personal experience.

One evening, Swamiji called us to gather around for an open air kirtan session. Swamiji played the harmonium, and we accompanied him with cymbals, drums and other instruments. The soulful music began to draw us inwards, but we were soon distracted. The sky had suddenly grown very dark and heavy rain-filled clouds were threatening to disrupt the kirtan session. Swamiji noticed the group's restlessness, looked up at the sky, waved his hand and told us that the storm would pass. Incredibly, the dark clouds scudded away immediately, and the sky grew bright again. We continued the kirtans with renewed vigor and a great sense of awe at Swamiji's command over the forces of nature. About a half hour later, Swamiji stopped the kirtan and urged us to dig trenches around our tents, to drain away the waters of the rainstorm that was soon to descend. There was thunder and lightning and it rained heavily all night. The trenches kept out the water and our tents stayed dry.

5.
Training to be a Mantra Initiator

"When a student goes to a guru, he takes a bundle of dry sticks. With reverence and love, he bows and says, 'Here, I offer this.' That indicates that he is surrendering himself with all his mind, action and speech with a single desire to achieve the highest wisdom. The guru burns those sticks and says, 'Now I will guide you and protect you in the future.' Then he initiates the student on various levels and gives him the disciplines to practice. The guru imparts a word and says, 'This will be an eternal friend to you. Remember this word. It will help you.' Then he explains how to use the mantra. This is called mantra initiation."

Sadhana: The Essence of Spiritual Life

In mid 1972, Swamiji decided to train a small group of five to six students to become mantra initiators in the Himalayan tradition. I was fortunate to be a part of this group, which also included Charles Bates and Phil Nuernberger. Dr. Arya also sat in on these classes, and gave a lecture or two on initiation rituals. The early classes were held in the attic of Dr. Arya's home.

Swamiji told us that mantra is a compact prayer, a concise affirmation. Mantras were revealed to sages in their deep meditative states. The first teacher in the Himalayan tradition is Hiranyagarbha, the Golden Womb. The mantras are like seeds that bring forth hidden knowledge. Mantras help free the initiate from worldly desires. Every word has a sound, but not every sound is a word. Every word has a definite form. A word has sound, creates vibrations and hence a form in space that is never dissipated. Everything in this world is created by sound vibrations. Mantra has meaning, feeling and purpose, and all three aspects of the mantra have to be understood to reap the rewards of the mantra.

Swamiji described the various categories of mantras. There were Vedic mantras, like the Gayatri and Maha Mrtyunjaya mantras. Then there were apta mantras, mantras of the siddhas, revelations of the guru tradition. These mantras were words of power and blessing, that did not always have a lexical meaning. The bija or seed mantras, and *shakti* mantras were from the *tantric* tradition. Puranic mantras were associated with the deities, like Rama and Krishna of the puranas, the ancient stories of Indian mythology. There were also abhichara mantras, mantras of black magic, which we did not explore.

Swamiji told us that as initiators, we were conduits for the flow of the mantric energy, but we were not teachers or gurus by virtue of giving mantra initiations. Just as soil had to be tilled and prepared to receive the seed, initiators had to inspire and prepare the initiate. He assured us that the seed would never die, even if it did not sprout immediately. Only two things had the power to transform man: mantra and love. Even death had no transformative power. It merely changed conditions, without transformation.

Swamiji told us that the mantra should become a life companion, a trusted friend which would never desert one in times of need. He told us that at the time of death, the conscious mind begins to fail, and the subconscious mind, which is the storehouse of past impressions, takes over. If one has cultivated the mantra and assimilated it in the subconscious, then the mantra would come forward, and lead one through this dark period of transition at the time of death.

Swamiji divided people who came for initiation into four categories:

- Those with worldly problems
- Those who were mentally sick or emotionally unstable
- Those who wanted to become more dynamic and creative
- Those who were searching for higher knowledge

Swamiji told us how to judge persons in selecting the mantra to be given. We had to know how much to give, and to whom. He taught us how to meditate with the person seeking initiation, and how to look for subtle signs that would guide us in choosing the appropriate mantra. Intuition, rather than analytical thinking, had to be our guide. Swamiji asked us to fix up Mondays and Thursdays as preferred days for mantra initiation.

Swamiji held these mantra classes for the small group of initiators for several days, while he was visiting Minneapolis. He then had to leave for Chicago. The initiator group decided to travel to Chicago to continue the instruction. These Chicago classes were held at the Flamingo Motel, where Swamiji had taken up residence temporarily. Swamiji gave us an ashirvad (blessing) that only people whose karma needed us as an instrument would approach us for mantra initiation. He told us that those who receive mantra initiation are taken out of the stream of their previous karma, and that past karma is unable to affect them.

HIMALAYAN

INTERNATIONAL INSTITUTE

of Yoga Science & Philosophy

This is to certify that Shri प्रकाश केशविया Prakash Keshaviya has been trained, and is authorized to give Mantra Diksha to new initiates in accordance with Sanātana Dharma, under the guidance of our tradition of Gurus and the long line of Sages.

RISHIKESH, HIMALAYAS

ऋषिकेश Oct. 15, 1972

ACHARYA · H.H. SWAMI RAMA

Mantra Initiator Certificate

A few months later, I was surprised to receive a certificate in the mail, signed by Acharya H.H. Swami Rama and Pandit Dr. Usharbudh Arya, certifying that I had been trained and authorized to give mantra diksha to new initiates, in accordance with *sanatana dharma*, under the guidance of our tradition of gurus and the long line of sages.

6.

The Sannyasi's Complaint

"The master's ways of teaching are many and sometimes mysterious. He teaches through speech and actions, but in some cases he may teach without any verbal communication at all. The most important teachings have their source in intuition and are beyond the powers of verbal communication."

Sadhana: The Essence of Spiritual Life

In the summer of 1973, we received a phone call from Dr. Usharbudh Arya, asking us to provide hospitality to a visiting *sannyasi,* Swami Ramtheertha, from Rishikesh. I was asked to pick him up from the Greyhound bus depot in downtown Minneapolis and host him for a few days. Vijaya and I agreed to do so, and left that night to pick up Swami Ramtheertha from the bus depot. He arrived late that night from the West and we took him home.

As it was rather late, and knowing that swamis are very disciplined about meal times, I assumed that it was too late to offer him supper and he went to bed after having a glass of warm milk. The next morning, Vijaya, knowing that he was from South India, decided to make a South Indian specialty for breakfast, masala dosa, a crepe-like pancake filled with a potato curry. She had also made the traditional accompaniment of sambar, a soup-like, lentil and vegetable preparation. Unwittingly, Vijaya had used onions in the potato curry. The swami was scandalized, and reprimanded us for not knowing that swamis refrained from *rajasic* foods like onions. In consternation, Vijaya made some new dosas sans the filling, that is, plain dosas and served them with the sambar. The swami had his breakfast and left for the Meditation Center in Minneapolis. He did not return, and we presumed that he had resumed his travels.

Soon after, I left for a conference, the Gordon Research Conference, held each summer in New England. I presented a paper related to my Ph.D. thesis topic of red cell destruction due to fluid stresses in artificial organs. That night, I called home to make sure that all was well. Vijaya told me that Swami Rama had come to town and that our guest, Swami Ramtheertha had complained to Swamiji about the poor quality of his students, who did not know how to receive and host a swami. Swamiji had sought an explanation from Vijaya, and upon hearing the full story he had remained quiet. When I heard about the complaint, I was really upset and could not sleep all night. I kept blaming myself for the lapse, and realized that my friends would have gotten better hospitality at my home than did the visiting swami. At the back of my mind was also the unspoken fear that an irate swami's curse may have serious consequences for us.

I returned to Minneapolis about a day later, and Vijaya met me at the airport. One of her first questions was whether her telling me about the swami's complaint had upset me, and caused me to lose sleep. I was surprised at her question, and admitted that that had indeed been the case. She then told me that she had gone back to see Swami Rama the next day, and the first thing out of his mouth was a reprimand for having told me about the sannyasi's complaint. He then mentioned that the incident had troubled me a great deal and caused me to lose sleep.

We were both flabbergasted at Swamiji's intuitive awareness of what was happening to one of his students a thousand miles away. The incident brought back memories of how Swamiji had bailed us out when we got stuck in Paris on our return from India a year and a half earlier. It was clear to us that time, space and causation are of no consequence to the man of realization, because of his conquest of duality and his constant dwelling in the One. As Swamiji had told us in his lectures, the infinite universal library is available to such a one.

Though I had serious misgivings about our poor hospitality, due to our relative ignorance of sannyasi protocols, I thanked Swami Ramtheertha from the bottom of my heart, for having provided us an opportunity to discover the universal consciousness that Swamiji inhabited, and his great concern and compassion for his students. As a post script, I must add that Swami Ramtheertha returned to Minneapolis a couple of times after that, and we had opportunities to host him and compensate for our lapses on his subsequent visits.

7.

Time to Start a Family

"You should accept the responsibilities of parents from the beginning. If you understand that God has created you as instruments to give birth to someone, it should be a joy for both of you. You should have the attitude that if the Lord wants you to serve someone, you will serve him or her with all your heart and mind. Accept whatever God gives you and learn to love your duties toward your child. Then you will enjoy your child. Birth is not an accident. Parents do not understand this fact and do not prepare themselves to meet and appreciate the uniqueness of the person in their newborn child."

Let the Bud of Life Bloom:
A Guide to Raising Happy and Healthy Children

Swamiji was in Minneapolis and staying at the home of Dr. Arya. Vijaya and I went to see him. He was very kind and talked of many things. Then he suddenly excused himself, and went into an inner room. He came out soon thereafter, and suddenly announced that we would have three children, two boys and a girl. The suddenness of the announcement surprised us. Swamiji then explained that he had just received a vision, courtesy of his guru *Bengali Baba*, in which he saw us with a family of three children.

I had long wanted a photograph of Swamiji for our meditation altar, and requested him to allow us to photograph him. He permitted us to photograph him.

I had hoped that his eyes would remain open so that we could gaze upon his beautiful, shining eyes when we sat to meditate. That was not to be. He closed his eyes for the photograph. He then told us that this photograph was for our personal meditation use only, and should not be copied and handed out to others. I readily agreed. He then told us that the photograph contained not just him, but also other sages of his lineage. I was very excited and could hardly wait to get the film developed. It turned out to be a beautiful, peaceful photograph of Swami Rama with eyes closed. Try as hard as I may, I have yet to discover the other sages in the photograph! This reminds me of a story in Justin O'Brien's book, *Walking with a Himalayan Master*, where Ann Aylward's mentally-challenged aunt Kitty was able to see five other sages in a photograph of Swamiji, whereas to everyone else, there was only Swami Rama in the photograph. Swamiji explains to Ann that her aunt, whom they all felt sorry for, was a realized saint, who had come back in that body to help Ann spiritually. Being realized, the aunt was able to see Swamiji and his five teachers in the photograph.

We framed our photograph of Swamiji and put it upon our meditation altar. For many years, no one else had seen the photograph. A few years later, I was asked by Dr. Arya to initiate and counsel an American family consisting of the parents and their two children, who were just out of their teens. One of the children, a young man, had had a very troubled life with difficulties relating to his family and peers as well as problems with drugs. I was very moved by his story and felt that he really needed the help of the sages of our tradition. With that in mind, I decided to give him a copy of Swamiji's photograph that was on our altar. I knew that I was disobeying Swamiji, but I hoped that he would pardon me, considering the circumstances. I have lost touch with the family, and can only hope that they are being guided by Swamiji and the sages of our tradition.

About a year after Swamiji had had the vision of our future family, he asked Vijaya and me whether we had considered starting our family. We told him that we had begun to think of a family, and he strongly supported our plan. Soon after this, Vijaya became pregnant. Around the same time, Ammaji (Mrs. Arya) was also pregnant with their third child. Vijaya would baby sit for Ammaji sometimes, and once, in Vijaya's presence, Ammaji asked Swamiji whether Vijaya would have a boy or a girl. He replied that whether it was a boy or a girl, it was for the best. Secretly, Vijaya was hoping for a son while I was rooting for a daughter.

The pregnancy went well, though the baby was often restless and moved about a lot. At classical Indian music concerts, Vijaya noticed that when the drum solo began, the baby would start kicking vigorously. The due date came and passed, without Vijaya going into labour. She was two weeks overdue, and getting worried. Swamiji reassured her that all was well; the baby knew when to come into the world. Vijaya went for a periodic checkup with her gynecologist, who decided to admit her right away and induce labor. Vijaya protested that she had not brought her clothes and other necessities, but the doctor dismissed her protestations, and admitted her to the Metropolitan Medical Center in downtown Minneapolis. I rushed home to get Vijaya's suitcase that was packed and ready. When I returned, I found that they had just started an intravenous drip on her. Before they could administer drugs into the drip to initiate labor, Vijaya started having contractions on her own, much to our relief, as we did not want a drug-induced labor.

It was a long eighteen hours of labor. Vijaya's back hurt a lot, and I tried my best to massage her lower back and make her comfortable. Finally, at 3:00 a.m., our son decided to emerge into the world. As his head and face appeared, I was filled with feelings that just cannot be described. Never had I felt such feelings of joy mixed with relief mixed with pride. The time of the morning when he was born is known in India as Brahma Muhurtam, the time of Brahman, which is most auspicious and conducive for spiritual practices. It was the fourth of July, America's day of Independence. It was also Guru Purnima, the full moon day dedicated to the guru. As Swamiji had reassured us, the baby knew when to come into the world. He had waited patiently for two weeks for this auspicious arrival!

Vijaya asked me to inform Swamiji about the baby's arrival, and to request him to name the baby. Swamiji suggested the name 'Rakesh,' connected with the full moon. I accepted his suggestion, but Vijaya reacted with dismay. She said that it reminded her too much of the Sanskrit, 'rakshas,' for demon! She wanted me to call Swamiji back to ask for a different name. I was rather reluctant to do so, but Vijaya was insistent. Plucking up my courage, I contacted Swamiji again, and described the situation. He listened to me quietly and then told me to call him back in a few hours. When I called him back, before revealing the new name, Swamiji extracted a promise from us that we would keep that name alone and not change it. He told us that he had contacted his guru Bengali Baba, who had given us the new name. We were thrilled to accept the name 'Mayank' for our son; Swamiji told us that the name was that of an ancient *rishi,* and that it was also connected with the full moon. He said that there were several other meanings as well, but did not elaborate. After a short stay in the hospital, Vijaya came home with Mayank.

8.
Ministering to Mayank

"Concerning the child's health, the mother should educate herself in preventive methods and natural healthcare rather than allowing modern physicians to blast the child's tender system with various drugs and sedatives for every minor ailment. Excessive drugging has adverse effects on the child's sensitive system. All drugs have possible side effects and may systematically affect the nervous system or result in impaired hearing or bad eyesight or they may generally weaken the immune system.

"Another source of conflict between mother and child can arise if the child is not allowed to sleep in the same room as the parents. These days there is a theory that the child should not sleep in the parent's room. The doctor tells you not to allow your child to stay in your bedroom because it will disturb your and your husband's sleep and that it is unhealthy for your relationship. Does it seem reasonable to put a newborn baby in a separate, dark room for your personal pleasures?"

Let the Bud of Life Bloom:
A Guide to Raising Happy and Healthy Children

Mayank was about two months old, when Swamiji happened to come to Minneapolis. He asked Vijaya and me to bring Mayank over to the Meditation Center on University Ave. N.E. He told us that he wanted to do a bhuta shuddhi (purification of the five bhutas or elements) for Mayank. Dr. Arya was also present in the room. Asking Dr. Arya to hold Mayank, Swamiji dipped a gold pen in honey and wrote a purificatory mantra on Mayank's tongue. Afterwards, Swamiji said something to Dr. Arya in Hindi about Mayank's future.

Mayank came into our life without an instruction manual. The combination of our inexperience, and his problems with colic, made the first few months very difficult. We would put him to sleep at night with great difficulty, often taking him for a long drive in the car, in order to lull him to sleep. He would wake up easily, even when the car stopped at traffic lights. After a long drive, when we thought he was fast asleep, we would head home, only to have him wake up as we got him out of the car! At night, he would wake up and start crying long and loud, much to the annoyance of our neighbours upstairs, who would keep banging on our ceiling to express their feelings. In order to avoid annoying our neighbours, and tired of hearing the landlord's complaints, we finally moved out of the apartment into our own first home in Robbinsdale, a western suburb of Minneapolis.

In the new house, Mayank had his crib in his own room, as advised by our pediatrician. Mayank had other ideas, and would wake up crying bitterly; the intensity of his crying would cause him to throw up all over the crib and carpet. Vijaya, never a heavy sleeper, would wake up at the slightest whimper from Mayank, and we would attend to him before he got upset enough to throw up all over. We were very troubled with Mayank's problems and consulted Swamiji. Though my conscious intention in calling Swamiji was to express my concern about Mayank's health and his crying, Swamij, unearthing the unconscious frustration we were experiencing, reprimanded us in no uncertain terms for being inept

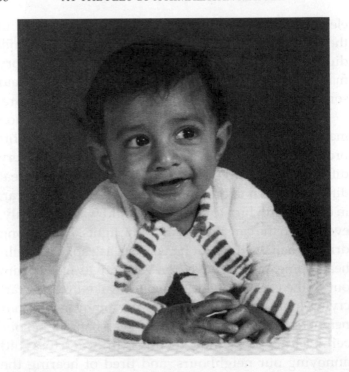

Baby picture of Mayank

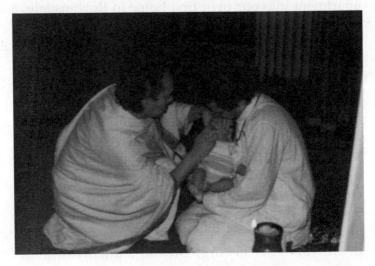

Bhuta Shuddhi ritual for Mayank

parents who had no patience with a child's natural tendencies. He indicated that he was aware that when we tried to put him to sleep by patting him on his back, sometimes, our anger at the situation would be expressed in rather vigorous patting! However he did explain that Mayank was crying so much because he remembered his past life. He was filled with remorse at the fact that his past actions had resulted in his present embodiment and he felt trapped in that small body.

A baby is usually colicky for three to six months. Mayank's colic continued even after his first birthday. He had also become susceptible to mid-ear infections, and was slightly anemic. The pediatrician had prescribed a rather strong medication to induce sleep at night. She also informed us that the only remedy was a stiff shot of Scotch, for the parents! Suddenly, one day, out friends Terry and Cathy Cullen called upon us, and told us that they had visited Swamiji in Chicago and that he had sent a message for us. The message was clear: "Stop drugging your child."

We called Swamiji in Chicago and he urged us to bring Mayank to Chicago, to be treated by Dr. Rudy Ballentine with homeopathic rather than allopathic medications. Dr. Ballentine's homeopathic remedies proved very efficacious. Mayank improved his hemoglobin level and got over the recurrent ear infections. We were overwhelmed by Swamiji's concern and compassion, and realized that physical distance is of no consequence where Swamiji is concerned. He was aware of Mayank's problems and our inexperience, and while he wanted us to handle our problems by ourselves, he intervened when he deemed it appropriate and necessary.

9.
A Death in the Family

"We grieve the deaths of those close to us, and fear our own passing. There is a period of mourning, and a time to let go. This is why cultures around the globe and throughout history have devised customs of letting go, of mourning and of putting death into perspective. These customs help people to go on with their lives and prepare for their own deaths. Human life is a cycle of coming and going, birth and death. The death of the body is not the end of the soul. The Self is unchangeable. Therefore, grief beyond the limits of its own time is unwise."

Sacred Journey:
Living Purposefully and Dying Gracefully

I was one of four children, with two older sisters and a younger brother. My brother Vishwanath was three and a half years younger than I, and had also come to the West for post-graduate studies. He spent about a year in Germany. I then sponsored his coming to Kentucky, to do his Master's degree in Chemical Engineering. He then went on to get an M.B.A. Soon after this, he found employment in Canada. Vishwanath came to visit us in Minneapolis, a few months after Mayank was born. During his visit, Swamiji was in Minneapolis and was due to give a lecture in the basement of a Minneapolis church. I wanted my brother to come along to meet Swamiji.

He was not particularly keen on coming, but allowed himself to be persuaded.

Swamiji gave a very inspiring lecture on *prana* and the *nadis*. I clearly remember that in this lecture Swamiji stressed the importance of applying *sushumna* before meditation. He told us that when sushumna is opened, the result is sukha mana, or joyful mind. Swamiji had taught us the technique of sushumna application earlier, but we had missed its significance. He now pointed out that the reason why our meditations were sometimes joyful and sometimes merely mechanical, was related to whether sushumna had been opened or not. Having experienced this varying nature of meditation, I was thrilled to learn how to make meditation less boring and mechanical, and more filled with joy and peace.

After the lecture, my brother was able to meet Swamiji briefly. Swamiji invited my brother to visit him in Chicago. Sensing some reluctance on my brother's part, Swamiji remarked jocularly that he was a modern swami and had no objection to my brother bringing along his girlfriend. I was amazed and amused at this interlude.

A little less than a year later, my wife and I had just returned from dinner with some friends at a restaurant, when the phone rang. It was a call from a hospital in Canada telling me that my brother had been killed in an automobile accident. I was stunned. In my grief, I kept imagining my brother struggling for life, while I was out enjoying dinner with friends. This painful thought haunted me again and again. I phoned Swamiji to tell him of my brother's tragic death, and he expressed shock at the news. I told him that I was flying to Canada the next morning to identify the body, to perform the final rites and to settle my brother's affairs. Swamiji asked me to stop in Chicago on my way back.

My brother and I had been very close growing up. However, we had drifted apart a little when I left home to live in the college hostel. My brother had joined the same college for his engineering degree, but with our differing schedules and living in different hostels, it was never the same as when we were growing up. Then I left for the U.S. and a few years later he went to Germany. Upon his coming to Kentucky, we were able to visit each other, and tried to make up for lost time. As I flew to Canada, I dwelt on old memories and regretted not having had more time with my brother in recent times. My reading and re-reading the *Bhagavad Gita* on the flight helped, but my heart was weighed down by the tragic turn of events, and I could not unburden myself. I went to the hospital morgue, identified the body and arranged for its cremation.

I learnt that my brother had been a passenger in a friend's car. The friend was taking my brother to his home for Thanksgiving, to express his gratitude for the great help that my brother had rendered him. The car spun out of control, my brother fell out of the car and his head hit the pavement, resulting in his death. The hospital was a few hours drive from the apartment where my brother lived. I went to his apartment, where his friends arranged a short prayer meeting. Hearing the tributes of his friends and colleagues, I was moved to tears, and again regretted not having spent more time with my brother when he was alive.

I hired a lawyer and requested a friend of my brother to help with legal formalities. I then flew back with a short stopover in Chicago. Swamiji sent one of his students to bring me from the airport to the Glenview center. Swamiji was resting when I arrived, and I waited in an anteroom that was rather dark and matched my mood. Suddenly, Mama, Ann Aylward, came to the anteroom, wondering why I was waiting and had not gone in to see Swamiji. She ushered me in to Swamiji's presence. I entered his room with a very heavy heart. Swamiji greeted me with a tight embrace. As soon as he hugged me, my heart grew light, the heaviness lifted and was dissipated. The suddenness of this change was remarkable. Swamiji then consoled me with kind words and arranged for me to go back to the airport for my flight to Minneapolis.

My brother was only 27 years old at the time of his death. My parents were totally devastated by the tragedy. They had had very high expectations of him, and had a very hard time reconciling themselves to this cruel stroke of fate. Swamiji's taking on my grief and lightening my heart, gave me the courage to go home to console my parents. My father accompanied me to Haridwar to consign my brother's ashes into the holy Ganga. A flock of beautiful white birds hovered around us as we performed the ritual. Seeing the birds, my father felt comforted, sensing that my brother was present there.

10.
"I am dealing with your situations one by one."

"The truth is that the relationship of guru to disciple is indescribable. The relationship extends to the realm beyond the world, transcends death, and stretches far beyond the limited karmic bonds associated with family and friends. A mother and father help sustain the body of their child, and nurture and guide the child through the formative years of life to adulthood. Guru sustains, nurtures, and guides a soul through lifetimes to ultimate liberation.

"There are different heavenly realms, lower and higher, depending on the purity and impurity of one's mental constituents that remain even after the physical body is dropped. For the ignorant, death is a long and deep sleep, interspersed with dreamlike heavenly or hellish visions. Those who claim to communicate with departed souls are either hallucinating or lying. When someone is in deep sleep, it is not possible to communicate with anyone. Only enlightened souls can communicate with others after death because they remain fully conscious all the time."

Sacred Journey:
Living Purposefully and Dying Gracefully

A few months after my brother's passing, Vijaya, Mayank and I visited Swamiji in Glenview. He was very kind to us, and we talked about my parents and how they were handling their grief. When we returned to Minneapolis, Swamiji wrote to us. (A copy of the letter is on page 46.) In this letter, Swamiji writes, "My love for you is eternal and I am dealing with your situations one by one." I was not sure what to make of this cryptic remark. Also, at the end of the letter, Swamiji writes, "Give my blessings to your child, Vijaya and your mother-in-law. I was happy to see blessed Mayank." This was also confusing, as he refers to our child, and later mentions Mayank by name.

A few days later, Vijaya went for a medical check-up, as we suspected that she might be pregnant. The pregnancy was confirmed but it was only three weeks into her pregnancy. As soon as we returned home, the phone rang and Swamiji was on the line. He asked me, "So now you know?" I pretended to be dumb and asked, "Know what, Swamiji?" He countered, "Didn't the doctor tell you?" I was amazed at the timing of the phone call. Swamiji had waited to phone us, until we just got home from the doctor's office. I then realized that when Swamiji had mentioned the 'child' in his letter, he was referring to the newly conceived baby. I calculated that Vijaya was only a week pregnant when we had gone to see Swamiji. Even sophisticated medical tests are unable to detect pregnancy that early!

During Vijaya'a pregnancy, we visited Swamiji in Chicago. He let us in on a profound secret. He told me that being aware of my grief at being separated from my brother, he had gone to the subtle realms that souls go to between death and the next birth, and had put in very strenuous efforts to bring my brother back into our family. I was deeply moved by Swamiji's compassion and his arduous efforts on my behalf.

Vijaya's pregnancy went well, especially with her mother living with us. A few days after Christmas, we rushed to the same hospital where Mayank had been born. Unlike the first delivery, the labor was short, and

HIMALAYAN INTERNATIONAL INSTITUTE OF YOGA SCIENCE & PHILOSOPHY
1505 Greenwood Road   Glenview, Illinois 60025   (312) 724 - 0300

April 29, 1976

Prakash Keshaviah
3707 44th Avenue North
Minneapolis, Minn. 55422

Most Blessed Prakash:

God Bless You. Now you should learn to be strong from
within and not to be affected from the turmoils created by
the world. The flower of meditation will bloom when you learn
to live in the world and remain above. The technique of meditation needs a sound philosophy to support it.

My love for you is eternal and I am dealing with your
situations one by one. Your duty is to go to the silence in
meditation and my duty is to give you the message. I pray
for you and you should never feel neglected. Give my blessings to your child, Vijaya and your mother-in-law. I was
happy to see blessed Mayank.

God Bless You.

Thy Own Self,

Swami Rama

Letter written by Swamiji mentioning Vijaya
and the child

that afternoon, our daughter, Aparna, came into our lives. Aparna was born with two strawberry marks, one on her back and one on the top of her head. She also had a skin condition on the top of her head called cradle cap. The strawberry marks were absorbed and disappeared in a few months, as did the cradle cap condition. To me, they seemed to be vestigial marks of the traumatic death experienced in the previous body. Strengthening this belief was the strange fear Aparna exhibited, when she was only three or four years old. Each time we got into the car to go anywhere, she would insist on our locking all the doors of the car. As the yogis say, the *samskaras* of past experience are the seeds of future personality traits and attitudes.

Prakash's brother Vishwanath
who was killed in a car accident

Baby Aparna

11.
Raising the Kids

"Tender loving care should be the first step in the education of the child. When children are given care and love, they will definitely be self-disciplined, and they will return that love. If selfless love is freely given to children, they will respond spontaneously with love. Adults underestimate the ability of children to understand and respond to love. If you really love your children, the first step that you will have to take is to teach them through your example, not through your words. Parents think that unless they tell their children something, they will not understand. That is false. The best method of communication is not through the mind or through speech; the best communication is through the heart."

Let the Bud of Life Bloom:
A Guide to Raising Happy and Healthy Children

In previous chapters, I have talked about the circumstances surrounding the birth of our son Mayank and daughter Aparna. The two kids were diametrically opposite in many ways. Mayank was a very intense baby who cried a lot. Aparna was a happy baby, who smiled a lot, and was quite easy to take care of. One was born in the heat of summer, the other during the cold winter. One was born early in the morning, the other in mid-afternoon. One was intense and introverted, the other easy going and extroverted.

Vijaya's mother came to live with us for several months at a time, and the kids had a strict but caring grandmother who taught them about their roots and culture. However, when she left to spend time with her other grandchildren, it was difficult juggling two kids, with both of us working. Vijaya had trained to be a computer systems analyst, but did not pursue her career until the kids had started going to school. But with the kids growing up, there were other demands on her time with music and dance lessons, swimming, skating, and softball. Swamiji had forecast that we would have three kids. Realizing the difficulties we were facing with just two kids, we, one day, beseeched him to reconsider his prophecy. We told him that with two kids we had our hands full, and having had both a son and a daughter, our family was complete. He made sure that we had considered the matter carefully, and then gave his assent. We were successful in limiting our family to two kids.

Swamiji helped us a great deal in raising our kids. He was very emphatic in pointing out that young kids should not be subjected to a lot of discipline. He said that for the first five years, kids should only experience love and no discipline. Once they were secure in their parents' love, they would respond better to discipline. He advised Vijaya to take the lead in disciplining the kids. But even about discipline, Swamiji insisted on our not resorting to any form of physical discipline. He did not believe in the old adage, 'Spare the rod and spoil the child.' He told us that merely looking at the kids disapprovingly should be enough to deter them from disobeying their parents. He always told us that we should never rob the children of their childhood with too many dos and don'ts. They should enjoy the freedom of childhood. He would always ask the kids if I beat them, and made sure that I did not. I took his guidance to heart and refrained from using corporal punishment. Swamiji also advised us that as the kids got older, we should relate to them as friends rather than as parents. He also advised both Vijaya and me to separately take one of the kids at a time for outings, ensuring that the child got the full attention of the parent.

Swamiji would also always ask my wife if I was treating her well, and often cautioned me against male chauvinism and ego. He told me that he did not want me to be the 'typical Indian husband.' He once asked my wife how the three kids were doing. Seeing that she had not understood, he laughed and told her that he was referring to her two kids and the third of her mother-in-law. This then became a standard joke of his!

There was a phase in Mayank's life when he was terrified of spiders, and could not fall asleep if he spotted a spider on the walls or ceiling. Our reassurances about spiders being harmless creatures did little to calm his fears. We had not mentioned this to Swamiji. We were attending one of Swamiji's seminars in Honesdale. After Swamiji had delivered his lecture in the auditorium in the basement of the building, we were walking with him along the hallway leading to his apartment. I was walking slightly ahead, and Swamiji, Vijaya and the kids were just behind. Suddenly Swamiji reached down, took his slipper off, and turning to Mayank pointed to a spider on the wall of the hallway. Swamiji ordered Mayank to swat the spider with his slipper. Mayank hesitated, and said that he did not want to kill it. Swamiji told Mayank that the spider's time had come, and ordered him to kill it. Mayank had no choice but to obey, though his swat was hardly very forceful. After this incident, Mayank lost his fear of spiders. I had been walking ahead of Swamiji and Mayank, and had not seen any spiders on the wall. I began to wonder if the spider had really been there, or had been 'manifested' by Swamiji, in order to teach Mayank that unless he learnt to face his fears, he could not overcome them. Self-preservation is one of the four primitive fountains, the other three being food, sleep and sex. Of the four fountains, self-preservation is the hardest to regulate. Swamiji taught us that most of us do not want to examine our deep-seated fears. Unless we examine our fears, they will grow and grow to enormous pro-portions. How then can we enjoy life under the pressure of such enormous fears?

In the Indian tradition, when a young boy is around twelve years old, he is invested with the sacred thread and initiated into the sacred Gayatri mantra. Swamiji told us that he would like to perform this ritual for Mayank at Honesdale. Mayank was about fourteen years old when Swamiji fixed the date for this sacred ritual. We invited a number of our relatives and friends to Honesdale to participate in the celebration. Swamiji was kind enough to reserve a number of rooms for our guests, and they were served breakfast in a separate room from the Institute's dining hall. Swamiji made a personal appearance while our guests were having breakfast, in order to greet them and make them feel at home. I was very touched by his kind graciousness.

The ritual was held in the auditorium, and as the ceremony included a yagna or fire sacrifice, the resi-dents of the Institute rigged a canvas canopy over the area to protect the ceiling from smoke damage. Both Dr. Arya and Pandit Rajmani officiated at the cere-mony. The assembled audience of relatives, friends and Institute residents were spellbound, listening to Dr. Arya, explaining in English, the symbolism of the ritual and the meaning of the mantras being chanted. Sud-

Mayank's sacred thread ritual at Honesdale

Mayank gets a big hug from the Master

denly Swamiji walked into the auditorium, and motioned to Pandit Rajmani and Dr. Arya to get on with
the ceremony. They hurried up with the rest of the
ritual and Mayank was initiated into the sacred Gayatri
by Pandit Rajmani. Mayank, Vijaya, Aparna and I went
to Swamiji's apartment to seek his blessings. Vijaya
and some of her friends had cooked up a real feast in a
kitchen adjoining the main Institute kitchen, and we
were all served the meal, seated cross-legged in rows
on the floor of the auditorium.

In 1985, Swamiji came to our home in Plymouth,
a western suburb of Minneapolis. Mayank was eleven
years old then. Swamiji predicted that we would have
some trouble with Mayank in his teen years. He would
be rebellious and argumentative and would frustrate
us. Swamiji said that it would be good for Mayank to
take a year off after high school. Mayank did well in
high school and was accepted at Dartmouth College.
He and his friend Bruce wanted to take a year off to
travel around Europe on their bikes. They planned to
carry their tents, cooking stoves, sleeping bags and
camping gear on their bikes, as they biked through
eight or nine countries over the course of a year. We
agreed to the proposal, but our Indian friends thought
we were mad and not very solicitous parents, to let
someone so young go off on so risky a venture. We
chose not to be persuaded by our friends, and were
reminded of Swamiji's prediction. We requested
Mayank and Bruce to include a flight to India as part
of their trip. We also advised them to return a few
months before school started in the fall, so as to earn
some money to help pay off some of the expenses of
the trip.

With bikes packed into oversized cartons and
overstuffed backpacks, Mayank and Bruce set off for
Paris, en route to Delhi. After a short stop there to drop

off their bikes, they proceeded to Delhi. Swamiji was in Delhi, and put them up at the guesthouse in Malviya Nagar. The summer heat was fierce, and Swamiji had them follow him to Rishikesh. He then arranged for them to visit Uttarkashi and Gangotri. The scenery was spectacular, but their enjoyment of the trip was marred by having to travel in rickety, smoky buses, packed with people and poultry. Mayank and Bruce decided to cut short their stay in India and proceed to Paris for the start of their biking adventure. Swamiji wanted Mayank to stay on, and I tried, over the phone, to persuade him, but to no avail. I apologized profusely to Swamiji for Mayank's stubbornness, but he just dismissed the issue, telling me that the time and circumstances had not been right for what Swamiji had in mind for Mayank.

Mayank and Bruce started their trip in France and then biked to Switzerland, Italy, Spain, England, East and West Germany, Sweden and Denmark. They biked about a hundred kilometers a day, starting early in the morning, packing lunch for the road, and reaching their campground or the field of a friendly farmer before it turned dark. They cooked dinner over their camping stoves. In the mornings, their fingers were numb as they brushed the frozen dew off their tents and packed up their gear. They encountered inclement weather, tire punctures and even a crushed wheel from crashing into a construction cone. They sometimes spent nights sleeping on railway platforms, and encountered suspicious and surly immigration officials at border crossings. It was a rigorous test of their resolve and they emerged victorious. The trip matured Mayank and helped him increase his self confidence. He left home a boy, and came back a young man.

As a teenager, Mayank had a poster on his bedroom wall, which showed a beautiful chateau with expensive cars parked in the foreground. The tag line on the poster was, 'Justification for Higher Education.' At that time of his life, Mayank did aspire for the good things of life, and wanted to retire wealthy, at a relatively young age. Once, Swamiji remarked to Vijaya and me that though Mayank might want to be a Birla (wealthy Indian tycoon), he wanted Mayank to become a Tagore (Nobel Laureate in literature). Mayank was not aware of Swamiji's statement. Mayank is now in his mid thirties, has two Master's degrees, one in Education and the other in Dramatic Writing and has tried his hand at many careers including financial analyst on Wall Street, dot-com entrepreneur, primary school teacher, playwright and director, drama critic and SAT coach and curriculum developer. He has had the courage to make dramatic career changes, always seeking passion in his career, unmindful of the financial sacrifices he has made, and the years spent in pursuing his passion. He is still seeking that which will be the consuming passion in his life, and with Swamiji's blessings, we hope he finds fulfillment in his quest.

When Aparna was less than a year old, Swamiji predicted that she would be an accomplished dancer. On one of our visits to India, Aparna had watched a young cousin of hers demonstrate her dance skills. On going home, we were amazed to discover that young Aparna could reproduce the dance steps of her older cousin very gracefully. When Aparna was six years old, she began dance lessons with a dance teacher of Indian origin who was teaching the classical South Indian dance form called Bharatanatyam. As the name suggests, Bharatanatyam is the synthesis of *bhava* or feeling, raga or melody and tala or rhythm. Bharatanatyam uses movements of the hands, feet and eyes to express emotions and tell a story. Aparna took to Bharatanatyam as a fish to water and made rapid

Swamiji sitting with Mayank and Aparna

Aparna in a
dance pose

progress. She won awards at the Minnesota State Fair and other dance competitions. Aparna had her debut dance performance (Arangetram), an important milestone, when she was sixteen.

In 1987, Swamiji invited Aparna, her dance teacher and the teacher's daughter, also a good dancer, to perform at the Annual Congress of the Institute. The auditorium had filled up to capacity, and I came on stage to act as the M.C. for the show. When I introduced the dance teacher and the two dancers, I did not mention that Aparna was my daughter. Swamiji, in the audience, pulled me up and asked me to tell the audience who Aparna was. Introductions done, I went backstage, and as the curtains were drawn, in the darkness, I knocked over a glass that was on stage behind the curtains. The glass shattered to pieces all over the stage. I was shocked at my clumsiness and froze. Swamiji immediately jumped out of his seat and took control of the situation. He had the Institute residents bring brooms and mops. He had them meticulously clean up the mess, making sure that no shards were left behind, as Bharatanatyam is performed with bare feet. I had recovered my composure by now, and told the audience that before such events in India, we usually break a coconut on stage. Not having a coconut, we had to make do with a glass. The show was a hit, and when Aparna performed a dance about the saint Meera's love for Lord Krishna, Dr. Arya was so moved that there were tears flowing down his cheeks.

Swamiji told us that as Aparna would grow up into a beautiful and graceful young lady, there would be inducements for her to take to a career in acting or modeling. He advised us to discourage her from such career choices, as such a life would only bring her unhappiness in the long run. He exhorted us to send both Mayank and Aparna to the best schools possible and not skimp on their education.

Aparna received her Bachelor's degree in Mathematics from Duke University and her Master's degree in Biostatistics from the Harvard School of Public Health in Boston. Aparna is pursuing a successful career as a biostatistician, having distinguished herself in breast cancer research, and is also pursuing a career in dance, which includes research, choreography and teaching. Aparna was recently awarded a Fulbright grant in dance. She did her research in India on Bharatanatyam, surveying hundreds of dancers in three major cities, to understand the nature of 'tradition,' and using statistical analysis to reveal the diversity that is characteristic of a dynamic, living art form. She recently accepted a research position at the Massachusetts General Hospital, to do research on a range of psychiatric disorders and health outcomes.

12.
Are you an Insider or an Outsider?

"A spiritual master's ways of teaching are many and sometimes mysterious. To one student the guru may show much attention, spending much time with a student, even doting on a particular student. Another student may be utterly ignored by the master. It doesn't matter. Each student is getting a teaching, and because of the insight of the master, just the right teaching at the right time. The guru is not in a student's life to give a student what the student thinks he wants, but rather to give what is needed to progress spiritually."

Sacred Journey:
Living Purposefully and Dying Gracefully

In the early years, Swamiji spent a fair amount of time in Minneapolis, and we had fairly easy access to him. Many evenings were spent with Swamiji discussing philosophical doctrines and conundrums like destiny versus free will, the unreality of both the waking and dream states, and whether we were already realized and did not know it, or whether we had to make efforts to achieve realization. As Swamiji's mission in the West began to expand, the number of students increased many-fold, and Swamiji spent more time traveling to other cities to set up yoga centers. Swamiji got so busy that sometimes, when his visit to Minneapolis was very brief, we got to know of his visit only afterwards.

On one such brief visit, we learnt that Swamiji was staying at the apartment of one of his American students near downtown Minneapolis. With some effort we got permission to go see him. As I felt free to address any issue with Swamiji without restraint, I started to complain to Swamiji about the lack of accessibility, and how there were so many barriers when we tried to contact Swamiji. I told him that I had considered myself an insider, but it was increasingly obvious that I was becoming an outsider.

Swamiji deftly turned the tables on me with his play on my words. He told me that the more I became an insider, that is, the more I went within myself, the less I would feel that I was an outsider. It was a profound teaching, but I just felt frustrated at how deftly he had distorted my complaint!

As is true with many gurus, the guru starts by being very sweet and kind to the student, making him feel special and important. That is the honeymoon phase, until the student is truly hooked. The student's ego gets inflated, when suddenly, the guru pricks the balloon of ego with harsh words and seemingly unjustified criticism. The student is caught totally unawares and sometimes resentment builds up, as the student goes away to lick his wounds in isolation. The guru is ever watchful and makes sure that the testing is not so severe that the student never returns. The scolding and criticisms are still bearable, because the astute student realizes that the guru cares for him very deeply and is trying to reform him. The next phase, however, is that of total indifference. That is the unkindest cut of all. It is indeed a severe test of the student's steadfastness of purpose and sincerity.

It was inevitable that we would soon face this severe test of total indifference. Swamiji became totally inaccessible to us even when we knew where he was.

We were not able to see him nor could we contact him by phone. Having tasted so much love and attention earlier, we had a very hard time accepting this situation, and could not easily apply the earlier teaching of learning to be insiders.

Then, one night, I had a very vivid dream. Vijaya and I were in a bookstore browsing, when Swamiji entered the store. We ran up to greet him, but he ignored us and kept walking to the back door of the bookstore. Before leaving the store, he turned back, looked at us and asked, "Do you know why I have been ignoring you? It's because you have become too dependent on me. I want you to stand on your own feet." The stark reality of the dream hit me, prompting me to introspect deeply about the truth of the dream message.

A few months later we visited Swamiji in Chicago. He repeated, verbatim, the message he had given me earlier in the dream. I was thunderstruck, and blurted out to Swamiji that he had already given me this message in a dream. Swamiji acknowledged that he had to sometimes teach me through dreams. I was truly in awe of one who could permeate my waking, dream and deep sleep states.

Now, even after Swamiji has dropped his body, many of us continue to receive instructions in dreams and look upon them as true teachings and not mere products of the churning of the subconscious mind. As Swamiji once told one of my guru brothers, Pandit Hari Shankar Dabral, one can dream of Swamiji, only if he wills it, not otherwise!

13.
The Guru Knows All

"Many times students come to the guru with a preconceived idea of what the guru should be like. They come with expectations of what the guru is there to do for them. Perhaps the students think the guru should give them much attention, or make decisions for them, or take on troubles they have created for themselves. Sometimes the students think the guru should behave in a certain way. When these expectations and preconceived images are not met, the student becomes upset and may even leave the guru.

"This is not the proper way to approach a teacher. A student should not be filled with expectations and preconceived images, but with a burning desire to learn, and with firm determination. Then there will be no difficulty. The guru and the disciple can do their work accordingly."

Sacred Journey:
Living Purposefully and Dying Gracefully

I was visiting Swamiji in Honesdale. I flew into Newark, rented a car and drove towards Honesdale. Justin O'Brien happened to be at Newark airport and I gave him a ride into Honesdale. The next day, I had to return the rental car at Scranton airport, and Justin agreed to drive his car up to Scranton to give me a ride back to Honesdale. I had a 4:00 p.m. appointment with Swamiji and I was keen to return to Honesdale in time for the appointment. However, Justin was delayed in our starting off for Scranton, and at 4:00 p.m. we were still on our way back from Scranton. Justin tried to reassure me, saying that he would explain it all to Swamiji. Suddenly, some michievous thoughts entered the monkey mind of mine. I reasoned that Swamiji had never seen me on time, so my being late would not matter. Even if he were on time, Swamiji had often kept me waiting; it shouldn't matter too much, if he had to wait, just this once, for me!

I came back an hour late for my appointment with Swamiji. Justin ushered me into Swamiji's presence. Swamiji told me that he had had people looking all over for me. I was perplexed, as Theresa O'Brien was with him at that time, and she knew about Justin and me going to Scranton to return the rental car. Even before I could apologize for the delay Swamiji sarcastically remarked, "Yes, yes, I have kept you waiting many times before, so today you have kept me waiting!" I was stunned and mortified at his having read my errant thoughts as we were returning from Scranton. There was no point in apologizing for my disrespectful mind, when Swamiji knew it all. Since that episode, I have tried hard to discipline my mind from thinking such disrespectful thoughts, always aware that one cannot hide anything from the guru. It is amazing that the guru can love us and extend his grace, in spite of our disrespectful and despicable behavior.

Samskriti, whom I first met during the Minnesota retreat of 1972, had moved to Chicago to be a part of Swamiji's mission. She once told me an interesting story of her Chicago ashram days. Swamiji, having given a group of the ashramites some routine work, had gone upstairs to his room. After a while, the monotony of the assigned work prompted the group to start talking as they worked, resulting in some loss of concentration. The phone rang. It was Swamiji on the line telling them to quit the gossip and get on with the work. They were taken aback and got back to work. After some time, without thinking, they again started to talk as they worked. Again the phone rang, and it was Swamiji reprimanding them for their lack of discipline. This story also reminds me of the time Swamiji was in Topeka, Kansas and discovered that Dr. Arya, in Minneapolis, was reading the newspaper at the meditation time that Swamiji had given him. With undisguised glee, Swamiji got on the phone, berated Dr. Arya in no uncertain terms and hung up, chuckling about the shock he had delivered to Dr. Arya.

When we are unable to tame our own egos, the guru, in his grace, intervenes. And the intervention can be rather painful. I was going through a phase when I could do nothing right in Swamiji's eyes. He mercilessly exposed all my warts, and traced all my relationship problems to my ego and to the unrealistic expectations I had of others. I am generally not that emotional, but Swamiji would reduce me to tears, with his laying bare my egoistic ways. It reached such a point that I began to rue the day that Swamiji came into my life. I kept telling myself that life was much simpler before Swamiji entered our lives.

Soon after this, I happened to visit India with Vijaya and the kids. When we were in Bangalore, we heard interesting stories about a yogi called Shiva Bala Yogi whose ashram was not far from where we were staying. As the story went, Shiva Bala Yogi was once meditating on the banks of the Godavari River, when the river began to flood and submerged its banks. When the waters receded, Shiva Bala Yogi was discovered, still seated in deep meditation, oblivious to the flood. We decided to visit Shiva Bala Yogi's ashram in Bangalore.

Shiva Bala Yogi had spent so many years in the cross-legged seated position that his legs had atrophied; he had to be carried from his inner chamber to the hall where he gave public audiences. He was impressive looking with large glowing eyes and matted locks. Though we had only gone to meet him, his enthusiastic disciples tried to convince us to take mantra initiation from him. In spite of our protestations, we were lined up for initiation. When the mantra was imparted, I kept my own guru mantra going without pause as fast as I could, trying to block any other mantra! Later, during the public audience, many of the yogi's disciples began to dance spontaneously in a trance-like state, moving across the hall with eyes closed, without bumping into each other, or into the pillars of the hall. The yogi brought them out of the trance, by rubbing sacred ash on their forehead at the eyebrow center.

On this same visit to Bangalore, we had an opportunity to meet another celebrated spiritual leader called Satya Sai Baba, who sported a huge Afro hair style and was known to materialize sacred ash, lockets with his picture, rings and other material objects, by the mere waving of his hands. He was regarded by his disciples as God on earth, and huge crowds gathered to merely have his *darshan*, even from a great distance. He had established educational institutions and many other enterprises, for the social welfare of the less fortunate. He was going to be at a suburb of Bangalore called Whitefield, where a new educational institution was under construction.

A large crowd had gathered and was eagerly awaiting the arrival of Satya Sai Baba. He appeared clad in silk robes, and spent a fair amount of time

Shiva Bala Yogi

inspecting the new construction. He walked among
the people who had gathered, greeting some of the
familiar faces. He passed by us, but we had no interaction with him. The feeling of worshipful emotion he
evoked in the gathered crowd was indeed amazing.

Though my meeting with these spiritual figures
was juxtaposed in time with my despair at the way
Swamiji was treating me, I was not consciously seeking another guru. However, the next time we met
Swamiji upon our return from India, he jocularly asked
me, "Hey, how was your guru shopping in India?"
Needless to say, my jaw almost hit the floor. The guru
knows all.

Swamiji's inspiring classic, *Living with the Himalayan Masters,* was completed while Swamiji was still
at the Glenview Center. Swamiji narrated to me an
interesting episode associated with the completion of
this book. Swamiji had just finished penning, in his
own beautiful handwriting, his poetic dedication, 'At
Thy Lotus Feet,' addressed to his master Bengali Baba.

Suddenly, the door opened. Swamiji looked up and smiled. A short while later, the door closed. Swamiji told me that Bengali Baba had come into the room, in his subtle form, to bless the completion of the book and then left, closing the door behind him! I have read and re-read this fantastic book several times and still discover something new each time I read it.

14.
The Guru's Healing Touch

"Guru is not a physical being. Those who think of the guru as a body or as a man do not understand this pious word. If a guru comes to think that his power is his own, then he is a guide no more. The guru is tradition; he is a stream of knowledge. That stream of knowledge goes through many channels. Christ also said this when he healed people: 'This is because of my Father; I am only a channel.' "

Sadhana: The Essence of Spiritual Life

As narrated earlier, my younger brother was killed in an automobile accident when he was only 27 years old. My father had bottled up his grief at the tragic loss of my brother. Within a year, he was stricken by a rapidly progressive rheumatoid arthritis which laid waste the joints of his knees, hips and wrists, rendering him bedridden for the last five years of his life.

One day, in Minneapolis, I was suddenly afflicted by pain in my knee which made walking, especially climbing stairs, painful. It came on very suddenly and I began to wonder if there was a familial tendency for rheumatoid arthritis which was now affecting my knee joint. Swamiji happened to visit Minneapolis, and I asked him about my knee problem. He told me that the problem was not in my knee, but in my mouth! I was taken aback, and sought further explanation. He told me that I had a dental problem that was responsible for the knee pain, and advised me to see my dentist. As it turned out, an oral infection was the source, and the knee joint was the target. My knee pain resolved quickly after the dental problem was taken care of. I was amazed at Swamiji's intuitive diagnosis of my knee problem.

Another time, when we were in Honesdale, Swamiji wanted to throw a party for some visiting guests. He asked Vijaya if she could prepare masala dosa for his guests. Swamiji was aware that Vijaya was suffering from severe pain in her left hand, the result of carpal tunnel syndrome. Swamiji told her that he would take care of the problem in return for her masala dosas! Happening to hear this, I, half-jokingly, tried to make a deal too. I told him that as I was going to help Vijaya with the cooking, would he take care of my tennis elbow? I loved my weekend tennis game, but tennis elbow was making it difficult to enjoy the game. Swamiji smiled at my guile.

Swamiji's guests loved the masala dosas and Swamiji thanked Vijaya for her hard work. Gradually the pain in her left hand faded away. I had not taken my healing request all that seriously, but the tennis elbow too resolved fairly quickly, and no longer prevented me from enjoying my weekend tennis.

Just before I left the shores of India for Minnesota, I had begun to develop a rash on the back of my neck, which was not only uncomfortable from the itching, but also made me self-conscious. I tried some Ayurvedic remedies but to no avail. The allopathic physician in India prescribed a rather strong steroidal oral medication. When I consulted the American physician at the University of Minnesota Health Service, he was shocked, and asked me to go off the strong medication at once. I gradually got used to the rash, but it did not improve.

Swamiji was imparting training in Homeopathy to some of the Western physicians who were studying with him at Glenview. The excellent book for home prescribing, *Homeopathic Remedies,* was compiled by these physicians, based on Swamiji's training. Once, Swamiji had me show these trainees the rash on my neck, and there was some discussion, but I did not receive any treatment for it. A few years later, Swamiji suddenly asked me what happened to the rash on my neck. I told him that it was still there. He then asked me to apply pure mustard oil on the affected area daily. Purchasing a bottle of mustard oil from one of the Indian grocery stores in Minnesota, I followed Swamiji's instructions. I was thrilled to find that the rash responded to the mustard oil; soon the rash was replaced by smooth unblemished skin. I had suffered from this rash for more than 10 years, and now, the simple remedy of mustard oil had eradicated the rash. About a year or so after this, Swamiji again asked about the rash and I told him that the mustard oil had completely cured it. He just nodded and made no comment. I wondered if the rash was the karmic consequence of past actions, and I had to endure the problem until the right time for a cure presented itself.

I was in Washington D.C. to attend a meeting at the National Institutes of Health in Bethesda. After the meeting, I decided to visit Honesdale over the weekend. Swamiji had the troops out for his spring 'rocks and roots' cleanup of the Institute grounds. I too pitched in, but soon realized that my sedentary desk job had not prepared me for the rigors of the project. I persevered, but the warm weather and my blistered palms were making the going tough. Suddenly Swamiji called out to me, told me that his dog needed a drink of water, and asked me to take the dog back to his apartment for some water. I was glad to have this break, and accompanied the dog back to Swamiji's apartment. To my surprise, the dog was not thirsty and refused the water I offered it. I was initially perplexed, but it soon hit me, that Swamiji had created this diversion for my benefit, not for the 'thirsty' dog. I was bowled over by the guru's grace and compassion.

15.
The Guru's Protection

"He (the guru) wants nothing, for what he is doing is his duty, the purpose of his life. If he guides you, he is not obliging you, he is doing his work. He cannot live without doing his duty. Genuine gurus cannot live without selflessness, for selfless love is the very basis of their enlightenment. They radiate life and light from the unknown corners of the world. The world does not know them, and they do not want recognition."

Sadhana: The Essence of Spiritual Life

Every year, we, as a family, made it a point to visit Swamiji in Honesdale, Pennsylvania. At the end of one of our visits, we went to Swamiji for his permission to leave for home that evening. We had planned to stop over for the night at a cousin's home at the western end of Pennsylvania, before driving on towards Minneapolis the next day. The cousin had made plans for us to have dinner with him that night. When we talked to Swamiji about our plans, he, without any explanation, forbade us leaving that evening. He said that we should wait until the next morning for our departure, no matter how early we left the next morning. I called my cousin to tell him about the change in plans, but could not give him a satisfactory reason for the change, being reluctant to admit that we were acting on our guru's directions.

We left at 4:00 the next morning, and bundled the kids, still in their night clothes, into the back of the station wagon where we had spread out their sleeping bags. The meditation time that Swamiji had given us was 5:00 a.m. At that time, we pulled off the road near a clearing of trees, and spent a few minutes in meditation. We then drove on and joined the main highway out of Pennsylvania. It was now raining heavily and visibility was decreasing with the mixture of heavy rain and fog. Driving very carefully, we made it to a gas station to fill up. I talked to the attendant at the gas station about the poor driving conditions. He remarked that the driving conditions had improved a great deal, compared to the previous evening, when one could not even see the front end of one's own car. Suddenly, Swamiji's injunction against our leaving the previous evening became clear to us, and we offered up our silent thanks to the guru for his grace and protection.

This incident reminded us of other times when the guru's intervention and protection had averted a calamity. Before I got married, I had saved up enough to buy a used Chrysler car. In the beginning the car served me well, but after a few years, the repair bills began to mount. One afternoon, Vijaya and I were driving down Franklin Avenue in Minneapolis. As we approached the intersection, the light turned yellow. I applied the brakes, only to discover that the brakes had failed completely. A huge truck was just about to enter the intersection at right angles to our car. I stepped on the accelerator, and ran the red light, in order to clear the intersection without colliding with the truck. I was desperately pumping the brakes, and tried to apply the hand brake to slow down the car. The next intersection loomed ahead and the light had turned red. There was no indication of the car slowing down. Just before I approached the intersection, I noticed a driveway leading into the parking lot of a liquor store. I steered hard into the driveway, and used a concrete parking lot curb to bring the car to rest. Our amazing reprieve from disaster left us breathless.

A few years later, I was driving to work and was in the inner lane. A school bus was in the outer lane, and without any warning, the bus tried to make a sharp right turn at the intersection from the wrong lane, my car being between the bus and the intersection. I emerged from the car, shaken but unhurt. Looking at the damage inflicted by the bus on the car, I was amazed. The rear lights of the car were broken, the rear door had caved in and there was damage to the front fender of the car. The only part not damaged was the front door adjacent to the driver's seat! The bus was being driven by a trainee driver, who had not observed my car when he tried to make the turn from the wrong lane. I was not only unhurt, but was also calm enough to exchange details of insurance and driver's license before continuing my drive to work.

Then there was the time one winter, when my car skidded on an icy patch and climbed up a high snow bank on the road divider, coming to rest at the top of the snow bank. I looked down and saw the stream of cars speeding past in the opposite direction beyond the divider. A little faster skid and I would have climbed over the snow bank and right smack into the opposing traffic. I waited for the traffic to go by, before slowly driving down the snow bank and turning onto the highway on the other side. That was a very close shave and again revealed the guru's protection.

Thinking of averted road accidents brings one more incident to mind. I was driving down one of Minnesota's highways at about 100 kilometers per hour (60 miles per hour) in the inner lane. My mind was distracted briefly by a magazine that lay on the passenger seat next to me. In that brief instant, the traffic ahead had suddenly come to a halt. When I looked up, I was heading straight for a crash with the car ahead that had stopped. I braked hard, and my car spun out of control. If it had spun into the outer lane, I would have been hit by the incoming traffic in that lane. My car spun around facing the traffic, but safely on the shoulder of the highway. My heart was racing as I tried to calm down. I offered prayerful thanks for the protection given, admittedly undeserved. I felt very repentant for having troubled the guru with my carelessness.

Many years later, when I was complaining to Swamiji, as was my wont, about his not spending much time with me, he replied that he spent a lot of time on me, and asked me to think about the many times that I had been protected from accidents. Years earlier, a friend of mine who knew palmistry, had remarked about the shortness of my life line. An astrologer, visiting Minnesota from India, told me that the guru's influence was very strong in my horoscope. He remarked that my longevity, and all that was auspicious in my life, was attributable to the guru's grace.

16.
Bio-magnetism, Drug Use and Other things

"There is a vast difference between an ordinary teacher and a spiritual master or guru. That which dispels the darkness of ignorance is called guru. In the West the word guru is often misused. In India this word is used with reverence and is always associated with holiness and the highest wisdom. It is a very sacred word. It is seldom used by itself, but always with its suffix, *deva*. Deva means 'bright being.' An enlightened master or guru is called gurudeva."

Sadhana: The Essence of Spiritual Life

Swamiji was visiting Minneapolis and was giving a small group of us some yoga lessons. He suddenly said that he had something to show us. He asked for a needle and thread, and had us close all the doors and windows in the room, to keep out any air currents. He tied the thread to the middle of the needle, and suspended the needle from the thread. He then told us that he would give us a demonstration of bio-magnetism. He gently rubbed together the tips of the fingers of his right hand. He then bunched together the tips of the fingers of his right hand, and held them close to the needle tip, without touching the needle. To our amazement, the tip of the needle was repulsed, and swung away from his finger tips. He now said that he would change the polarity of the bio-magnet. This time, when he held his finger tips near the needle tip, the needle was attracted and swung towards his fingers. He told us that this was not difficult to do; all it required was one-pointed concentration on the tip of the needle, and having the needle do what one wanted it to do. I decided to give it a try, and concentrated very hard on the needle tip. Nothing, not the slightest movement of the needle tip; I walked away from the experiment with a horrendous headache!

Another interesting demonstration of Swamiji was related to detecting drug use. In the seventies, many young, and not so young, people turned on with drugs, and tuned out the world. Swamji often lectured about the harmful effects of drugs, and advised students to take up meditation instead, for predictable and sustainable results. Swamiji made a young bare-chested man lie down on his back. He then asked for a piece of string. With the string he measured the distance between the navel and the right nipple. He then showed us that the distance from the navel to the other nipple would be the same in one who was not on drugs, but would be a different measurement for a habitual drug user.

On another occasion, Swamiji was seated on a chair with his feet planted on the carpeted floor. He asked me to observe his feet and feel them. Swamiji had beautifully-formed, warm, rosy pink feet. He asked me to look again. One of his feet had become a sickly yellow, and when I touched it, it was cold like dead flesh, remaining dimpled where I poked it with my finger. However, the other foot remained pink and warm. When I looked at the changed foot once more, it had resumed its pink, healthy look. I asked Swamiji how he did this. He said that there were three ways. One way was through pranic control of the smooth muscles of the blood vessels. Another way was to use the concentrated mind, but easiest of all was through one's will power or *sankalpa* shakti.

Swamiji was once teaching me about the 10 openings through which the soul leaves the body at the time of death. They are the two eyes, the two ears, the two nostrils, the mouth, the navel, the urinary orifice and the rectum. He then told me that yogis, who voluntarily drop their bodies, do not use any of these 10 openings, but leave through the 11th opening, the fontanelle of the skull, called *brahmarandhra* in Sanskrit. He said that this opening was there in the skulls of very young babies, but as they grew older, the bones of the skull fused together, closing this opening. Swamiji then asked me to touch the top of his head at the fontanelle. The skull was hard and did not yield to the pressure of my fingers. He then asked me to try again and this time, the fingers went in a little, indicating a gap between the skull bones. There was no indication of any strain or effort on his part!

Swamiji was once visiting Minneapolis and gave a talk at the Meditation Center. There was an Englishman in the audience. At the end of the lecture, during the question and answer session, this man expressed his great frustration at Swamiji having given him the slip at each place that he had tried to meet up with Swamiji. Swamiji was quite amused and asked if the reason for his visit from England had been fulfilled. The Englishman admitted that his quest had been successful. Swamiji responded that then, there was no problem, and added that when he sometimes got really busy, he delegated his work to a network of helpers!

17.
The Ramana Maharshi
Book Project

"The guru does not operate from what seems fair, or outwardly appropriate. He is not constrained to such cultural amenities. He can seem harsh, even brutal. He will put students in situations that make no sense, or are very uncomfortable. He will say things that won't make any sense for months. He will ask things of students that students think are impossible. Everything the guru is doing is for the growth of the student. The student only need have faith in that fact."

Sacred Journey:
Living Purposefully and Dying Gracefully

Not long after Swamiji came into my life, I came across that most inspiring book, *Ramana Maharshi and the Path of Self-knowledge,* by Arthur Osborne. Reading the book filled me with great joy; I had to interrupt my reading of the book every few pages, to savor the joy I was experiencing, and to meditate upon the experience.

Ramana was a young boy of 17 who was, one day, suddenly assailed by the fear of death. Being of an intellectual disposition, he decided to find out what the experience of death was like. He lay down, and stiffened his body to simulate the rigor mortis of death. He realized that he was still breathing, and held his breath. This made him aware of the thoughts passing through his mind, and being ripe for the experience, he was able to still his mind. Becoming aware of the 'I' thought, he sought its source, and immediately transcended the ego and realized the Self. All of this happened in a matter of a few seconds, and the Self-knowledge he gained remained with him permanently.

Ramana was then divinely guided to the temple town of Tiruvannamalai, abode of Arunachala, the fiery hill, considered to be *Shiva* himself, manifest on earth. Ramana took up residence in an underground vault in the temple, and was totally indrawn and unmindful of the insects and vermin feeding upon his young body. Passersby force fed him, and he was subsequently taken out of the vault to nearby shrines and orchards, and looked after by pilgrims who were impressed by the saintly young man who was steeped in meditation, totally unaware of his body. He remained in silence for a few years, and then slowly began to respond to questions with written answers, sometimes scrawled upon the sand. He gradually returned to normal body awareness. Soon disciples gathered around him, inspired by his direct and profound answers to their spiritual questions, as well as by the deep peace and joy they experienced in his company. His direct teaching, born of his own experience, was that if one were to seek the source of the 'I,' one would, in time, transcend the ego, and become established in the Self.

Ramana took up residence in various caves on the holy hill, finally settling down at the base of the hill, where his disciples established an ashram. Ramana lived in this ashram, until he dropped his body in 1950, having spent a total of 54 years in the small town of Tiruvannamalai, to which he was divinely guided after his experience of the Self. Though Ramana never left Tiruvannamalai, spiritual seekers from all over the world came to him. Many of them settled down in the ashram for the rest of their lives, being drawn to Ramana as iron filings to a magnet.

Reading Arthur Osborne's inspiring biography of this modern day rishi filled me with deep bliss. Swamiji told me that, in our tradition, we look upon Ramana as the reincarnation of that great philosopher-saint, Adi Shankara, of the eighth century A.D. Being a great admirer of Shankara and his works, this revelation of Swamiji thrilled me, sending shivers down my spine. Swamiji encouraged me to learn more about Ramana's life and teachings. This advice of Swamiji was easy to follow as I was naturally drawn to Ramana and his philosophy of Self-enquiry. Swamiji also told me that he had witnessed how Ramana had assisted his mother's absorption into the Self, by placing his right hand upon her heart and his left hand on her head, during the last two hours of her life. Ramana accelerated the ripening of her karmas, having her experience in consciousness, all her future life experiences, thus eliminating the need for rebirth. Her face indicated the pains and pleasures that she was experiencing, during this period of accelerated experience. I went home, and upon checking, discovered that Ramana's mother had passed away in 1922, about three years before 1925, Swamiji's stated date of birth. The next day, I asked Swamiji how he had witnessed something that took place before his birth. He revealed that his master had recreated the scene of the passing of Ramana's mother, in order to teach him and his monastic guru brothers about this process.

Not long after I read Osborne's book, I had a beautiful dream. I was standing on the banks of a river with my brother and sister, when I noticed Ramana swimming in the river. He swam towards the bank and beckoned to me. He asked me why I was worried about the success of my *sadhana*, when he had touched me. I was overwhelmed, and asked him to also bless my brother and sister. He nodded in assent. Interestingly, at the time of this dream, I had not known that Ramana could swim. Only years later did I find out that Ramana, even as a young boy, had been an expert swimmer.

Not soon after, Swamiji told me to start working on a book on Ramana and his philosophy. He gave me a tight schedule for completing the book. I soon gathered as many books on Ramana as I could find, and wrote to Ramanashram for permission to quote from their publications, which was readily given. I perused the publications and began to compile my book on the life, philosophy and writings of Ramana *Maharshi*. After several reminders from Swamiji, I laid my manuscript upon his desk. Swamiji seemed to approve of my efforts, and gave the book to his editor Arpita for review. I discussed the manuscript with Arpita over the phone, and several phone calls later, she returned the manuscript to me with her editorial comments and suggestions. Arpita wanted me to add a section on some of the important disciples of Ramana and their experiences with the master. This was soon done, and I visited Honesdale to complete the editing with Arpita. One night, we worked on the manuscript into the wee hours of the morning, and Swamiji, on his nightly rounds, came by and seemed pleased with our efforts. I gathered photographs of Ramana, the holy hill and the ashram for the book, and was in discussion with the press at Honesdale on the cover design.

Suddenly, without warning, the manuscript went into cold storage. Arpita left Honesdale and nobody seemed to take charge of the manuscript. Every once in a while, Swamiji would ask me what happened to my book, and my standard answer was that it was still with him and his editors. He created a drama of calling various people to ask about the book and the need to get it into print soon, but nothing seemed to happen beyond the drama. Some years later, Shanta became the editor of Honesdale publications, and she was asked to edit the book for publication. Shanta tried to get some others like Phil Nuernberger to read the book for critical review, and I got some superficial feedback from Shanta and Phil, but nothing definitive.

I was content to forget the whole thing, but Swamiji would not let me, often asking me what had become of the book. I was truly perplexed, but could not make much headway in determining the cause of the delay or the reason for his constant goading. I did some introspection on the whole incident, and realized that Swamiji was testing me and my motivations. I was thankful to Swamiji for having set the task for me. It had motivated me to study Ramana's life, writings and philosophy in depth. This had been part of my sadhana. I also realized that I had nothing really original to offer, as the book had been compiled after studying and digesting the many existing books on Ramana. It was a case of regurgitating what was already available, albeit in my own words and with the filtering of my mind.

The next time Swamiji asked me about the book, I confessed that the book was not worth publishing because it lacked originality, and was only a compilation based on the other books on Ramana. That was the last time Swamiji asked me about the book. He had accomplished his purpose. The manuscript is still with me, and reminds me of Swamiji's teaching that most knowledge is secondhand, a case of putting old wine in new bottles. True knowledge is not gained through books and lectures, but only through personal experience.

Ramana Maharshi

Many years later, I had another significant dream of Ramana. I was kneeling before Ramana. With anguish in my heart, I asked Ramana when I would achieve success in my sadhana. With a gesture, he motioned to someone behind me. I looked back and saw my mother standing behind me. He indicated that I had to wait until my mother came to him. I understood from this, that I would have to wait until my worldly responsibilities towards my mother were fulfilled.

18.
Visiting Hansda Ashram

"Maintain a balance between the internal and the external worlds. Do not be caught by the rigidity of external observances, which are actually nonessentials. Do not be affected by the suggestions of others, but learn to follow your own way that does not hurt, harm or injure anyone."

Sadhana: The Essence of Spiritual Life

We were in India in 1983 visiting parents and relatives. We came to Delhi and knew that Swamiji was in India at that time. We contacted some of the people in Delhi known to Swamiji, to find out about Swamiji's whereabouts. Our search lead to Chandan Swarup, who needed some time to contact Swamiji, and asked me to call her back. When I called back, I was thrilled to learn that Swamiji was in Delhi and staying at the India International Centre. We were told that we could visit him the next morning. Vijaya and I arrived at the India International Centre and were ushered into his room. Swamiji was happy to see us, and ordered up a great breakfast of masala dosas and coffee for us. We told Swamiji about our recent visit to Ramanashram in Tiruvannnamalai, and our having circumambulated the holy hill, Arunachala. He showered us with a lot of praise for our piety, much to my embarrassment. He then sprang a delightful surprise on us. He told us that he was leaving for Nepal the next morning, and asked us to join him. He instructed Chandan Swarup to arrange flight tickets for us, our two kids Mayank and Aparna, and my mother-in-law. We arranged to meet him at the Delhi International airport the next morning.

Swamiji showed up at the airport, elegantly dressed in a closed collar suit and wearing stylish shades. On the flight, I was happy to be seated beside Swamiji, but wished the flight to Kathmandu had been a little longer. They served lunch, and we had requested a vegetarian meal. At first, Swamiji refused lunch, but when he saw my vegetarian meal, he requested one as well, and seemed to enjoy it. When we landed, we had to wait in line to go through immigration and customs, but Swamiji, an honored guest, was quickly whisked away without being subjected to many formalities. Swamiji asked us to check in at the Yak and Yeti hotel and arranged for a young lady from a Delhi travel agency to show us around Kathmandu that day. He invited us to his new ashram, Hansda Ashram, the next day. He also exhorted us to visit the famous Shiva temple, the Pashupatinath temple. Swamiji then drove off to Hansda Ashram.

I knew that Swamiji smoked, but he had never smoked in our presence, presumably because he realized that we were not comfortable with his smoking habit, and did not want to cause us any discomfiture. I had often wondered about Swamiji's smoking, especially as I had been brought up to look upon smoking and drinking as particularly bad habits. I also realized that surrender to the guru is essential for spiritual growth, and that while one may not understand the guru, one should learn to unconditionally accept the guru. I decided that the time had come for me to test my capacity for surrender.

There were duty free shops at the airport, and they had Swamiji's favorite brand of cigarettes, Dunhills. I bought a carton of Dunhills, and sent it to Swamiji at Hansda Ashram with one of his students. I was bashful about personally handing the carton to Swamiji. Swamiji graciously accepted my symbol of surrender, but never mentioned it. However, after that, Swamiji did not hesitate to smoke in my presence.

The Yak and Yeti was a very comfortable hotel, and the kids were particularly thrilled with the great breakfasts the hotel served up. We enjoyed the sights of Kathmandu. I particularly remember Kumari Ghar, the temple of the Kumari (virgin), considered to be a living Goddess. At a certain time each day, the Kumari granted public audience from an upper story carved wooden balcony. The Kumari was heavily made-up and decked out gaudily. She seemed to have rather sad eyes, despite the forced smiles she exhibited to the fawning public gawking at her, who regarded her as a symbol of divinity. I decided not to pass judgement on something I did not understand. Vijaya enjoyed the colorful markets of Kathmandu, well-stocked with smuggled Japanese and Chinese goods. We picked up some shawls made of yak's wool and some brass figurines. The kids found a great board game, involving fearful sheep and a marauding tiger, the board and pieces all being made of brass.

The next morning we visited the ancient Pashupatinath temple. As no leather items were allowed into the temple, we had to deposit our camera case and belts in lockers outside. The sanctum sanctorum was crowded, and we were quite far from the main deity, the Shiva *linga*, which is worshipped by pouring holy water over it. We were conversing in our mother tongue Kannada, the language of the South Indian state of Karnataka. One of the temple priests, also from

Karnataka, overheard us, and was very happy to hear
his native tongue spoken so far from home. He located
us, and cleared a path for us to get very close to the
deity. We enjoyed the ritual worship, and unwittingly
became objects of worship ourselves! The enthusiasm
of the worshippers, and our proximity to the deity,
resulted in our being drenched by the holy water meant
for the deity.

Finally, it was time to visit Swamiji's ashram,
which was about twenty kilometers from the city. The
young lady from the Delhi travel agency arranged
transportation for us, and we reached the base of the
hill on top of which the ashram was built. We began
our ascent on foot, carefully traversing a log bridge to
get to the ashram. The kids loved the bridge, and
couldn't get enough of it. Swamiji welcomed us
warmly, and showed us the great views from the top
of the hill. He pointed out the clinic that he had set up
on the main road at the foot of the hill. The local
population was very grateful to Swamiji, for having
established this clinic with free medicines.

Dr. Agnihotri, the father-in-law of Pandit Rajmani, was staying at Hansda Ashram when we visited,
and he entertained us with inspiring stories of his
association with Swamiji. The issue of Swamiji's
smoking came up for discussion, and Dr. Agnihotri
told us that this habit was responsible for Swamiji
remaining anchored to the body. He told us that if
Swamiji did not smoke, he would end up dropping
his body, because of his total detachment and non-
identification with the physical body.

A simple but tasty lunch of mountain greens was
served, and after lunch we relaxed with Swamiji in
his cottage. Unlike us, the kids were not in awe of
Swamiji, and clambered all over him with great glee.
Swamiji played the role of doting grandfather, and

seemed to be enjoying the kids' games as much as they were. I marveled at Swamiji's ability to be as much at ease with young children as with royalty, ambassadors and politicians. I realized that this came naturally to him, because he saw the One in all and all in the One. We enjoyed hot cups of tea, watching the sun go down, seated in the thatched gazebo of the ashram. It was the perfect end to a perfect day. We returned to Delhi the next day, inspired and contented.

Hansda Ashram, Nepal

Vijaya and
her Mother
with
Swamiji
at Hansda
Ashram

19.
Sadhana

"All sadhanas, all practices, are meant to purify and strengthen the mind that disturbs your being and prevents you from being aware of the Reality that is within you."
Sadhana: The Essence of Spiritual Life

"Without training, *manas* assumes too much power, ignores the *buddhi,* and acts independently, when it is not reliably capable of doing so. Manas is full of conflict within and without. Without the help of purified buddhi, manas is a source of uncertainty and misery. Over time, the actions of manas become habits. This is one reason Indians repeat the famous Gayatri mantra. A portion of the mantra asks the Almighty to enlighten the intellect, which is to say to improve the functioning of the buddhi: *Dhiyo yonah prachodayat.*"
Sacred Journey:
Living Purposefully and Dying Gracefully

I had been initiated into the Gayatri mantra when I was invested with the sacred thread as a teenager. Until then, I had not known about this mantra, as my education had been more western-oriented, rather than steeped in Indian culture and traditions. I went to schools run by Jesuits, so I knew more about the Bible and the parables of Christ than I did about the Bhagavad Gita, *Ramayana* and *Mahabharata.* Yet, once I started doing Gayatri *japa,* I felt a strange kinship with the sounds of the mantra and felt elevated by the japa. I did not understand much about mantras, but had been told that the Gayatri was a mantra of purification and intellectual development.

I was accepted into the Indian Institute of Technology (I.I.T.) in Madras, one of the institutes of higher education in India. As the entrance exam was highly competitive, I found myself in a group of incoming students who were all at the top of their class. I kept up the practice of the Gayatri mantra despite the pressure of studies. Imperceptibly, the practice was helping my intellectual development. In my second year at I.I.T., I made it into the Merit Scholarship list. Also, my new life away from home in a hostel, surrounded by teenagers with raging hormones was unsettling. The Gayatri practice had a calming and purifying influence, and I was less swayed by hormonal influences than my fellow students.

After graduating from I.I.T. in 1967, I accepted a job in Bombay (Mumbai). One day, I saw a poster advertising classes in Transcendental Meditation (T.M.). I enrolled and was initiated into a mantra and taught a basic meditation technique. Bombay was a concrete jungle. Despite the noisy traffic, I would practice meditation in public parks. Soon after my initiation, I was told that the founder of T.M., Maharishi Mahesh Yogi, fresh from his triumph with the Beatles in England, was arriving in Bombay. I was invited to attend his lecture at the T.M. headquarters. After the lecture, a few of us had a personal interaction with the Maharshi. I found him to be a very interesting personality, flower garlands, giggles and all.

I did reach a certain depth of peace with the T.M. practice, but after a few months, I felt that I had hit a plateau. Soon after, in the fall of 1968, I left the shores of India for the U.S. and in that first hectic year of graduate school at the University of Minnesota, my sadhana was put on hold. About a year later, as narrated in Chapter 1, I attended Swami Rama's lecture at Coffman Union in the fall of 1969. I started the raja yoga course with Dr. Arya in the summer of 1970.

Early in 1971, Swamiji directed Dr. Arya to give me mantra initiation, and specified which mantra I should be given. I was initiated by Dr. Arya in the attic of his home. I was very grateful to be linked to the tradition of Himalayan sages through the mantra initiation. Soon thereafter, Swamiji took over as my spiritual teacher. He came to Minneapolis fairly often and held small group classes in Dr. Arya's home. He taught us several spiritual practices such as the tense-relax exercise, the 61 point exercise and mental worship in the heart lotus. During the 61 point instruction, Swamiji looked at the quickly drawn figure in my notes, and remarked humorously to Dr. Arya, "Look, Prakash has created a ghost." Swamiji also taught us the technique of alternate nostril breathing for nadi purification and how to apply sushumna. I have preserved my lecture notes from these early classes with Swamiji, and cherish the memories of those intimate small group sessions. I particularly remember the meditative depth we experienced when he taught us the practice of mental worship in the lotus of the heart.

One evening, I witnessed a scene that has never been repeated to the best of my knowledge. Swamiji allowed Dr. Arya to perform the traditional act of worship or puja offered to him as the deity. Swamiji remained seated impassively in a chair, while Dr. Arya applied vermillion to his forehead, garlanded him with a flower garland and performed the aarti or waving of the light around him. Swamiji's impassive face was like that of a granite statue in a temple's inner sanctum.

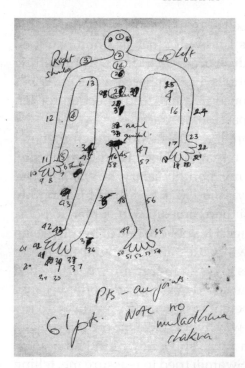

61 point exercise for the ghost created by Prakash

Swami Rama lecturing in Minneapolis

He conducted himself with majestic dignity during the ritual. Knowing as I now do, that Swamiji shunned rituals and often discouraged students from getting too immersed in rituals, his acquiescing to Dr. Arya's puja request, demonstrated his deep affection for Dr. Arya and his compassionate grace.

One day, Swamiji asked me how much money I made as a half-time research assistant at the University. When I mentioned my monthly salary, he was shocked and added that my salary was less than his monthly phone bill. Swamiji then came up with a plan to boost my monthly earnings. He spoke to one of his physician students in the Twin Cities and arranged for me to teach yoga postures to his church group. I was touched by his kind offer, but could not accept the offer because I did not feel competent to teach yoga postures. In my way of thinking, it was hypocritical for me to pose as a yoga teacher when I was still a novice in hatha yoga, the physical yoga. Swamiji tried to reassure me, telling me that the competence would develop once I started teaching, but my faith was limited and I stubbornly declined his offer. Little did I realize that if I had begun to teach, Swamiji would have ensured the rapid honing of my hatha yoga skills. To this day, I regret my lack of faith and stubbornness.

In 1971, Vijaya and I got married in Delhi, and flew to Kashmir for our honeymoon. It was the month of August, when pilgrims make their way to the mountain shrine of Amarnath, to see the naturally formed linga of snow that takes shape every year, in a cave high up in the mountains. We were in Gulmarg, and were surrounded by crowds of joyful pilgrims returning from the Amarnath cave. They were distributing *prasad* (sanctified offering) of halwa from the Amarnath shrine, and we were fortunate to partake of this prasad. We then sat on a grassy knoll near a mountain stream, watching the setting sun. I noticed a bearded *sadhu* with long matted hair, immersed waist-deep in the mountain stream, offering his evening prayers to the setting sun. Suddenly, I was gripped by a very strong feeling of déjà vu, and of intimate familiarity with the scene. I could not explain the feeling and it soon passed.

I got married while I was still a Ph.D. student at the University of Minnesota. Because of my student visa, my wife Vijaya could not take up a regular job, though she did try to supplement our limited income with babysitting. Our paychecks were just enough to cover the rent, utility bills and food expenses. There was little left over for anything else. To make matters worse, I had a used car that was breaking down fairly often, and the repair bills caused me a lot of anxiety. Swamiji was very concerned with our financial difficulties, and did not want my financial worries to hamper our spiritual growth. He asked Vijaya and me to come over to learn a special practice that included *yantra* and mantra; he instructed us to perform this practice for a prescribed period. He told us that with this practice, we would always have enough material resources for our needs, and would never suffer from financial woes. To date, this has been absolutely true, and I ascribe our material comfort to the special practice and Swamiji's boundless grace.

Right from my early days with Swamiji, he would often tell me, "Prakash, do you know I pray for you?" Initially, I did not understand this oft-repeated statement. I interpreted it superficially as Swamiji telling me that he included me in his prayers to the Divine, asking for Divine Grace to guide and protect me. Only later did a different interpretation strike me. When he said he prayed for me, he was telling me that he was performing sadhana on my behalf. He was doing 50 percent (or more) and only the remaining part of the sadhana was my responsibility. It is said that rather than the student looking for the guru, gurus go looking for the students who are ready and meant to be guided by them. It has been written of Shri Ramakrishna, the divine mystic of Bengal, that the faces of his disciples had been revealed to him in mystic visions, but they were yet to arrive at his threshold. He longed for them, and at sunset, he would be found on the terrace of his dwelling, looking out upon the horizon, asking, "Divine Mother, where are my children, why have they not yet come to me?"

Early in my sadhana, Swamiji had given me a practice that involved visualization at one of the chakras (energy centers). I was struggling with the visualization, having a difficult time trying to decide whether I should view the chakra from above or from the front or from behind. I asked Swamiji about this when I visited him in Chicago. He curtly dismissed my question, telling me that if I had such doubts, I just did not get it. Rather than totally identifying with the visualized image, I had created a mental distance, a mentally-created space, which was leading to the confusion and questions of visual perspective!

I was visiting Swamiji in Glenview and that night, Swamiji allowed me to be with him in his room until almost 2:00 a.m. He then asked me to leave, as I had an early morning flight to Minneapolis. After about three hours of sleep, I was making my bleary way to the bathroom, when I passed Swamiji in the hallway. Swamiji had been up all night, and I could not help exclaiming at how fresh he looked, despite the lack of sleep. Swamiji responded simply, "Prakash, sleep is just a concept." I was struck by the profundity of his simple remark. However, I am still in the powerful grip of this concept.

In one of the early classes that Swamiji taught in Minneapolis, he once asked the class which earthly pleasure was the highest. Without any hesitation, both Dr. Arya and I blurted out that sleep was the highest pleasure. Swamiji smiled approvingly at our answer. In deep sleep, one experiences, though unconsciously, the sheath of bliss, anandamaya kosha. When one wakes up, one remembers the bliss experienced in deep sleep.

I once asked Swamiji about his being awake all night, and he told me that he spent much of the time clearing the garbage that his disciples put into their conscious minds. He told me that it took him about eight minutes to clear a month's garbage! On another occasion, he told me that from a distance, he could change the hand *mudra* of the disciple in meditation, if the mudra was incorrect. He also said he could deliver 'messages, bangings and beatings' from a distance.

Another special practice that Swamiji had me do in the early days required a small, polished wooden plank whose dimensions had to be exactly as Swamiji prescribed. Fortunately, a young 'hippie' craftsman had opened a small carpentry shop near our apartment on University Avenue, and he prepared the wooden plank at a cost I could well afford. Another practice I was given around that time required a lot of flowers. I was at a loss considering the prices at the neighborhood florist. Looking through the yellow pages, I found a wholesale florist in downtown Minneapolis, who offered me flowers without stems at an extremely reasonable price, allowing me to complete the practice without having to rob a bank!

Swamiji was invited to present an open air lecture in Minnetonka, one of the western suburbs of Minneapolis, arranged by Dorothy Hale, one of Swamiji's students. The weather was perfect, and it was a beautiful setting for a beautiful lecture. At the end, Swamiji allowed some time for questions. A middle-aged lady, probably of Indian origin, stood up, and without any hesitation asked Swamiji if he had realized the Self. Swamiji told her that if he said, "Yes," he would be considered arrogant and if he replied, "No," he would be lying. So, he concluded, "Let me just say that wherever I look, I see only God." This thrilling response sent shivers down my spine.

Swamiji had given me a *rudraksha mala* with beautiful small beads. I had used it for a few years, when it suddenly broke. I gathered up the beads and was quite upset at having broken the mala. The next time I visited Swamiji in Chicago, I mentioned the broken mala. He took the broken mala from me, and the next morning he returned the repaired mala to me. I was very thankful, but when he told me that one of the ashramites had spent the entire night re-stringing the mala, I felt very perturbed for having given so much trouble to this ashramite. The mala broke again a few years later. I happened to be in Honesdale, and decided to do the re-stringing myself. Swamiji had once mentioned that these rudraksha malas were made by certain families in Rishikesh, who undergo a rite of purification before stringing a mala, and also repeat a purifying mantra with each knot of the mala. I locked myself in my room for a few hours, and did the mala re-stringing using my guru mantra with each knot that I tied to hold the bead in place.

A couple of years later, Swamiji instructed me in a practice of manasa puja (mental worship) offered in the temple of the heart. Quite often, when offering this mental worship, I would see myself, in my mind's eye, as a bearded rishi-like figure with matted hair offering worship to various temple deities. When I asked Swamiji about this experience, he confirmed that memories of a past life were bubbling up from the unconscious mind into the conscious mind, being evoked by this practice. He added that I had fallen spiritually, and that was why he was being so strict with me now. This conversation helped me understand the sudden strong feeling I had experienced, while on our honeymoon in Kashmir, watching the sadhu in the mountain stream.

One day, my friend Howard Judt called to ask me if I would be able to host his guest, an astrologer from Bangalore, who was having trouble with the bland American diet. I agreed to host Mr. Shastri. *Shastriji* was an engineer by training, but he came from a long line of astrologers who had been trained in the interpretation of a particular astrological manuscript called the *Shuka Nadi.* This manuscript, in traditional leaf format, had been in the family for many generations. When his father was on his deathbed, Shastriji had promised his father to continue the family's astrological tradition.

Shastriji stayed with us for about a week, and did astrological readings for many clients who came to our home for their readings. At the end of his stay, he said that he would like to repay us for our hospitality, by doing a reading for me and my wife. He asked us for some basic data related to our birthdates and parentage, and found the page in the manuscript pertaining to us. In doing our reading, he made the significant remark that the influence of Jupiter (guru) was very great in our horoscopes, influencing longevity, our marriage, and career. He said that our destiny had been re-worked by the influence of the guru. We had not told Shastriji much about Swami Rama, our guru, and were amazed to hear his remarks.

In the early 1980s, Swamiji instructed Pandit Rajmani in Honesdale, to send me written details of a

fairly involved practice, which required me to memor-
ize several pages of Sanskrit mantras. I had never
studied Sanskrit, and the task of memorizing so many
mantras was very daunting; and my heart sank at the
task. Technology finally came to my rescue. I recorded
the entire practice on an audio cassette, and started
the practice with headphones on, mentally repeating
the mantras along with the recording. A few weeks
later, I was able to divest myself of the headphones
and was able to do the practice with memorized
mantras.

Although the audio cassette approach worked
with this practice, there were many other occasions
when I experienced strange failures. I tried recording
Swamiji's instructions for spiritual practices, but there
would often be only static noise on the recording. Once,
I was determined to succeed, by taking all necessary
precautions. I went into Honesdale to buy a new, high
quality cassette; I borrowed a good cassette recorder
from one of the Institute residents. Before the appointment, I set up the system in the room where we
were to see Swamiji, and successfully tested the set-
up. Inspite of these precautions, I did not succeed in
recording Swamiji's instructions. When I asked
Swamiji about it, he shrugged his shoulders, and said
that such things happened with others as well,
implying that the sages of the tradition were not in
favor of such recordings, as the tradition was an oral
tradition. Once I did succeed in recording Swamiji's
instructions, and took the prized cassette home to
Minneapolis. A few days later, my mother-in-law
mistook the cassette for a blank one, and recorded some
music over Swamiji's instructions!

About 10 years after I had been initiated into the
Himalayan tradition, Swamiji asked me and Vijaya to
undertake a purascharana (purificatory practice) of the

Gayatri mantra. Being mindful of the demands of career and family, Swamiji only prescribed a laghu (light) purascharana, which required us to complete 125,000 repetitions of the mantra. Swamiji instructed us on the 24 syllables of the mantra and the requirements of the practice. He asked us to inform him when the prescribed number had been accomplished.

It took us several months to complete the prescribed number of mantra repetitions. Initially, we were aware of the individual syllables of the mantra, and each mala of 108 repetitions took several minutes. As we continued the practice, our awareness was less on the sounds of the mantra, and more on the vibrations of the mantra. We were aware of the mantra being repeated, without conscious awareness of individual syllables. The time it took for a mala had become a lot shorter than when we started.

It was sometimes difficult to get hold of Swamiji on the phone, even when he was visiting Minneapolis. When we completed the Gayatri practice, Swamiji was in Japan. We got Swamiji's phone number in Japan from Kamal, and in spite of language barriers, we were able to contact Swamiji in Japan. He was very pleased to hear that we had successfully completed the practice. He told us that the traditional way to complete the practice was to perform a homa (fire ritual) and to make offerings of sacred herbs into the fire with each repetition of the Gayatri, with a certain prescribed number of repetitions. He told us to contact Dr. Arya, who had been brought up in the priestly tradition to help us conduct the homa successfully.

Dr. Arya kindly agreed to come home and help us perform the fire ritual as traditionally prescribed. Before starting the fire ritual, we invoked the blessings of the elephant-headed god Ganesha, the remover of all obstacles. We also invoked the blessings of the guru. An oil-fed lamp with a cotton wick was lit during the invocation. I missed Swamiji's physical presence at the ritual. Suddenly a strange thought entered my mind. I felt that Swamiji was present, in subtle form, as the light from the oil lamp, and I told myself that this would be borne out to be true, if the lamp stayed lit throughout the ritual, without the oil being replenished. The ritual took several hours, and I kept glancing nervously at the oil lamp. I was amazed and overjoyed to observe that the lamp stayed lit throughout the ritual. I thanked Swamiji with all my heart for having, so kindly, been present to bless the completion of the Gayatri purascharana.

I think that it was in 1993, the last time we were visiting Honesdale during Swamiji's lifetime; Vijaya and I got a call telling us that Swamiji wanted us to meet him at 10:00 p.m, and that we should bathe and change into fresh clothes before coming. We did as instructed. Usually, Swamiji gave us spiritual instructions downstairs in Room 6, but this time, we were ushered into Swamiji's upstairs apartment. Swamiji was reclining on his couch, and seemed quite excited about the practice he was going to give us. He confided that he had received permission from his master to give us the practice, and added that he got a tingling sensation in his spine, when his master communicated with him. We were thrilled to hear this. The practice he gave us was simpler than previous techniques. Swamiji told us that this would be our practice for many years to come. He also said that we would not be able to sit in meditation very long, only about 20–25 minutes, because of the subtlety of the technique. From Swamiji's excitement and instructions, it almost seemed that we had reached the culmination of the spiritual journey. However, we are still on the path, still striving to progress spiritually.

20.
Other Encounters with Swamiji

"Technically, the word vairagya means control over desires. As Buddha explained, desires are the cause of suffering in the world. Buddha meant desires in a broader sense of attachment as well. Desires hook and attach people to things and to others, making them dependent and defining the meaning of life. Suffering is the only result. Therefore, to rise above suffering, according to the Buddha, rise above desires. To rise above desires sounds impossible, or not even healthy or human, but it is possible to control and transcend desires."

Sacred Journey:
Living Purposefully and Dying Gracefully

"*Shaktipata* is only possible with a disciple who has gone through a long period of discipline, austerity and spiritual practices. Shaktipata on a mass scale seems suspicious to me. It is true that when the disciple is ready, the master appears and gives the appropriate initiation. When a student has done his sadhana with all faithfulness, truthfulness, and sincerity, then the subtlest obstacle is removed by the master. Those who do not believe in discipline should not expect enlightenment. No master can or will give it to them just because they want it."

Sadhana: The Essence of Spiritual Life

In the early days of Swamiji's stay in the U.S., he used to spend equal periods of time in the U.S. and

India. Once he established the Himalayan International Institute of Yoga Science and Philosophy and relocated it from Chicago to Honesdale, he spent about eight months of the year in the U.S., and only the winter months in India.

Swamiji had found a great property in Pennsylvania, near the town of Honesdale, to relocate the headquarters of the Himalayan International Institute. Funds were required to acquire this property. The Meditation Center in Minneapolis decided to arrange a $100 a plate dinner, hosted by Swamiji, to raise funds. The dinner was arranged near downtown Minneapolis, and Swamiji spoke before dinner was served. He told us about the project and the property and thanked all who had come for their generosity. One part of the talk that stuck in my mind was Swamiji saying that when one gives for a good cause, the giver is benefited more than the one who receives, because by giving, one is loosening the bonds of attachment that bind us all. He went on to add that the giver should be beholden to the one who receives, because of the opportunity provided for cultivating detachment. He also told us that if the fist were closed, there would be no flow of affluence, which required an open palm. It was indeed a unique perspective on giving. During the dinner, Swamiji, the gracious host, went from table to table, thanking each one individually for their generosity. It was a memorable occasion for me.

As described by Justin O'Brien in his book, *Walking with a Himalayan Master*, Swamiji had also conducted a marathon fund raising effort from coast to coast, by telephoning potential donors. We had been privileged to receive such a phone call too, and we were touched when Swamiji told us, over the phone, that he was approaching us with his begging bowl for a donation. For a great Himalayan yogi to have to do this saddened us. We asked Swamiji to name the amount he wanted us to contribute, and with his graciousness, he named an amount that we could contribute without mortgaging our house!

On our first visit to Honesdale, Swamiji instructed Mrs. Judt, who was the Chairperson of the Institute, to greet us personally and provide us with a really nice suite-like accommodation on the ground floor, near Swamiji's apartment, replete with flowers, a bowl of nuts and other amenities. I was very moved by Swamiji's gracious hospitality and his taking care of even minute details. Applying his philosophy to the situation, I was beholden to Swamiji and the Institute for helping loosen my attachment to material possessions.

In the 1980s and early 1990s, we tried to visit Swamiji at Honesdale once or twice a year, and also got a chance to see him when he visited Minneapolis. We also tried to catch his lectures and seminars in Madison, Milwaukee, Green Lake and Chicago. The Green Lake retreat was one of our favorites, as the group was small and intimate. I also got a chance to play tennis with Swamiji. I tried to inaugurate my very first video camera by recording Swamiji's lecture at one of the Green Lake retreats. I got permission from Nina Johnson to video record the lecture. Unfortunately, not knowing how long the battery would last, I ended up with only about half the lecture on video tape. It was also at a Green Lake Retreat in 1981, that Swamiji told us that he was leaving the U.S. never to return. We were all choked up, with tears streaming down our cheeks. We cursed ourselves for not having utilized our time with Swamiji better; the future without Swamiji was very bleak. Fortunately for us, Swamiji's life span was extended by his guru and he returned to our midst.

On one of my early Honesdale visits, I suddenly realized that I had never made the traditional offering of a bundle of twigs to the guru. The twigs symbolize one's accumulated karmas, and the offering symbolizes one's surrender to the guru, requesting him to take charge of your life and help burn your karmas in the fire of his *tapas*, thus clearing the way for your spiritual advancement. It did not take long to collect a bundle of twigs, given the wooded ambience of the Honesdale campus. Swamiji was visibly pleased with the offering, and I was overjoyed by his acceptance of the bundle of twigs, because it indicated his acceptance of me as a disciple. This was very significant, because on a few occasions, he had publicly declared in his lectures that he had many students, but very few disciples. Once he even said that he had only four disciples, and people were immediately trying to identify the four. When I approached him after the lecture and expressed my sadness at his having accepted so few disciples, he teased me by asking why I did not count myself amongst the four. With no attempt at modesty, I had to confess that I was not worthy, and that there were others more deserving, if he had only four disciples. A few days after the offering of twigs, I asked Swamiji about the offering, and he said that he had burnt them. I couldn't help asking, "All of them?" referring to all the twigs. Swamiji preferred to interpret the question as all my karmas, and he exclaimed, "Bapurey bap (Oh my Lord or Oh my gosh!), you want me to burn all your karmas?"

Though I had learnt some of the basic hatha yoga postures and had my routine, I never considered myself to be much into physical yoga and preferred to spend my time in meditation. Once, in Honesdale, Swamiji was demonstrating some postures on stage, when he suddenly summoned me up on stage to demonstrate some of the meditative postures. I was taken aback, realizing that more experienced teachers were in the audience. However, I did go up on stage and demonstrated two postures used for meditation — *siddhasana* and *swastikasana*. I made a subtle mistake during my demonstration, which I knew Swamiji had noticed, but probably not any of the others. To my considerable relief, Swamiji did not publicly pull me up and I got away with it! To my surprise, for many days after that demonstration, other students were coming up to me, asking me to check their postures. I was truly humbled.

Both Vijaya and I had been exposed to Indian classical music from an early age. In Minnesota, we sorely missed not being able to hear the Indian artistes who visited the U.S. and performed in larger cities like Chicago and New York. Some like-minded friends joined me in helping found the Indian Music Society of Minnesota. Not being able to afford lawyer's fees, we did all the work related to incorporation and tax exemption. We also applied for grants from local arts councils for seed money. As there were only a few volunteers to start with, we had to do a lot of work including picking up the musicians from the airport, hosting them, doing the required publicity, selling tickets, and recording the music. I once asked Swamiji if this was time well spent, and he encouraged us to continue our service to the community through sponsoring music concerts.

A famous North Indian musician, Pandit Jasraj, performed in Minnesota through the sponsorship of the Indian Music Society of Minnesota. When I told Swamiji about Pandit Jasraj's fantastic concert in Minnesota, he was excited and wanted me to arrange Pandit Jasraj's concert in Honesdale. It was a privilege to make the arrangements, and Swamiji thoroughly enjoyed hosting Pandit Jasraj, whom he had known well in India.

I was on my way to India, and the first leg of the journey was from Minneapolis to New York. Before boarding the transatlantic flight to London, I was waiting in one of the lounges at J.F.K. airport. To my great joy, Swamiji entered the lounge, and I realized that we were both on the same flight to India. When we reached London, Swamiji wondered if we could get a cup of tea while we waited for the onward flight to New Delhi. I gladly jumped up and made my way to one of the tea shops of the transit lounge. Unlike the U.S., where tea is served in a paper cup with a tea bag steeping in the hot water, tea service in England is a very cultured affair. The tea tray I brought back had a nice ceramic pot of hot tea, matching creamer and sugar bowls, and two china cups and saucers. Swamiji was pleasantly surprised to see all this paraphernalia, and remarked that all he had asked for was a cup of tea!

On the flight, Swamiji and I were in different sections. As the flight was approaching Delhi, Swamiji came back to where I was sitting, gave me his passport, and asked me to fill in his arrival and customs declaration card. I was happy to oblige. When I opened up his passport, I was surprised to see that it was issued in the name of Brij Kishore Sharma, Swamiji's given name. Under occupation, the passport tersely stated 'Saint'! The year of birth was 1925, but I learnt later that that was not the true year of his birth, but a date that had been made up by whoever went to the passport office to apply for Swamiji's passport.

When we reached Delhi, Swamiji had no trouble getting past immigration and customs. Before he left the airport, he gave me the address and phone number of his new apartment in Delhi, 704 Sarva Priya Apartments, Sarva Priya Vihar. Sarva Priya Vihar means the Abode of One Beloved by All. I was struck by how apt an address Swamiji had chosen. I left for my sister's home in a northwestern suburb of Delhi.

A few days later, I made my way from my sister's home to Sarva Priya Vihar in an autorickshaw, a three-wheeled vehicle powered by a motorcycle engine. It was a very long ride through the hot, dusty streets of Delhi. After asking around for directions, I found myself at Sarva Priya Vihar, and was happy to find Swamiji at home. As it was a hot day, Swamiji asked me to join him in his bedroom which was air-conditioned with a window unit. The room had a mattress placed on the floor, and Swamiji stretched out on the mattress. I admired his pink flushed feet which I had always considered to be so beautiful and worthy of worship. A sudden thought entered my mind: it would be so nice to be able to massage Swamiji's feet. Swamiji immediately stretched his feet towards me and asked me to massage his feet. I was thrilled to be afforded this privilege. Swamiji was a most gracious host and invited me to have lunch at his apartment before I went back to my sister's place.

Once, I was walking with Swamiji in Honesdale, and he stopped often to greet other visitors. He asked them about their spouses and children, often by name. I was amazed by these feats of memory, and expressed my amazement to Swamiji. Swamiji flatly declared that this was nothing. There was a time when the minute he saw someone, their past, present and future came up before his eyes. This proved to be too much of a distraction, so Swamiji deliberately turned off an inner switch to confine himself to the present life!

Swamiji often told us that things of the world were meant for us to enjoy, but that we should never make the mistake of thinking that they belonged to us, and we should avoid getting attached to them. Swamiji would give the example of how we enjoyed the use of towels and bed linens in a hotel room, but did not take them along with us, when we checked out of the room. He would tell us that we had come to this platform of worldly life for a short time, and should not have any regrets when it was time to move on. In another lecture, Swamiji gave the example of people taking home amenities like soaps and shampoos offered to hotel guests. I felt uncomfortable hearing this, and wondered if this was a message meant especially for me. I traveled a fair amount in my job at Baxter Healthcare, and stayed in hotels that offered such amenities. I had never thought it was wrong to take home some of these amenities. After Swamiji's lecture, I found an opportunity to discuss this issue with him. I tried to justify my actions, telling him that these amenities were included in the room rate, and so taking something home that one had paid for was not stealing. Swamiji quietly told me that he was not talking about stealing but about attachment. I was initially taken aback, but soon realized that he was right, especially when I noticed the collection of soaps and shampoos that had built up in my closet.

Often in Swamiji's lectures, after describing a practice, he would say that a good student could perfect the practice in a month, a middling student would need three months and even a poor student could accomplish this in a year. This may have been meant to inspire us but it often had the opposite effect on me. Swamiji had dangled the carrot of giving me the touch for many, many years, especially after every new practice he gave me. The tape at the finish line was constantly being yanked further down the track. First, I had to wait until I got married, then I had to finish my post graduate studies, after that I had to wait until the kids were older. I reached the end of my tether. On a visit to Honesdale, I told Swamiji that he was just leading me on. I argued with him and demanded that he give me the touch. After many attempts at dissuading me, Swamiji with some visible anger, ordered me to sit down before him. Seeing that he was angry, I wondered if getting the touch this way was worthwhile. I decided not to push it, and told Swamiji that I would wait until he thought I was ready. Swamiji seemed visibly relieved. He appeased me by telling me that he wanted me to experience the struggles and joys of walking the path on my own, rather than taking me to the end of the journey through the power of his touch.

If memory serves me right, I think that it was on this same visit to Honesdale that Swamiji unrolled a deer skin and gave it to me to use on my meditation seat. I was thrilled to receive this gift, especially when he told me that his guru, Bengali Baba, had sat on the deer skin. I reverently accepted it, but could not bring myself to sit on it, considering myself unworthy of sitting on it. I kept it by me when I meditated and when I slept. I was worshipping it rather than using it. I finally did start using it on my meditation seat, telling myself that I needed all the help that I could muster.

A few years back, I had a very vivid dream, in which Swamiji placed his hand upon my head. I immediately experienced a strong surge of energy rising upwards to the top of my head. Almost immediately, I discovered that the whole riddle of life had become very clear to me. I had cracked the code and it all seemed so obvious. There were no more questions. Unfortunately, when I woke up, I remembered the dream, but little else. The questions were all still there!

Swamiji visits our Plymouth home

Visiting Swamiji at Honesdale

21.
Swamiji Graces Our New Home

"A person walking on the path of self-transformation should be aware of the dangers of egoism. Even while practicing the great virtues of truthfulness and non-violence, a person can feed the ego. The ego related to the realm of spirituality is more subtle and injurious than the ego related to one's worldly success.

"A human being is miserable if he fails to unfold and use his inner potentials. In order to unfold his inner potentials, he must purify the ego or surrender it to the higher Reality. After renouncing slavery to the ego, he can emerge from the confines of body, senses, and mind."

Sadhana: The Essence of Spiritual Life

Over the years, we were fortunate to have had Swamiji visit all of the homes we lived in, even the humble rented apartment we occupied when I was still a student. In 1982, we bought a very nice home in Plymouth, a western suburb of Minneapolis. The home was across from a very small lake, aptly called Lost Lake. We had waited a few years for Swamiji to come and bless this new home, and he did in May, 1985.

Swamiji had recently had extensive oral surgery. He told us that every time he spoke, his tongue hit the roof of his mouth, causing him great pain. I was very touched that he had come to bless our home and counsel us, in spite of his pain. He told us that on his last visit to Minneapolis, he was aware that we were disappointed by his not visiting us. He told us that on that occasion, his mouth was sore, his face was swollen and he was unable to talk. This was why he did not visit us, knowing, as he did, that we wanted his guidance and teachings. I had experienced confusion and negativity when Swamiji did not come, thinking that he had become distant, and did not have the same feelings of affection for us as before. The thought of his pain, and my self-centered feelings, made me very ashamed of my selfishness and unreasonable ex-pectations. Swamiji acknowledged that he was aware of my feelings, and said that he knew how I felt because he had, at one time, experienced similar feelings towards his guru. That statement made a great impression on me, and made me feel a little less small for entertaining such negative feelings. I, however, realized that these negative feelings were damaging to my mind and sadhana.

I confided to Swamiji that my sadhana had become mechanical and meaningless. I felt that I was not making much progress. Swamiji told me that I was aware only of what was happening at the conscious level. That was not where the changes were taking place. He told me, by way of analogy, that I was aware only of the money in my hand, and was neglecting the deposits being made into my bank account. He told me, that my being too intent on having experiences in my meditation, was an obstacle to my sadhana. I told Swamiji that my hankering for meditational ex-periences was diminishing, and that I was now seeking tranquility, more than experiences. However, I did indicate the need for milestones, to give me some measure of my progress in sadhana. Swamiji said that the best milestone or measure was for me to stop meditating for a while, and to then observe how I fared. That would open my eyes to the value of my sadhana.

I did remark that I tried not to pray for anything or ask for things in prayer. He replied that when the reservoir was flooded and overflowing, was there need for more water? I had been blessed with so much. Why was I so discontent?

Swamiji remarked that of all of his students, I was one of the more obstinate. He said that his Gurudeva had told him that he had many obstinate students, and of these, there were three or four who were extremely obstinate. Swamiji mentioned that his Gurudeva had named me as one of these extremely obstinate students. Hearing this, I was overcome by conflicting emotions. On the one hand, I was thrilled that his Gurudeva was even aware of my existence, let alone my obstinacy. On the other hand, I wondered about the significance of the statement related to my sadhana.

Swamiji told me that I should look upon the time of sadhana as a sacred time, set aside from all worldly endeavors, a time I should selflessly dedicate to the tradition of sages and gurus. This time and effort were not my own, but had to be offered up as a sacrifice, with detachment. Swamiji said that he himself had not slept at night for the last 32 years, and had dedicated this time at night for such a sacrifice, and for unworldly endeavors. Swamiji advised me that if I cultivated this attitude, it would prevent me from being anxious about progress, results and experiences, for the efforts were not mine and should not be dedicated for my own welfare.

Swamiji indicated that he had wanted to give me the touch, but had refrained from doing so, because I was living in the world, and had technical knowledge. He felt that the power might be subject to misuse. He decided, instead, to allow me to experience the pains, the joys and the frustrations of my undertaking the journey. He said that he wanted to guide me systematically, and had many exercises that he wanted to teach me.

Swamiji had a meal with us, and this was a mark of his graciousness, because he went through the effort in spite of the obvious pain. He went around the house and remarked that it was very nice and right for us. I wanted to show Swamiji our meditation room, a walk-in closet, that we had converted into a meditation room. Swamiji told me that he knew our meditation room and did not need to see it! Swamiji also walked around the garden, and advised us on how to prune, water and care for the trees and shrubs. He asked us to plant some more flowering trees and shrubs in the backyard. He advised me not to change homes, and said that this should be our last home.

He phoned Honesdale for some homeopathic medicine for the kids, and advised us all to have regular medical check-ups. Swamiji advised us not to become 'dollar nuts.' Swamiji told Vijaya to only work on a part time basis. He felt that the kids deserved a lot of attention, and told us to be more selfless in looking after the kids and adjusting with each other. He warned me not to go on ego trips and blame Vijaya for my own faults.

We were overwhelmed by Swamiji's kindness, and the significant teachings he had given us. Our home was truly blessed by his visit. We lived in that home for 18 happy years, until we left Minnesota for the Himalayan Institute Hospital Trust in India.

22.
Pulverizing the Ego

"The relationship with the guru is based on the purest form of unconditional love. There is complete openness with the guru. The disciple should hold nothing back from the guru. This is why in the tradition, a student goes to the guru and offers a bundle of sticks to burn. The bundle symbolizes that everything the disciple has is offered unconditionally to the guru. Everything is offered to the guru so the guru can do the work of shaping the student spiritually. The disciple comes with full faith and entrusts his whole life to the guru. The guru takes that life and chops it and burns what is not necessary, and then carefully carves what remains into something sacred.

"In this chopping and burning, the guru is merciless. The guru's job is not to hold hands with the disciple and wipe away tears, but to cut into pieces the disciple's ego and all that stands between the disciple and freedom. The guru does not allow dependence. If the disciple becomes too dependent on the guru, the guru pushes the disciple away, insisting on independence. It is a remarkable expression of the deepest love."

Sacred Journey:
Living Purposefully and Dying Gracefully

The process started gently enough when Swamiji graced our Plymouth home for the first time. Swamiji had acknowledged that he was aware of my negative feelings, but had softened the blow by saying that he had at one time, experienced similar feelings towards his guru. That admission made me feel a little less ashamed for entertaining such negative feelings.

The next step was not as gentle. Vijaya, the kids, and I went to Honesdale that same year (1985) to attend the Annual Congress of the Institute. On the last day of the Congress, Swamiji asked me in to see him. As I sat waiting for him, I was overcome by all the negativity I was experiencing in my relationships with people—at home, at work and socially. I do not cry easily, but for some strange reason, rising emotions made me choke up with tears. I felt that only the grace of Swamiji could pull me out of this mire of delusion. I washed my face, hands and feet, and waited for Swamiji.

Swamiji came into the room and told me that I was doing my sadhana all wrong. He said that I was not punctual in keeping the assigned time for my morning meditation. Being an engineer by training, I was aware that all measurements had a certain range of error tolerance. In my case, I had decided that the assigned time plus or minus five minutes, was within the allowed tolerance. Swamiji reprimanded me for this lackadaisical attitude, and told me that I should go strictly by the clock, not by approximate time. He told me that when I did not appear at my meditation seat on time, I was keeping the sages of the tradition waiting, and this was not appropriate. I felt truly ashamed, not having realized the significance of adhering strictly to the meditation time.

Then Swamiji told me that I was not keeping my head, neck and trunk erect, and was bending forward. I had heard Swamiji emphasize the importance of keeping head, neck and trunk aligned, for almost 15 years. However, I acknowledged that I was unable to maintain the correct posture, and asked Swamiji if this was a physical problem with my spine. He said that it was not a physical problem, but a spiritual problem, related to past samskaras! He indicated that I had reached a sort of block, and that he was going to work with me and help me get over it. He advised me to make a contoured back rest, against which I could rest my head during meditation.

I then told Swamiji about negative emotions like anger, frustration and envy that had become more apparent in the last year or two. Swamiji said that these were not of recent origin. He had always been aware of them, and this negativity was a big problem for me. He said that the negativity came in the way of my relationships with him, with my parents, with my wife and kids and with people at work. Swamiji said all this as a statement of fact, without any manner of condemnation. Coming from anyone else, I would have perceived the statement as condemnatory, and my defenses would have been aroused. His way of stating it only revealed the magnitude of the problem, and his awareness of it.

Swamiji told me that he had long been aware of the negative thoughts I had towards him, and that had sometimes hurt him. He quickly added that more than the hurt, he felt sad at my attitude. He emphasized that he expected nothing from me — no money, no gifts or material objects, no favors. His was a selfless relationship, devoid of expectation. He was trying to introduce me to the long line of sages of our tradition, to link me up with this ancient tradition. He was satisfied with the fact that he was selflessly fulfilling this duty, even though I sometimes felt the absence of overt love and guidance. He told me that he was anxious to lead me to the state of samadhi, but that I was impatient for quick results and experiences. He wanted to teach me a lot, provided I was ready.

He then asked me to describe the details of how I practiced my sadhana. He corrected the sequence of practices, pointing out that some practices like the 61 point exercise, should be done at other times, rather than along with the meditation practice. He also stressed that the mantra should not be consciously repeated, but that I should be able to listen to its subtle sounds with *ajapa japa*. *Nada* would lead the mind to higher states. He said that mantra awareness would also guide one in the transition from life to death. Swamiji reoriented my sadhana practice, and asked me to continue with this practice for the next month or two. He said that he wanted to teach me seven or eight more exercises, and asked me to make arrangements to come back to Honesdale, around the middle of the next month, for a period of 10 days. He said that I would be provided with a room that had an attached bathroom to facilitate the practice. He said that he would spend time with me at night during this period, guiding my sadhana, teaching me new approaches, discussing problems and philosophic concepts. He said that I had some misconceptions regarding philosophy that he would rectify. He also indicated that the new exercises would take care of some health problems as well.

I came away reassured of his love and guidance, and with the hope that I could transcend the negativity, through the new disciplines he would prescribe for me. I made arrangements with Kamal for my stay. She asked me to call before I came, to make sure that Swamiji's plans had not changed.

We were all invited to lunch with Swamiji. It was a very nice lunch, except that Swamiji did not make a personal appearance! As we had to leave for our flight soon after lunch, we hoped that we would be able to bid Swamiji good-bye and receive his blessings. Swamiji had once told us that if three or more people concentrated their minds on him, he would be present. The kids and I decided to test our concentration. We were on the verge of disappointment, as the time for our departure was fast approaching, when suddenly, Swamiji appeared to bid us good-bye. The kids and I were overjoyed. Vijaya, however, became tearful, at the thought of leaving. Swamiji told her that he had adopted her as his daughter, and that it pained him to see her cry. As a father, he too felt bad about the parting. We had to drive away, however, as fast as we reasonably could, to reach Scranton in time for our flight to Minneapolis.

Soon after our return from the Annual Congress at Honesdale, I had three dreams, all on the same night:

In the first dream, I had walked and walked, and was now on the last leg of the long journey. My feet were all bandaged up and sore. I was asked to remove the bandages before completing the last leg of the journey. The bandages were closely adhered to the skin, and the skin had almost grown into the fabric of the bandage. I experienced great pain as the bandages were slowly peeled away. In thinking about the symbolism of the dream, I wondered if the bandages were symbolic of the ego, and the pain I had felt when Swamiji peeled away the layers of ego with his blunt words. At least it was comforting to believe that I was on the last leg of the journey!

In the second dream, Vijaya and I were told that we had to provide hospitality to a visitor. We were anxious to meet him and honor him. (Subconsciously, I may have remembered the debacle with another visitor, Swami Ramtheertha!) Great was our happiness in recognizing the visitor as Swami Satchidananda, disciple of Swami Shivananda. For many years, I had longed to be a host to him, and was thrilled at the prospect. I gave thanks in my heart to my guru, Swami Rama, for having sent us this distinguished guest. I had enjoyed Swami Satchidananda's lectures at the Annual Congresses as well as in Minneapolis. He had a wonderful way with words and a great sense of humor. I had also enjoyed a book about him called, *The Master's Touch*. Though I never got the chance to host him in real life, we did visit Swami Satchidananda's ashram in Yogaville, Virginia, many years later, and enjoyed our time with him.

In the third dream that I had the same night, I saw three or four sages seated in meditation. I recognized one of them as *Sant* Keshavdas, from the Temple of Cosmic Religion in California. (Sant Keshavdas had graced our home annually for several years, regaling us with his wonderful humor, melodious kirtans and inspiring *Harikathas*). I did not recognize the other sages. They were seated at different levels. I approached each one in turn and prostrated before them, and they, in turn, acknowledged my greetings. When I prostrated before the sage seated to the right of Sant Keshavadas, he pressed his hands to my head and gripped my head really hard. I felt a tremendous surge of vibrating energy emanating from his hands and passing through my head, permeating my entire frame. It was a very vivid experience. Was this the 'touch' that Swamiji always dangled tantalizingly before me in order to inspire me in my sadhana?

About a month later, I was back in Honesdale for the 10-day retreat with Swamiji. I arrived around 6:30 in the evening, and left word with Kamal to let Swamiji know that I had arrived. I was given a comfortable room with an attached bathroom, as Swamiji had promised earlier. I waited in my room for a call from

Swamiji, reading Swamiji's commentary on the Bhagavad Gita.

The next morning, I again approached Kamal, but there was no word from Swamiji. Soon after lunch, I encountered Swamiji in the hallway near the reception. He informed me that he would see me at 4:00 that afternoon. As narrated in an earlier chapter, I had to return the car that I had rented at Newark airport to Scranton. I was late for the appointment. Swamiji had discerned my disrespectful thoughts about him always making me wait, and had sarcastically reprimanded me for entertaining such thoughts. I was stunned and speechless. Swamiji spent a short while with me asking about Vijaya and the kids. As always, he reminded me not to go on ego trips in my dealings with Vijaya and the kids. I tried to defend myself, but Swamiji was not too convinced. He dismissed me, promising to see me that night.

That evening Swamiji played tennis and I went to watch. After he had played for a while, he asked me to take his place and gave me his racquet to use. The racquet was excellent and I enjoyed playing with it. Swamiji asked me how I liked the racquet and then remarked that I was playing well. Later, Shanta knocked on my door with the message that Swamiji would see me at 10:00 that night. Reviewing the conversation with Swamiji that afternoon, I felt very penitent about my having made Swamiji wait, and wrote a note addressed to him, apologizing for my behavior and praying for continued guidance and grace. I folded the note, and kept it in my shirt pocket, close to my heart, when I went to see him that night. He did not make me wait and saw me promptly at 10:00 p.m.! He appeared tired, but still took the time to teach me some new spiritual exercises. I was asked to do these exercises three times a day. The timings were such that I would miss dinner every day. He asked me to start the practice right away that night, and promised to see me again the next morning. I felt very calm doing the practice, but experienced great pain in my hips and lower back when I came out of it. I went to bed, peaceful and happy at the prospect of a new phase of my sadhana.

The next morning after doing the new practice, having breakfast and finishing my walk, I went to see Swamiji. He came out of his room briefly and said that he would see me at 10:00 that night. Virat came to my room that night, and said that Swamiji was waiting for us. I found myself as part of a small group that included Virat, Vimal, Leroy and me. Swamiji started to teach us about application of sushumna. He told us that proper application of sushumna results in the breath flowing equally through both nostrils, thus energizing both *ida* and *pingala* nadis. This, in turn, causes the central nadi sushumna to open up, allowing the sleeping serpent power kundalini to rise upwards to higher chakras, creating great bliss. An open sushumna creates sukha mana or blissful mind. Swamiji proceeded to demonstrate sushumna application, and asked me to check his pulse during the demonstration. I felt his pulse becoming fainter and fainter and being finally obliterated. I felt a click at his wrist when the pulse disappeared. When I announced my finding to the group, Swamiji explained that this was because of the breath becoming very, very fine and subtle, as one breathed equally through both nostrils, keeping breath awareness from the space between the nostrils to the eyebrow center and back.

Swamiji added other elements to the practice— the buttock roll, *agni sara* and the relaxation-tension exercise. For the buttock roll, he told us to pull the muscles upward and inward. When I tried it, in spite of great muscular effort, there was little inward movement. Swamiji then demonstrated the buttock roll, having me put the palms of my hands on his buttocks, one on each cheek. My palms came together by more than 12 inches! It was truly amazing. I'm still working on my buttock roll. Swamiji put all the exercises into the proper sequence, and left us to continue on our own. He said he would meet us the next morning.

The next morning's appointment was postponed for the night. I kept reminding myself not to be disappointed, but to surrender to the guru. I kept up the practice and experienced some soreness of the lower abdomen from trying too hard with the agni sara exercise. I also found myself taking long naps after lunch. I was looking forward to the night session with Swamiji, but that too was cancelled, and we were told that Swamiji would meet us at 9:00 the next morning instead. The next morning, Vimal and Leroy told me that Swamiji had cancelled the morning session and would see us at night!

He did meet us at night, and made me demonstrate the buttock roll. He slapped me on my bottom, telling me that it was too jerky, and should be done more smoothly. He then had me demonstrate diaphragmatic breathing, and again pointed out faults in my technique, advising me to practice with a 10 pound sand bag. I was ashamed at not being able to do even the basics to his satisfaction. However, Swamiji looked closely at my face and remarked that I was looking healthier. He told me that he would meet me the next afternoon, to answer any questions that I might have.

After Swamiji's displeasure at my not being able to do the basics right, I began to lose my self-confidence with these exercises. I was trying too hard. As a result, I would come out of the practice with my joints aching and with my neck, back and stomach sore. I grew despondent, and was prepared to throw in the towel, even though I had just reached the halfway mark of my 10-day retreat. The afternoon session was cancelled, and I was asked to come that night. I waited for about an hour to see Swamiji that night. Kamal, with a wan smile, came to tell me that Swamiji had company from India and could not see me that night either. As I was about to go back to my room, I heard Swamiji coming down the hallway to meet someone at the front door by the reception desk. I waited, hoping to have a word with Swamiji. He had a smile on his face, but as soon as he saw me, the smile disappeared. His face became grave, and he asked me with some impatience what I wanted to see him about. Sensing his displeasure, I told him that it could wait until the next morning, to which he readily assented.

I came back to my room, overcome by feelings of hurt, disappointment and self-pity. My throat choked up and sobs shook my frame. I began to cry, realized the childishness of it all, stopped, remembered the hurt all over again, and again resumed crying. My cheeks were stained by my tears and all kinds of thoughts passed through my mind — thoughts of violence, frustration and self-pity. I thought I should just pack up and leave. I wondered how I could let myself be manipulated so much by another. How could Swamiji be so cruel to me? He spent so much time laughing, joking, entertaining and eating with others. Why was he so harsh with me? Why was he punching my ego so hard, kicking it in the groin? Maybe I should look for another guru, who would be kinder and gentler to me. I was really, really, upset and had to do many malas of japa to calm myself down.

I read a few pages of Swamiji's commentary on the Gita, as well as the book, *The Master's Touch*, about

Swami Satchidananda. He often used to say, "No appointments, no disappointments." It was so apt to my situation. The missed appointments with Swamiji were leading to so much disappointment, because of my high level of expectation. Another quotation from the book that applied was, "Did you come here to get attention? Why did you come here?" And again, "I want you to be master of yourself and not dependent on anything or anyone for your happiness—not even on me. The sooner this happens the better. If you trust me, this can happen quickly. If you don't trust me, take your suitcases and go. You could remain here for 20 years with no results whatsoever." Oh, how pertinent to my situation! It was as if Swamiji was addressing me through this book. Another quotation that really consoled me, "Do you love me Gurudev?" — "I can't avoid it!" I decided to give up my rebellious thoughts, and tried very hard to surrender, but the sense of hurt remained.

The next morning, Kamal knocked at my door to tell me that Swamiji would see me at his cabin at 7:30 a.m. I opened the gates to Swamiji's cabin. His dog was outside, growling at me. I ignored it and went up and knocked on the door. Swamiji shouted out that I should wait and that he would join me. I sat with Swamiji in his Japanese garden. It was beautiful and tranquil with the soothing sound of flowing water and the chirping of birds. Swamiji told me to ask my questions. I had written down several questions and I began to read out my questions, with the prefacing remark, that I found it difficult to ask some of these questions.

Question 1: How should my attitude be towards you? Should I take all your statements with literal conviction? If I do not, how do I prevent myself from becoming cynical?

Answer 1: Swamiji said that I had to work out this question of attitude by myself. He told me that my resentment and negative vibrations did touch him. He would not help me in this regard. I had to work on the negativity myself, and develop the right attitude. He indicated that further discussion of this question was a waste of precious time. He added that he had given similar answers to Dr. Arya and Pandit Rajmani. He asked me why there should be negativity if he could not keep an appointment, because something else had come up. He did not expect anything from me. He was doing his duty selflessly with no thought of return. What more did I want? Was he not guiding me and giving me time?

Question 2: Is the fact that I do not have easy access to you important? Why are there distinctions? After knowing you for so long, why is there lack of intimacy?

Answer 2: The answer was a continuation in the same vein as with the first question. He said that he had great love for me, a pure, selfless love, and that he had said this in front of his master. He was giving me more time than anyone else. He said that he was intimate with me, and did not understand why I felt as negative as I did. He was satisfied in the performance of his selfless duty towards me. He plainly told me that he was guiding and protecting me. I asked if we had been linked before, and he assented, emphatically, that that was so, and that he knew me very well (from before). He said that I had very good samskaras and was a good person, but that I had to clear out the junk in the conscious mind, which I had gathered in this life. I had to work on my attitude and develop the right attitude towards my relationships, work and sadhana. The new practices he was giving me were the most important thing, not intimacy and his spending time with me. Success in sadhana could not be handed to me, dropped down from above, without the requisite effort.

Question 3: What are the future directions in my career? Should I make efforts to return to India?

Answer 3: Swamiji felt that I should remain in the U.S. for now, and that returning to India at the present time would create problems for Vijaya and the kids. He said that I should visit India as often as I could, but that it was best to stay in my present situation for now. He said that my work in the world would continue, as long as there was the desire for name and fame. Later, when the desire was fulfilled, the time would come for intense sadhana.

Questions 4 and 5: Please help me to become a better husband and father. Ego, anger, and frustration are the roots of my failings. Give me strength to conquer them. Please help me deal with the world outside with greater tranquility, love and joy.

Answer 4 and 5: My ego-centeredness was my greatest failing. It was when I got so wrapped up in my ego problem that I created problems for Vijaya, the kids and others. He said that selfishness was not my problem. It was anger and frustration. In spite of knowing what was right and what was wrong, my ego led me to say and do the wrong things. There had to be a clear separation between life in the world (the earth), and sadhana (the sky). I had to clearly divorce worldly problems from my sadhana and learn to let go, rather than struggle with these problems. Meditation was letting go (of thoughts, of emotions). *Rajas* made my mind very active, and all that thinking tired me out, leaving no energy for other things. He added with a smile, that though rajas was predominant, there was some *sattva* too! He said that others did not hurt me. It was my thinking that hurt me. I should learn to renounce all negativity and act selflessly. Then my actions would definitely bear fruit.

Swamiji asked me to reduce my salt and sugar intake, and recommended lemon tea rather than tea with milk and sugar. He also advised me to take some water with my meals as I did not chew my food properly. We walked for a while in the garden. He told me that mental overwork had to be avoided, and I should learn to let go in meditation. Though my path was not that of physical yoga, some physical yoga was necessary to make the body a fit instrument for mental practices. My health would be greatly benefited by practicing *shavasana*, diaphragmatic breathing and agni sara. I should gauge my capacity, and slowly expand it. Swamiji then asked me to go and attend to my other duties.

I had spent about an hour and a half with Swamiji in his Japanese garden. I was late for breakfast but managed to get some fruit and milk. After my fore-noon practice, I had lunch with Arpita, Vimal and Leroy under the trees. They told me that Swamiji also set them up with all kinds of games. They too fell for it over and over again! That night Swamiji took me up to the attic on the third floor, where he led the prayers and played the tabla. The group recited some prayers, including some verses from Shankara's *Saundarya Lahari* (Wave of Beauty), and then did some chanting. I was reminded of the kirtans that Swamiji led at the Minnesota retreat almost 15 years earlier. I was emo-tionally moved by the chanting and tears coursed down my cheeks. Swamiji met with our small group after the prayers and refined our practice. He told us that he would be lecturing the next day on breathing and emotions. His lecture would give us more insights. He again dangled before us the carrot of 'giving us the touch,' if he saw the appropriate signs and symptoms in us, indicating that we had perfected the practice.

Swamiji's lecture the next morning was on Breath, Emotions and Relationships. It was a beautiful, inspiring lecture. I felt that I was making a fresh start with the practice of breathing exercises, based on the insights received from this lecture. I will cover the highlights of this lecture in a subsequent chapter.

Swamiji had given us an appointment for 10:30 p.m., but Shanta informed us that Swamiji had cancelled all his appointments for the night. The next morning we had a short session with Swamiji, and he helped clarify many of our doubts regarding the practice. After lunch, I hiked with my Irish friend Martin to the waterfalls. The recent rains had swollen the flow making the falls an impressive sight.

We were informed that we would be meditating before Swamiji the next morning. We waited for him in Room 2. When he did not come right away, we decided to start our practice on our own. I was told later that Swamiji had come in, three separate times, to check our practice. The others were aware of his presence, but I was oblivious of his coming. I did feel someone tugging at my fingers, but did not respond thinking that Swamiji was easing the tension in my fingers. I was shocked by a ripple of vibration that passed through me at the touch. A little while later, there was another tug at my fingers, which I again ignored. I learnt later that Swamiji had asked Vimal to get me out of meditation with the tugging at my fingers! Finally, I felt a tickle in my throat, started coughing and came out of meditation. I was totally taken aback to see Swamiji and the others standing around me, and quickly got to my feet to greet Swamiji. Swamiji promised to teach me one more exercise, kundalini dhyana, separately, before I left for home.

After lunch, Pandit Rajmani invited me over to his house and I had a very intimate, instructive and inspiring conversation with him that I will cover in a subsequent chapter.

The next morning, after my practice and breakfast, I sat down to read Rabindranath Tagore's beautiful collection of song poems, *Gitanjali*. The spiritual longing, the aching heart, and the beautiful imagery moved me to tears. I finished most of the book in a single sitting, feeling very elevated. Late that evening, I saw Swamiji at the tennis court. He said he would see me later that night. Swamiji's call never came that night. The next day was the last day of my 10-day retreat. All morning, I kept looking under the door for a message from Swamiji. At breakfast, Swamiji came looking for me, but I was outside. I got the message that Swamiji wanted me to teach diaphragmatic breathing and the 61 point exercise to one of the guests. I was bemused by this message. Just a few days back, my technique had come in for a very critical appraisal, and now I had to teach the technique to someone else! I met with Swamiji briefly, and he stressed the importance of the practices and asked me to do the practices twice a day. The morning time of 6:00 had to be adhered to strictly. He did not say anything about the last exercise, kundalini dhyana, that he had promised to teach me. I did not remind him either, surmising that I was not yet ready for it. As I left, he gave me a big, warm, tight, long hug, and I interpreted it as a response to my complaints about lack of intimacy and overt show of affection. He sent his love to Vijaya and the children, and reminded me to be less bossy and more loving.

I went to join others at work on clearing the area around the pond. It was hard work and a copious flow of perspiration kept running into my eyes. I usually did not perspire very much, and wondered if the new practices had provided some cleansing, resulting in so much perspiration. Swamiji came to supervise, but ignored me completely. I had to leave so that I could teach the guest diaphragmatic breathing and the 61 point exercise. On my way out, I saw Swamiji and he approved of my departure. The lesson with the guest took a little less than an hour. The guest had earlier offered me a ride to the airport at Newark. I could clearly see Swamiji's hand in arranging the private lesson. It was to release me from any indebtedness for the ride to Newark. It was like 'singing for my supper!'

Much as I had enjoyed the retreat at Honesdale, I was looking forward to being back with Vijaya and the kids. I hoped I could retain the feelings and attitudes that Swamiji had evoked in me. I hoped that the world would not be too much with me.

Inner strength is necessary on the spiritual path. Too much reliance on the guru saps one's inner strength. The guru may keep the student at a distance, and deny himself the opportunity to show his love for the student, just to help the student develop self-reliance. Swamiji plainly told me that he was being harsh to me, to help me get back to the spiritual heights I had achieved in an earlier life. Despite my complaints, Swamiji always maintained that he was satisfied that he was doing his duty selflessly. He said that I could never imagine the extent of his love for me, and that he was always there to guide and protect me. In craving overt intimacy and attention, I was ignoring the precious gems he was offering me, and was instead enamored by glittering pieces of worthless cut glass. I needed to cultivate the right attitude of surrender, with the realization that the guru knows what my needs are, more than I, misled by ego, will ever know. I had to make myself a container worthy of holding and assimilating spiritual energy, rather than a sieve that allowed it to all leak out. When the container is deemed worthy, the appropriate guidance is given. Until then surrender, surrender, surrender!

The grating down of my ego was very painful and continued for a few more years. With time, my relationship with Swamiji mellowed with fewer hiccups. He was kind and compassionate, and spent time teaching me new practices. He never humiliated me publicly, even though I knew that he was aware of my many failings. The even tenor that developed in my relationship with Swamiji continued until the very end. After his passing, he has berated me sometimes in dreams, for my lack of intensity, but he has also provided the necessary guidance. Jai Gurudeva!

23.
An Inspiring Conversation with Pandit Rajmani

"To be on a spiritual path with a guru is not an easy thing. It is not pleasant. The guru tests the disciples, puts them in difficult situations, and creates obstacles for them. All the tests, difficulties and obstacles are meant to train and expand the consciousness of the disciple."

Sacred Journey:
Living Purposefully and Dying Gracefully

In my talk with Swamiji at the Japanese garden, I had asked him what the right attitude was with which to relate to him, and he said that I had to work that out for myself. He added that he had given the same reply to Dr. Arya and Pandit Rajmani.

During my retreat at Honesdale, Pandit Rajmani invited me over to his house, and I had a very intimate, instructive and inspiring conversation with him. I asked *Panditji* about the right attitude towards Swamiji. I mentioned Swamiji's appointments, my disappointments, his kindness to so many but his strictness towards me and the distance he kept me at. He gave me examples of his own experience, and also narrated some inspiring stories which I reproduce here:

Panditji said that in not keeping appointments and causing disappointment, Swamiji was trying to kill expectations in us, so as to release us from subsequent frustrations. Further, he felt that Swamiji wanted us to realize him in the true form of the guru, and not in the physical form. Panditji had also experienced the disappointment of cancelled appointments. Once, for two months, there were appointments and subsequent cancellations. Then Swamiji left for India, and was away for a whole year! The next year, Swamiji himself brought up the issue of giving Panditji some advanced practices. He told Panditji that he had been denied the teaching in the previous year because he had not shown enough eagerness and desire for the teaching. When Panditji asked Swamiji whether he was evincing greater desire for the teachings the next year, Swamiji remained quiet. Later, when they were both playing a game of volleyball, Swamiji left the court asking Panditji to follow him. Swamiji walked towards the trees, and appeared to be getting ready to urinate. Panditji stayed back, thinking it was inappropriate to follow. Swamiji beckoned him on. With one hand on his zipper, he outlined very casually and quickly a *Sri Yantra* technique, and specified the time for this practice. Panditji found the practice to be very powerful and rewarding, despite the informal manner in which it had been imparted.

One day, when Panditji had taken the effects of the practice for granted, and felt that he had reached a plateau, he had an interesting experience. He had not put on his ear plugs for his practice that day. There was a loud noise which caused him to experience separation from the physical body, and from above, he could see his body lying below in shavasana, and his wife Meera lying on the bed. Assuming that he was dead, he got very upset, thinking of the unfulfilled worldly and spiritual responsibilities. He then 'saw' Swamiji, who reassured him, and made him descend back into his physical body. He then came out of his meditation, woke up Meera to ascertain if it had all been a dream and whether Meera had heard him crying. She had not heard anything. The next time he went to visit Swamiji, Swamiji opened the door even before he could knock, and asked him to come into the room, using the same words with which he had pushed Panditji back into his physical body. Swamiji then advised him not to remove his ear plugs during the practice. That convinced Panditji that Swamiji had been with him during the experience, and that it was not just a dream.

Regarding Swamiji's apparent kindness to some and strictness with others, Panditji told me that there were some students who spent 24 hours a day with Swamiji, eating with him, watching movies with him, and joking around. Yet, they changed very little spiritually. Others, who were kept at a distance, and given only a few minutes with Swamiji, manifested great changes. So it was not the quantity of time, but the quality that mattered. Often, those students who spent a lot of time with Swamiji, were sent by him to Panditji for spiritual instructions. When Panditji wanted to give them higher practices, considering their close association with Swamiji, Panditji was specifically asked by Swamiji to give some simple practices, only to keep them occupied. Panditji was of the opinion that physical distance had its advantages and enhanced spiritual growth. The distance created greater reverence for the guru, the one who could unclog the blocks to spiritual flow, whereas, too much familiarity bred more familiarity, and reverence for the guru was lost. Casual familiarity was not conducive to the descent of spiritual grace. Panditji felt that if one started taking Swamiji for granted, it could have disastrous consequences as evidenced by the following story:

A Mr. B., a big shot in the Police Department in Rishikesh, had been of great assistance to Swamiji in the construction of the Rishikesh ashram. He had a lot of reverence for Swamiji and was, in turn, well regarded by Swamiji. Once, however, he forgot his reverence, and demanded to see Swamiji at the ashram. Swamiji was there, but told one of the residents to say that he was not around. Mr. B. was not convinced, and started getting belligerent. Swamiji appeared upon the porch, and in a loud, emphatic voice ordered the trusted devotee off the premises immediately. Mr. B. was later filled with remorse and expressed his penitence, but was kept away for two years. After the two year period, Swamiji himself visited the home of Mr. B. and spent a loving evening with him. After this incident, Mr. B. was careful not to do anything that bordered on disrespect for the guru.

Swamiji was very human in many ways—in his tennis playing and his playing with children—but at times the divine aspects were revealed, sometimes terrifyingly. A disciple of Swamiji and his family came to visit Swamiji at the ashram. As Swamiji was not there, they went for a drive to pass the time. During the drive, the car was involved in a terrible accident, and the man and his son-in-law were killed. When the bodies were brought before Swamiji at the ashram, the man's widow, insane in her grief, started accusing Swamiji of having allowed the tragedy to occur, and went on to blame Swamiji for having caused the accident, by maneuvering events. Swamiji remained silent. Rumors began to fly about, and the truth got distorted. There were threats of lawsuits and court cases. A large group of people came in strength to confront Swamiji. A few days before the group came, Swamiji, who had until then maintained silence about the accident, started talking about the tragedy, wondering why his Gurudeva had allowed such a tragedy to occur in the vicinity of his ashram. He began to wonder why trusted devotees had now become so irrational. When the group arrived to confront Swamiji, he emerged to meet them. Swamiji's eyes were fiery red, and seemed to emit flames like the third eye of Shiva. Swamiji told the group to take the case to any court of law, and to then come to him with the verdict. The vehemence and authoritative nature of his statement, and the fire in his shining eyes, made the crowd disperse very quickly, never to return. Things quietened down completely. The incident had revealed the Rudra aspect of Swamiji.

Gurus may seem to discipline their disciples harshly, but they always do it out of selfless love, and for the welfare of the disciple. In *Living with the Himalayan Masters*, Swamiji tells the story of his having had to go without food for several days, and of a hand emerging out of the water to hand him a bowl that filled up with any desired delicacy and never emptied. Swamiji was thrilled with this gift and began to misuse its power. Swamiji's guru was furious, and decided to punish him. Swamiji was banished to a solitary place for 11 months of penance; he had to renounce all his possessions including his clothes. Swamiji had to live on grass and leaves and endured much pain and suffering. However, the penance greatly increased Swamiji's inner strength and self-reliance. Never again would he beg for food or come to depend on it. The following incident illustrates the inner strength he gained from his penance. Swamiji was crossing a torrential river on a narrow rope bridge, which was only wide enough for one person at a time. At that time, he used to walk looking down at the ground. Suddenly he came face to face with a tiger on the bridge. Swamiji had always been told by his guru, that in all that he attempted in life, he should always move forward with conviction, and never look back or step backwards. Now, if he did not retreat, he had the choice of either being mauled by the tiger or being pushed into the torrential waters below. He resolutely moved forward. He had been in silence for many months, and could only produce an authoritative grunting sound. This scared the tiger into retreating, allowing Swamiji to cross the bridge.

24.
An Inspiring Lecture

"So prana is like our mother. Mind is like our father who discriminates. Mother and father live together, they have a close relationship. Breath and mind are called twin laws of life. To understand the mind, you will have to understand your breath. To understand your breath, you will have to understand your mind."

OM the Eternal Witness:
Secrets of the Mandukya Upanishad

During the 10-day retreat, Swamiji gave a lecture on Breath, Emotions and Relationships. It was a very instructive and inspiring lecture. Some highlights of the lecture are presented below:

Habits are formed in childhood. Parents need to teach children the basics of good posture, diaphragmatic breathing, nutritious food, proper chewing of food and toilet habits. The body builds toxins from bad food, bad posture, bad habits and bad thinking.

The breath is more vital than food. The respiratory system directly or indirectly influences all other body systems. To be successful, one needs to build a strong bridge between external life and internal life. Breathing techniques can help build this bridge.

The four bad habits of breathing that need to be avoided are:

Shallow breathing, with inhalation and exhalation being unequal
Jerky breathing
Noisy breathing, caused by blockage of the nostrils
Pause between inhalation, exhalation and the next inhalation

Breath is the vehicle, the horse. The vital energy or prana is the rider. Prana enters the body through the breath. Breath is life. All the body cells are floating in air. There is air within and without. Breath awareness and other breathing techniques help overcome lassitude and create energy. During sleep, if breathing is bad, one does not get good rest.

The techniques of *pranayama* produce many beneficial results. Diaphragmatic breathing is helpful during an emotional crisis. With diaphragmatic breathing, if one were to put the hands on the lower part of the ribcage, the spaces between the fingers would expand and contract as one inhales and exhales. There should be no chest or belly breathing. The crocodile posture is a good posture to learn diaphragmatic breathing. One should practice diaphragmatic breathing, twice a day, for 15 minutes per session.

To open up a blocked nostril, exhale through the blocked nostril and inhale through the free nostril. The pause between inhalation and exhalation is death. If there is an extended pause, it causes coronary artery disease. The yogi who controls the pause controls death. Swamiji practices prana bath three times a day, allowing the perspiration, thus produced, to cleanse all the pores and remove toxins.

Bhastrika or bellows helps shake the jars of the lungs, clearing the inaccessible corners of the lungs. Alternate nostril breathing also helps in controlling emotions and should be practiced before sushumna application. Sushumna application is essential for a tranquil and joyful meditation. Without sushumna application, meditation is a joke! With sushumna application, the breath becomes very fine and subtle. As a consequence, all involuntary muscles like the muscles of the heart and internal muscles get rested.

According to the science of swarodaya, study of the ripples, waves and currents of life, the right nostril should be activated before any vigorous physical activity. The left nostril should be open before passive, relaxing activity. Before meditation, both nostrils should be activated by alternate nostril breathing, followed by sushumna application.

All of the body is in the mind and not the other way around. The mind and breath arise from the same source. Mind and breath are inseparable like the letters 'q' and 'u.' In studying the mind, one finds that underlying the thinking process are emotions. Emotions rise up from desires. Desires are the products of the four primitive fountains of food, self-preservation, sleep and sex. As breath and mind are two sides of the same coin, one can work on emotions by working on one's breathing.

To develop relationships, one needs to develop the right attitude. This comes from the right philosophy of life:

All things are meant for me. I have the right to enjoy them, but not to possess them. Non-possessiveness helps develop detachment. Only then can one have complete enjoyment.

25.
Career Conundrum

"Lacking in foresight, people consider their present condition and circumstances alone to be truth. Taking their present condition for granted, they refuse to explore the possibility of other states of existence. The conscious part of mind fails to grasp that which lies beyond the spheres of time, space and causation."

Sadhana: The Essence of Spiritual Life

Swamiji had advised us not to skimp in any way, as far as the education of the kids was concerned. When Mayank was ready to enter the ninth grade, he had to change schools. Until then he had received an excellent education in the public school system, but when we visited the public high school he was due to join, we were not impressed by the school or the teachers. We decided to enroll him in a private school, for the last four years of his schooling, so as to better prepare him for entry into a good college. We settled on The Blake School near downtown Minneapolis.

Until then my career had been in academic research at the Minneapolis Medical Research Foundation. It had been a very satisfying career, but the money was not as good as in the corporate setting. Further, research grants were becoming scarce, and we had been forced to accept industrial grants to keep the research team together. These industrial projects were mere bread and butter projects, and did not involve much originality or challenge. The writing was on the wall, prompting me to consider a change in career. A corporate job would help pay for Mayank and Aparna's private schooling, as well as the college tuitions that would inevitably follow.

On a trip to Chicago, I was approached by a multinational company, Baxter Healthcare, to consider taking the position of Director of Research in their Renal (Kidney) Division. The job was attractive, and I was eager for a new challenge after 15 years in academia. I had lived in Minneapolis for 20 years, and despite the harsh winters, it had been a great place to raise a family. We loved the parks, lakes and warmth of the people. The job at Baxter would require us to relocate to Chicago. I was excited about the career change and was prepared to move to Chicago.

I returned to Minneapolis from Chicago, eager to discuss the new opportunity with Vijaya and the kids. They heard me out, and then all three voted with their thumbs down. No way would they move to Chicago. I could not convince them and was stymied. The job was too good to turn down, but I did not want to displease the family with the relocation. The thought of my moving to Chicago, alone, leaving the family behind, was not a great option. I decided to ask Swamiji for advice.

Swamiji heard me out patiently, and agreed with Vijaya and the kids that we should not move out of Minneapolis. Having said that, he added cryptically that the job offer was a good one, and I should seriously consider the offer. I was perplexed. Swamiji had thrown me a curve ball. I had to introspect on this haiku posed by Swamiji.

I did a lot of introspection, and then an interesting idea struck me. Why not create a job opportunity with Baxter in Minneapolis itself? I put together a seven page proposal, recommending the start up of a new research laboratory funded by Baxter, in the campus of the Minneapolis Medical Research Foundation, utilizing the clinical resources of the Foundation, with the aim of creating advanced products for Baxter. The idea was good, but I gave myself only a 30 percent chance of Baxter accepting an extramural laboratory, especially with all new players. To my surprise, the President of the Renal Division of Baxter decided to come down to Minneapolis to discuss the proposal with me and the Minneapolis Medical Research Foundation. The discussions went well, and in a very short time legal contracts were drawn up and signed. The Baxter Clinical Engineering Laboratory was born.

Swamiji had not made it easy for me by suggesting a solution, or making the decision for me. He had always wanted me to stand on my own two feet, and not use him as a crutch. With his carefully chosen words, he stimulated me to work out a solution, thus encouraging my independence and growth.

As a post-script, Baxter provided the funds required for expansion of the facilities and personnel of the laboratory. Over the 10 years of its existence, the laboratory performed well, filing several patents and winning a number of awards. The laboratory was closed when I decided to leave the United States to come to the Himalayan Institute Hospital Trust in India.

26.
Our Last Meeting with Swamiji

"The realized individual remains fully aware in all conditions—while living in a human body and during the state of death. The knower of Brahman does not go to any realm or heaven, nor does the knower become anything other than what it has always been—the Atman, the Self of all. After dropping the physical garment, the realized soul remains in a state of perpetual bliss and happiness, and infinite love and wisdom."

Sacred Journey:
Living Purposefully and Dying Gracefully

Once the hospital project in India got underway, Swamiji started spending eight months of the year in India. After 1993, Swamiji did not go back to Honesdale, and spent most of his time in Jolly Grant, India, establishing the Himalayan Institute Hospital Trust which included a tertiary care hospital and medical college.

I had been visiting the site of the Himalayan Institute Hospital Trust at Jolly Grant from its early inception. As my father in Delhi was not in good health, I used to visit India more often than before, and always made it a point to visit Swamiji in Delhi or Rishikesh or Jolly Grant. I visited the hospital site when they had only the two-room outpatient clinic, and Swamiji used to rest in what was then the Administrative building. It has now become a shrine with pho-

tographs of Swamiji. I visited again, when the first building called the Research Building, housing the biofeedback equipment, was constructed. It is now the guest
house. I was also there the day that Swamiji moved
into his upstairs apartment below which we now have
the Meditation Hall and *Mahasamadhi* room of the
Swami Rama Centre. They say that things move slowly
in India, but the bustle of activity I saw that day amazed
me. He was the guiding force. Carpenters were fixing
the pelmets and curtain rods, tailors moved into the
apartment with their sewing machines, hard at work
sewing the drapes and curtains. Visitors were coming
and going, and Swamiji, while directing all this activity, was still the consummate host.

On another visit to the hopsital site, through
miscommunication, I made the road trip from Delhi
to Rishikesh, while Swamiji, also traveling by road,
was going from Rishikesh to Delhi. I'm not sure where
on the road our paths crossed. After reaching Rishikesh
and not finding Swamiji there, I turned around and
returned to Delhi, and met Swamiji at his Sarva Priya
apartment. On another occasion, I was once booked
on the morning Vayudhoot flight, but a midnight
phone call informed me that the flight was cancelled. I
had to hustle to make taxi arrangements to go by road.
I did meet Swamiji, and waited for his blessings for
the return trip. Even though he usually rested after
lunch, he interrupted his siesta to give me his blessings.

I think it was on this same trip that our return to
Delhi happened to be on the day dedicated to the
founder of the Sikh faith, Guru Nanak. I made it to
Haridwar, but there the traffic started piling up, and
we were told that the highway had been closed off, to
control the crowds coming in to Haridwar for this special occasion. My intrepid driver decided that he could
take a shortcut across a dry riverbed. The wheels of

the taxi got stuck in the riverbed sand. It had turned
dark as we were trying to push the taxi out of the sand.
The previous night, I had had dinner at a fancy Thai
restaurant in Delhi, with gleaming silverware, candle-
lit tables covered with snowy-white table cloths, and
a live orchestra. A day later, I was trying to dislodge
the taxi from its comfortable bed in the river sand, with
the stench of human wastes assailing my nostrils. I
remember thinking that only in India, can one experience such contrasts within the space of 24 hours! Seeing a figure approaching us in the darkness, I appealed
to him to help us push the taxi out of the sand. He
asked us where we were from, and why we were up
to such activity so late at night. He told us that his hut
was not too far away, that his wife would make us hot
chappatis (flat wheat bread), and that we should spend
the night there, and work on the car the next morning.
I was overwhelmed by the hospitality and generosity
of this total stranger, who was willing to share his dinner with us. We thanked him, but requested him to
help us push the taxi out. Soon we succeeded, and
made it back to the highway with its bumper to bumper
traffic. I did not make it back to Delhi until 2:00 a.m.

In 1991, Garhwal experienced a very severe earthquake, which devastated many villages of the state.
The relief efforts of the Government were delayed and
meager. Swamiji mobilized medical teams to help with
earthquake relief, and personally visited many of the
earthquake hit areas. He was appalled by the apathy
of the Government, and organized rallies to make the
public aware of this. He also threatened to stage a fast
unto death in Delhi. Swamiji also urged all of us, in
the U.S. and other countries, to send faxes to the Prime
Minister's office to protest governmental apathy. We
too got into the act, and tried to send faxes to the number we had been given, but were unsuccessful in hav-

ing the fax go through. We later learnt, that the Prime Minister's office was so inundated by the incoming faxes that the fax machine had been turned off. Swamiji's efforts bore fruit, and the relief efforts of the Government improved considerably. Swamiji also raised a lot of funds for relief efforts, and helped re-build many of the destroyed rural dwellings. There is also a plaque at the main Shiva temple at Uttarkashi thanking Swami Rama for his help in repairing the damaged temple.

In January of 1996, Vijaya and I visited India, deciding to spend a couple of months there. We made it to the ashram at Rishikesh, only to discover that Swamiji was out of the country, probably in Nepal. No one knew when he was returning. We waited at the ashram for a few days, when suddenly, without any prior information, Swamiji returned from his trip. I was shocked when I saw how much weight Swamiji had lost. Gone was the imposing mighty frame. I asked him about the drastic change. His simple reply was that the body was 'jada' (inert), so how did it matter? He told us that he had cut short his trip when he realized that we were waiting for him.

We found that Swamiji was leaving the ashram in the morning for the hospital site, returning only late at night, or sometimes not at all, staying overnight at his apartment there. As we wanted to maximize the time we spent with him, I asked his permission to move to the hospital campus. He said that it was up to us, but that the ashram was a better place for sadhana. In spite of this, we moved to the hospital guesthouse. No sooner had we done this, than Swamiji started leaving the hospital site and returning to the ashram early each evening! Surrender, surrender, surrender!

I climbed to the guesthouse terrace each morning, waiting for his car to come into the campus by the main access road which, at that time, was just across from the guesthouse. After visiting the construction sites of the campus, Swamiji, wearing his broad-rimmed straw hat, would usually sit in the warm sun on the lawn of his apartment. That was a good opportunity to spend time with him. Swamiji treated all alike, and he would sometimes call out to one of the passing gardeners or security staff, and ask about them and their families. His love encompassed all and everyone felt that they had a very special relationship with him. Once, he pointed to the hills in the distance behind his apartment, and told us that in the future, our campus would reach those hills. Though the medical faculty at the hospital at that time must have been numbered less than 100, Swamiji told Vijaya that the faculty was 2,000 strong! For one who has transcended time, the future and the present are indistinguishable. On another occasion, Swamiji handed me a paper bag, filled with Indian currency notes, which someone had given him. He asked me to count out the money for him. He watched carefully as I sorted the notes into the various denominations, and then tallied the total. Again, I felt that he was testing me to see if I would feel any attachment, as I handled the money.

One Monday, Swamiji instructed us not to eat until he had given us a new spiritual practice. We waited all day, missing breakfast, lunch and dinner, expecting Swamiji's call which never came. Knowing that Swamiji usually gave spiritual instructions only on Mondays and Thursdays, we were faced with having to fast two more days, until Thursday. Sheepishly, we sent word to Swamiji through Maithili, asking if we should continue our fast. Maithili was surprised at our temerity, but did as requested, and came back to tell us that we could break our fast. We tried to meet Swamiji that day or the next in his apartment, but were told that he was busy and could not see us. Hearing this, the iron seemed to have entered my soul; I decided that I would not leave his apartment, but would wait as long as it took to see him. Dr. Barb Bova was surprised at my stubbornness, but let me stay on. Soon after, Swamiji appeared and I fell at his feet with tears in my eyes, asking him what we had done to displease him, and why he was not giving us the practice. With great love, Swamiji explained that, sometimes, he too needed time to prepare himself for the spiritual instruction. With his busy schedule, he had not found time for preparation. He asked me to come back on Thursday. On Thursday, Swamiji called us and made some subtle changes to our spiritual practice.

Swamiji's health was causing a lot of concern. He submitted himself to Ayurvedic, Homeopathic and Allopathic treatments. There was talk about Swamiji's kidneys being affected by the high level of mercury in his Ayurvedic medications. There was also talk of Swamiji's symptoms changing location and character from day to day, causing his physicians a lot of confusion. We were all wondering how much, and whose karma, Swamiji was taking upon himself. We were all aware of Swamiji's prowess in healing others, his ability to control involuntary body processes, and about his having ingested toxic substances like arsenic and mercury without apparent harm. We, therefore, fondly hoped that Swamiji's ill-health was transient, and that he would soon heal himself. We also wondered if Swamiji was merely testing the physicians and equipment of the newly-founded hospital, a sort of dry run! Little did we know.

Our son, Mayank, was also in South India at that time, taking time off from his courses at Dartmouth College, to study Sanskrit and South Indian classical music. We left Jolly Grant after a few weeks, to visit our son in Bangalore. We returned to Jolly Grant, bringing Mayank back with us to meet Swamiji. Swamiji was very happy to see Mayank and to spend time with him.

One day, Vijaya and I were with Swamiji when he told us that, as our children had grown up and become independent, we should consider returning to India, to help in the development of the hospital. He told me that the basic departments of the hospital had been set up, and now it was time to start on the next phase, with facilities like dialysis. He asked me to go to the U.S., set my affairs in order, and return to India within six months to be a part of his mission. Over the years, I had asked Swamiji, on numerous occasions, about returning to India, especially to fulfil my responsibilities towards my aging parents and to intensify my sadhana. Swamiji had always responded with, "Not now, not now." Finally, the time for our return to India was at hand, after 30 years in the U.S.

We returned to our room, and shared this information with our son, Mayank. He was taken aback, and grew quite upset. We had always discussed with our kids our desire to return to our roots one day. They had looked upon this as an abstract concept, and now, with only six months to go, Mayank could not accept the reality of the situation. He hurried to speak to Swamiji, and told him that he and his sister still needed their parents, and could not let go so quickly. Swamiji listened to him patiently, and then, with a smile told Mayank that he would give the kids a two-year extension, but no more. Mayank and Aparna had to learn to be independent, as he needed us in India. Mayank was mollified and accepted Swamiji's proposition. Before we returned to the U.S., we went to get Swamiji's permission for our leaving. He confused me by telling me to come back in six months. I kept thinking about the two-year extension and was not sure if Swamiji had forgotten his promise to Mayank. Only later, did I discover the significance of his remark. It was the end of March, and six months would have put it at the end of September. However, we returned to Minnesota, and I began to formulate plans for our winding up our affairs in the U.S.

27.

Returning Home

"As a human being, do you lead a liberated life or a life of bondage? If you study the lives of great men, there is one characteristic that you will find in their lives. They were all selfless, every one of them. Those who practice, practice this point first. I'll be totally selfless. Once you become selfless, you are free from all attachments. There is freedom on many levels.

"There are two laws, the law of contraction and the law of expansion. Hate others, you are going through the law of contraction. Love all, you are going through the law of expansion. Learn to love, that is the law of expansion. What does love mean? It means to give, without any expectation, to your own people."

Conscious Living:
A Guidebook for Spiritual Transformation

On at least two other occasions, I had made serious attempts to return to India, and had been thwarted by circumstances. Swamiji had also asked me to wait until the kids were older. Now, we had a definitive blueprint for the return to India, after a sojourn of 30 years in the U.S.

When we left for the U.S. after visiting Swamiji in India, there was no definitive diagnosis, but his health continued to deteriorate. The physicians were confused by the changing constellation of symptoms. Soon after we left for the U.S., a biopsy confirmed that

Swamiji had cancer that had metastasized throughout his body. The primary focus was not known. I used to call Dr. Shobha Lal from Minnesota for updates on Swamiji's health and the news was not good. Then in May, Swamiji left for some treatment in Malaysia. He came back much improved, and Dr. Shobha told me that Swamiji had started going on campus walks again, and I was reassured. As a consequence, my calls to India were less frequent, as I wrongly deduced that the crisis had passed, and Swamiji was beginning to heal himself.

In October of 1996, Vijaya and I were visiting Singapore for a dialysis conference, organized by the National Kidney Foundation of Singapore. Coincidentally, Dr. Vijendra Chauhan, an orthopedic surgeon of the hospital, who had visited us in Minnesota, was also in Singapore for an orthopedic conference at a different hotel. He heard from one of the medical representatives that I was in Singapore, and came looking for me. I was tied up in the conference, and he left without meeting me. To this day, I regret the circumstances that prevented our meeting. If we had met, he would have updated me on Swamiji's condition, and I would have changed travel plans and come to India. But it was not to be.

On November 14th, 1996, Vijaya called me at work, and as I was out of my office, a pink telephone slip was left on my desk by my secretary, asking me to call home. As luck would have it, new papers arriving on my desk camouflaged the pink telephone slip. I discovered it at the end of the day, around 5:30 p.m. As I was about to go home anyway, I decided not to call, and made my way home. As soon as I reached home, Vijaya gave me the shocking news that Swamiji had dropped his body on the night of November 13th, 1996. One of the other disciples from Minnesota had called her with the sad news. I was stunned and physically collapsed in the kitchen. I sat sobbing for some time, and then called Dr. Shobha to confirm the news. It was sadly confirmed. I then called some of the Minnesota disciples like Shivnath Tandon, to find out if there was a group going to India. It was late in the evening, and the group had left. I could not get any flights that night, and if I left the next day, I would arrive in India only after the cremation. I spoke to Swami Veda Bharati (formerly Dr. Arya) who happened to be in London. He confirmed the details of the cremation. He was leaving right away for India. Now the significance of Swamiji's remark, asking me to return in six months, struck home. I kept kicking myself for not having understood, and also for having missed Dr. Chauhan in Singapore.

Having missed the final rites, I waited for Pandit Rajmani to return to Honesdale. Vijaya and I went to meet him, to get some measure of consolation. He described the final rites, the 16th day feeding of sadhus, and mentioned a particular sadhu, who was unusually familiar with his wife Meera. The sadhu had addressed other disciples also very familiarly, just like Swamiji used to address them. We speculated about Swamiji, the expert of para-kaya pravesha, having taken the sadhu's body, to witness the final rites of his own physical body! Panditji then also narrated some amazing experiences, of seeing Swamiji in cosmic form, when he accompanied Shri Roshal Lal to immerse the ashes in holy places like Uttarkashi and Gangotri.

In January of 1997, I got time off from work to visit Jolly Grant. I visited the other disciples to hear their stories of Swamiji. I was desperately seeking some consolation. Kamal described the last minutes of Swamiji's physical life, his being supported to sit up and the last breaths he took before dropping the body.

I also visited the special cremation spot in Haridwar where Swamiji's body had been cremated. This area was not used for other cremations. I saw some remnant ashes still on the ground, and taking a handful, I went to the holy Ganga nearby to disperse the ashes, praying to Swamiji for continued spiritual guidance.

My heart was still very heavy and I felt the need for spiritual satsang. I had come across a beautiful book called, *Wake Up and Roar*, a compilation of satsangs with Shri H.W.L. Poonja, a spiritual master who was a direct disciple of Ramana Maharshi. I did not know if Shri Poonja was still alive or not. On a sudden impulse, I bought a train ticket from Delhi to Lucknow, as the book had been published in Lucknow. I took a cycle rickshaw from the railway station to the center of town, and went to a large bookshop there. The bookseller had published Shri Poonja's books, and gave us directions to Indiranagar, where Shri Poonja lived. By the time I arrived, Shri Poonja had retired for his afternoon rest. However, a kind Western lady disciple, hearing of my quest, went in and got permission for me to get the blessings of Shri Poonja in his bedroom. I was touched by his graciousness. He asked me to come back that evening, and invited me to watch a cricket match with him. He also arranged for my accommodations, at the home of the same disciple who had ushered me into Shri Poonja's bedroom.

That evening, I went to watch the cricket match with Shri Poonja, and a whole host of disciples, many of them from Israel, who were lustily cheering every run scored in the cricket match. I had the sudden realization that Shri Poonja, by inviting me to watch TV with him, was fulfilling a long-cherished unfulfilled desire of social intimacy with Swamiji. Interestingly, in Shri Poonja's presence, without any conscious effort on my part, continuous ajapa japa of my guru mantra was maintained for several hours, in spite of the loud cheering of the cricket match by Shri Poonja's disciples. After the cricket match, Shri Poonja invited me to have an early breakfast with him the next morning, at 5:00, my meditation time. Shri Poonja was diabetic, and had ulcers on his feet, that needed dressing. After breakfast, I had an opportunity to lightly massage the feet of Shri Poonja. Once more, I felt that the guru was fulfilling my desires through Shri Poonja. I had to leave for Kanpur that same morning. Shri Poonja kindly dropped me off at the bus station on his way to the bank. My grief was slowly yielding to the graciousness of the guru.

I left Lucknow for Kanpur to meet Dr. Sunanda Bai, an early and devoted disciple of Swamiji. Swamiji had always spoken of her devotion in glowing terms. She had sponsored Swamiji's visit to Japan in the late sixties. Dr. Sunanda Bai was a highly respected gynecologist of Kanpur, who was head of obstetrics and gynecology in Kanpur's medical college. She had retired, and spent her days in seclusion. She lived in the house that Swamiji had built for her; on the first floor, the room that Swamiji used to occupy when he visited her, had been maintained like a shrine. I had been told that Dr. Sunanda Bai was very strict, did not indulge in loose talk and did not suffer fools gladly. I was, therefore, a little nervous about meeting her. The meeting had been arranged by Dr. Renu Kapoor, sister of Maya Tandon. Shivnath and Maya Tandon were good friends of ours from Minneapolis. Shivnath had known Swamiji from a young age, and had had many interesting experiences with Swamiji. Maya's father had studied with Swamiji at the University of Allahabad, and Swamiji had been a frequent visitor to Maya's home.

I took a taxi to Kanpur, had lunch with the Kapoors, and then took a cycle rickshaw to the home of Dr. Sunanda Bai. One of the first things I noticed about Dr. Sunanda Bai was her brown eyes, that seemed to have a warm glow, as if lit from within. Her eyes did not shine from reflecting the light, but the light in her eyes came from an inner source. Rather than the very strict lady she had been made out to be, I found her to be very kind and hospitable. She served us hot tea and South Indian snacks. She then told me some interesting stories about Swamiji.

She told me that in her previous life in North India, she had been with Swamiji and his guru Bengali Baba. In a rebellious outburst, she had decided to leave them, and had gone off with a visiting group of pilgrims to South India. As a consequence, she had taken birth in South India, and had to come back to the North to continue her discipleship with Swamiji and his guru. She told me that the house we were in had been built for her by Swamiji, much against her wishes. She was not at all attached to the venture, and had not cared to visit the construction site even once. When the house was ready, Swamiji had persuaded her to move in. A special room upstairs was always ready for Swamiji. He often stayed there. At times, even when he was alone in the room, Dr. Sunanda Bai would hear other voices and conversations, as if some meeting were taking place in the room.

The contractor who had built the home, approached her soon after she moved in, and kept troubling her for more money. She told Swamiji about the contractor's demand. He grew very angry, and asked her for a large vessel filled with water. Swamiji shut himself up in one of the rooms for some time. When he came out, his eyes were glowing red, and the vessel was now filled with currency notes. Dr. Sunanda

Bai was asked to pay off the contractor, and to warn him to never again darken her threshold with his shadow. Being with Dr. Sunanda Bai, and hearing her talk of Swamiji, made me aware of her great devotion to the guru. It was also clear to her that though Swamiji had dropped the physical body, he was ever-present and would continue to guide his disciples. I was consoled, and thanked her for her graciousness and hospitality.

Though Swamiji has dropped his physical body, he continues to guide us through dreams. When we heard that Swamiji had dropped the physical body, and we were unable to make it for the final rites, I was quite dejected. Soon after, I had a dream that helped me get over my dejection. In my dream, Swamiji appeared all dressed in white, like he used to in the early years. He had a bowl containing kheer, a sweet porridge-like milk-based preparation, which he was holding behind him. Kheer is the sanctified offering given in temples to devotees. There were disciples around him waiting to receive the offering. I came up from behind, and tried to help myself to some kheer. He smilingly reprimanded me for my impudence. Trying to interpret the dream's symbolism, I wondered if it represented my desire for success in sadhana, without due effort. However, I was comforted by seeing Swamiji, looking like he used to many years earlier. I was also reminded of his saying that we could not dream of him, unless he willed it. It was nice to know that he willed us to dream of him, even after he had dropped the physical body. In another dream that I had after Swamiji had dropped the body, Swamiji told me that my lack of success in sadhana was related to my lukewarm attitude. I had to intensify my efforts in order to succeed. Sadhana had to take precedence over other activities.

I had made a commitment to Swamiji to return within two years, to start a dialysis program at the hospital. Swamiji was no longer physically present; notwithstanding the advice of others, Vijaya and I decided to fulfill our commitment, and made arrangements for winding up our affairs in Minnesota. I informed Baxter Healthcare about my decision, and they, in turn, decided that it was no longer necessary to maintain the research laboratory in Minneapolis away from their Chicago headquarters. The laboratory had been set up to accommodate my desire to stay on in Minneapolis, even after joining Baxter. So, in addition to winding up my personal affairs, I had to shut down the laboratory, and took it upon myself to help members of my research group find other jobs. It was a very hectic time for us.

Our son, who now worked in New York, came home for the weekend, as he felt very sentimental about our selling the house, which contained many of his childhood memories. Our daughter was away in Spain for her semester abroad. Our friends threw some going away parties for us. Many wondered about the foolish venture we were about to embark on. Vijaya's brother began taking bets with other relatives about how long we would last in India! He gave us a year, maybe two, at the most.

We were selling our home in the winter, not the best time for open houses and other real estate activity. To keep our deadline of being in India before the end of February 1998, we took the easy way out, and sold our home and most of the furnishings, to a young handyman who had helped us finish our basement and done other fix-it jobs on our house. He had, at one time, been an air traffic controller, but had lost his job when President Reagan terminated striking air traffic controllers. He had to sell his home before he could buy ours. He purchased our home at a bargain price, because of my desire to sell quickly, burning all our bridges behind us when we left for India. I could have rented out our house, and taken a year off from work, in order to ease the anxiety of returning to India, after a stay of 30 years in the U.S. If I had done that, my commitment might have been lukewarm, with the possibility of my wanting to return to the U.S. at the slightest provocation. As I told someone, it was like the difference in commitment between two people getting married rather than living together!

We arrived in Delhi, and soon after made our way to Jolly Grant. We had to stay in the guesthouse for a few months, as no quarters were available. For two of us, and our four suitcases, the guesthouse was rather cramped, but we had no choice in the matter. I contacted the engineering department and started planning the layout of the dialysis unit on the second floor, above the library. I also contacted vendors and ordered the equipment required for the dialysis unit. Fortunately, the hospital's investment for starting dialysis was greatly reduced by a generous donation of three hemodialysis machines, three peritoneal dialysis machines and a two-year supply of disposables by my former employer, Baxter Healthcare.

I had hoped to start dialysis in about six months, based on my U.S. experience; it took about 14 months instead. I had not taken into consideration the rather laid back attitude of the workforce (engineers, masons, electricians, plumbers and carpenters), sons of the soil, for whom time was always stretchable, and who did not believe in doing today what could be postponed to tomorrow. It was quite a challenge, and remembering Swamiji helped me through the low points of the project. To save time, while the construction work was still on, I started a six-month training program for five dialysis nurses. The nurses had finished their training by the time the dialysis unit became operational. In the beginning, very few patients showed up for dialysis. I was getting a little discouraged. Early one morning, at my meditation time, I took a photograph of Swamiji, visited all the rooms of the dialysis unit, lit some incense sticks and prayed to Swamiji to bless the project. A few days later, patients started coming in for dialysis. By the end of the year, three months later, we had completed 100 dialysis treatments. The dialysis team celebrated the milestone at a Dehradun restaurant. Now, about 10 years later, we do 100 treatments approximately every three to four days. In 10 years, the number of dialyis treatments has grown more than sevenfold. A kidney transplant program has also been initiated, and to date we have completed 14 transplants.

After the initial plans for the dialysis unit had been completed, we took three months off to visit our children in the U.S. We also packed our personal effects, and arranged for them to be shipped to India. In the fall, we occupied a newly completed two-bedroom flat, and waited for our personal effects to arrive. We received notice of the arrival of the shipment, and I proceeded to Delhi for customs clearance. I had very little experience dealing with the Indian bureaucracy, and initially, the customs officials gave us a hard time. While I waited for them to decide whether they would allow the shipment under transfer of residence rules, I sent up a small prayer to Swamiji, telling him that I was in India in accordance with his instructions, and that he had to smooth the way. Soon after, the customs officials agreed to clear my shipment under transfer of residence rules, and after paying reasonable customs duties, my shipment was cleared and on its way to Jolly Grant.

In the beginning, communicating with our children in the U.S. was extremely difficult and frustrating. The phone connections were poor. There was only one public phone on the porch of the old administration building, near the guesthouse. Sometimes, on cold winter nights, we would have to wait for hours past the agreed time, for a phone call from our kids. Dr. Shobha Lal, Head of Urology, was generous with her hospitality, and allowed us to use e-mail at her home. The bandwidth of the dial-up connection was very narrow, the phone connections were bad, and it sometimes took hours to send or receive e-mails. When we did succeed, we received long e-mails from our son, telling us how much he missed us, and accusing us of having abandoned him. His sister was away in Spain, and he had no one with whom he could share his troubles and loneliness. Now, years later, Mayank has gotten used to our absence. Nowadays, we eagerly look forward to e-mails and phone calls from Mayank and Aparna, which are few and far between. In the early years, we visited the U.S. every year to spend time with Mayank and Aparna. Now the visits are less frequent. The kids have also visited us at Jolly Grant.

At the time of this writing in May, 2009, we have been at Jolly Grant for more than 11 years, far exceeding the year or two that our friends and relatives in the U.S. had predicted. I have never regretted our decision to leave the U.S. and return to India. Our life at Jolly Grant is fulfilling. I feel that our attempts at serving others selflessly are part of a purification process, which will complement our sadhana.

Swamiji had promised to take us with him into the mountains. Living in the Himalayan foothills, we have had opportunities to visit Tarakeshwar, Uttarkashi, Gangotri, Gomukh, Rudraprayag, Devprayag,

Karnaprayag, Jageshwar, Auli, Badrinath and Tung-nath. I have also been blessed by being able to visit Manasarovar and Mount Kailash in Tibet. The ease with which we have been able to visit these sacred places, and the protection we have received, suggest that Swamiji has indeed taken us with him into his beloved Himalayas.

We have witnessed the tremendous growth of the organization: the construction of many new buildings, the startup of post graduate degrees and diplomas in several medical disciplines, the maturing of the nursing school into a college, the granting of university status for the medical college, the start up of new departments and facilities in the hospital, and the expansion of the activities of the Rural Development Institute, with its new building, tele-medicine and tele-education programs.

Despite all the construction activity and expansion of services, the campus continues to be an oasis of green serenity. When we go on our evening walks, the fragrance of the flowers, the twittering of the birds and the beauty of the sunset, remind us powerfully of Swamiji, his grand vision, and his compassionate grace in bringing us home and giving new meaning and purpose to our lives. We do miss Swamiji's physical presence; we are trying to become insiders. We hope that in time to come, the distinction between inside and outside will become less relevant.

Part Two:
Kamal's Narrative

Kamal

Kamal (Patrice Hafford) first met Swami Rama in 1979 when she was living in the Sufi community, Light of the Mountains, in Leicester, North Carolina. Struggling to earn a living as a classical bassoonist, she met Swami Rama during one of the community-sponsored conferences on holistic health. Having recognized her master, she joined his service in 1980 by moving up to the Himalayan International Institute of Yoga Science and Philosophy of the USA, in Honesdale, Pennsylvania. Kamal remained at the Himalayan Institute for 13 years serving as Swamiji's personal assistant. In 1993, Swamiji brought her to his ashram, Sadhana Mandir Trust, in Rishikesh, India. After Swamiji's mahasamadhi in 1996, Kamal remained in India, taking up residence on the campus of the Himalayan Institute Hospital Trust in 1997. Swami Rama Centre was established at the place where Swamiji took mahasamadhi. Kamal was appointed Director of Swami Rama Centre, a position that she continues to hold.

1.

My First Encounter with Swami Rama

When I met Swami Rama for the first time in November 1979 at the Sheraton Hotel in Asheville, North Carolina, I had no idea what a towering personality he was. At that time, I was living in a Sufi community called Light of the Mountains, which was spread over 90 beautiful acres of God's country outside of Asheville, along the creek known as Sandy Mush. We were a tight-knit, hard-working group of seven adults, with the goal of building a community based on Sufi beliefs and holistic living. John Johnson was the head and spiritual guide of the community. We plowed fields, built houses, ate and prayed together. In addition, each of us worked outside the community to help pay for food and other expenses. Being a struggling musician, I took whatever part-time work I could find, from painting houses to factory work, and occasionally playing the bassoon in local orchestras. Life was simple, and the community was slowly but steadily prospering.

For more significant expenses, such as the mortgage on the land, we raised money by periodically sponsoring New Age conferences on spirituality and holistic health. One of the doctors from our community had recently visited the Himalayan International Institute of Yoga Science and Philosophy in Honesdale, Pennsylvania. One of the main reasons he had gone to Pennsylvania was to personally invite Swami Rama, the spiritual head and founder of the Institute, to speak at our upcoming conference to be held in November. John had a high opinion of Swamiji and said he was a very great rishi. Pir Vilayat, the head of the Sufi Order of the West, and Swamiji were close friends. Swamiji had kindly accepted the invitation, and was scheduled to deliver a lecture on the science of breath.

One of my assigned duties during the conference was to cook for Swami Rama, a duty that was to continue for many years. In the Sufi tradition, the role of the cook is so important, that traditionally the teacher cooks for the disciple, not the other way around. Needless to say, I was both excited and apprehensive about cooking for Swami Rama.

With this awesome challenge in front of me, I was determined to prepare the food following all the recommendations that had been sent by his personal cook at the Institute. Just to make sure I didn't commit any major blunders, I telephoned his cook in Pennsylvania to confirm the instructions.

Some friends told me that Indians were very conservative and expected women to keep their arms and legs covered. They advised me to wear a long dress and pull my hair back in a ponytail. I was careful to follow these guidelines and found a dress made out of Indian material that adequately covered me from my neck down to my feet. (Years later, I was to learn that what I wore was like an Indian nightgown, hardly appro-priate attire for the occasion!)

When the day finally arrived, I took a bath and cleared my mind before I entered the kitchen. As I prepared the food, I remembered my wazifah (Sufi mantra) and observed silence. The meal consisted of steamed broccoli, brown rice, red lentils, green salad, and unpeeled fruit salad. To this day I wonder what

Swamiji must have thought, when I served him such a simple meal, dressed in an Indian nightgown.

All the guest speakers were booked at the Sheraton Hotel in Asheville. As lunchtime approached, I brought the food that I had prepared to the hotel and put it all on a cart that I borrowed from the hotel kitchen. I wheeled the food up to his room, and stood silently at the door for a few moments to compose myself. When I finally knocked, the door instantly flew open and there stood all 6'1" of Swami Rama with his 42" paunch. I was rendered speechless. My heart flew up into my mouth, and I couldn't say a word. In my life of 23 years, I had seen only one other Indian man — a sitarist performing in a concert at the university. He was a small man wearing a turban, sitting on a platform, aloof from the audience. And that is what I expected of Swami Rama — a tiny Indian man, sitting on a pedestal, deep in samadhi, in a room densely saturated with incense. To my astonishment, what I found instead was a huge man radiating an over-whelming presence, dressed in a white Nehru suit.

He shook my hand warmly and said, "You have gone to so much trouble."

I placed my other hand on top of his, and then, with a piercing look, he also put his other hand on top of mine.

I remember thinking, *What a big nose you have.* Then looking at his paunch, *And what a big stomach you have!* Still speechless, I could only grin from ear to ear. He repeated, "You have gone to so much trouble." Then he moved aside as I rolled the cart into the room.

"Why do you not eat with me?" he asked, as I began placing the dishes and utensils on the counter. I had not expected this and quietly refused. Even when he repeated the invitation, I felt far too shy to accept. However, once I had laid everything out on the table,

I thought to myself, *Maybe I'll accept if he asks me one more time.*

Sure enough, he boomed out forcefully, "Why do you not eat?!"

So I accepted.

Woody Allen could not have crafted a better script. Swamiji pulled out a chair for me and spread a towel on my lap. He dished the food onto my plate and then served himself. I noticed that the ashtray on the table was filled with cigarette butts, and I thought it was strange that a master of pranayama would smoke. There was also a bottle of vitamins on the table, and I wondered why a healer would need to take vitamins. I smiled and accepted it all in light of the Sufi tradition of dervishes, knowing that their ways were truly mysterious.

As we were eating, Swamiji questioned me inter-mittently: "How young are you? Are you married? Do you have a job? Where did you go to school?" And so on. I answered the questions to the point, still grinning like an idiot, thoroughly captivated by the novelty of the moment.

After a few moments of conversation, he lapsed into a prolonged period of silence, while staring intensely at the TV screen. WWF (World Wrestling Federation) was on, and the grunting, sweating men had thrown each other down in the arena, their slippery bodies pressed against each other. Again I remembered Woody Allen. Finally, I looked at Swamiji and asked, "Do you like to watch TV?"

He looked at me oddly, and said, "No." Then he again proceeded to stare intently at the TV screen.

After we had finished eating, as I was gathering up the dishes and putting them onto the cart, Swamiji told me I should go to India. He said that he went every year, taking a few students with him, and that he would be leaving soon.

I have to honestly admit that before this, I had never considered going to India. I just looked at him and said, "It takes money to go to India."

He said, "Money comes."

I said, "Yes, but not enough." I was remembering my struggles to make enough money to survive as a musician and odd-job worker.

He told me to let him know whenever I wanted to go to India; he would write letters of introduction for me to be received in India. Then he sat on the bed, opened up his briefcase and pulled out an Indian leather wallet.

"This is for you," he said as he handed it to me.

It was very nicely crafted and I was happy to receive it. As I look back, ever since Swamiji gave me that wallet, 'money comes,' and I have always had enough for my needs.

I had made some fresh orange juice for him, because it was on his list of food items; as he drank it, he said he loved orange juice. Then someone came to drive him to the lecture; I took the cart and left. I went back to the kitchen, made a quart of orange juice for him, and left it in his room.

Coincidentally, Dr. Elmer Green was also lecturing at the conference. Dr. Green talked about his findings from the scientific experiments that were conducted at the Menninger Foundation on voluntary control of involuntary states. Swami Rama had been an integral part of that research as he was an authority in that field. Swamiji demonstrated, under strict laboratory conditions, his voluntary control over involuntary states and changed the threshold of what science considered impossible. The results of that research formed the basis of what became popularly known as biofeedback.

One of the most amazing feats that Swamiji performed in the laboratory was to put his heart into atrial flutter, thereby preventing his heart from pumping blood for 17 seconds. An ordinary person could have died. After the experiment, Swamiji went out and delivered a lecture.

In another experiment, to demonstrate his exquisite control over the autonomic nervous system, he produced a difference of 10 degrees F. in adjacent areas of the palm of his hand. One of the most demanding experiments was his demonstration of psychokinesis. He made a steel knitting needle assembly mounted on a spindle to rotate 10 degrees, three times in a row, merely by the force of his willpower.

During the time that Swamiji was at the Menninger Foundation, he took part in many experiments that studied alpha, theta, and delta brain waves. Delta brain waves are associated with states of deep sleep. When Swamiji was hooked up to the monitoring equipment, he produced delta brain waves. Later he was able to recall conversations coming over the intercom with 85 percent accuracy.

These groundbreaking experiments in the field of mind over matter were taking place at a time when American society was in the grip of social revolution and transformation. Meditation had taken the young hippie generation by storm, and through drugs, they were experimenting with altered states of consciousness.

Swami Rama came to plant the seeds of holistic living in this fertile American soil. He taught conscious control of unconscious states, without the use of any drugs or props, through a scientific approach to spirituality. Humanity was on the brink of a leap in evolution, and Swamiji arrived to tip the scales, to help form a simple yet profound approach to life and living, the foundation of what would later come to be known as holistic health.

The scientific community was amazed and full of praise for the findings of this research. The experiments were published in scientific annals like the Nature Science Annual of 1974, the 1973 Britannica Encyclopedia, World Book Encyclopedia, as well as in many newspapers and scientific journals.

In the spotlight, Swamiji was featured on the Phil Donahue show in 1979. He became a national figure, and with that momentum propelling him, he established the headquarters of the Himalayan International Institute of Yoga Science and Philosophy of the USA, in Honesdale, Pennsylvania.

Initially, the scientific community enthusiastically supported Swamiji and his groundbreaking research. But soon thereafter, a few scientists became insecure and felt that he was a threat to their Christian beliefs. They tried to undermine the work that he had undertaken; it was too late because the results had already been published and could not be recalled.

There are many interesting accounts of these experiments. Doug Boyd's book, *Swami: The Mystic Saints of India*, is probably the best firsthand account of that time. *Beyond Biofeedback*, by Drs. Elmer and Alyce Green is another excellent book. *Walking with a Himalayan Master*, by Justin O'Brien (Swami Jaidev) gives some interesting insights into events that led to Swamiji's abrupt departure from the Menninger Foundation. *A Multi Splendoured Sage*, by K.S. Duggal, also sheds some light on Swamiji's relationship with the Menninger Foundation in later years.

I attended Swamiji's lecture, but did not meet him again, until he came to Asheville several months later, to lecture at one of our other conferences.

2.
New Beginnings

Light of the Mountains held another conference on spirituality in May of 1980. This conference was held at Black Mountain in a retreat center not far from Asheville. Wallace Black Elk and Grace Spotted Eagle were among the speakers who were invited along with Swami Rama.

I often thought about Swamiji for several months after our first meeting; but this time I felt uneasy about meeting him again. The organizers of the conference had decided that I should cook for Swamiji, but not personally attend on him this time. But as soon as Swamiji was received at the airport, he started asking for me and wanted to see me. My assigned duties included taking care of the other speakers as well.

Meanwhile, to organize my time better, I had prepared Swamiji's food in advance. This time when I brought the food, I also brought a list of names of people attending the conference who wanted to meet him. When I knocked on his door, Swamiji opened it dressed in what I presumed to be his bathrobe. Actually, it was a Yukata, a Japanese style robe that he often wore in private to be comfortable. In public, he wore western style clothes.

I don't remember much of what he said on this trip because it was so overwhelming. He said that his secretary (Samskriti) in Honesdale was expecting a baby, and that he needed a new secretary. He offered me the job, and asked me to come to the Institute. Swamiji talked to me for a long time. At one point, he said very quietly, "Don't come unless you are prepared to be burned," then looking me straight in the eye added, "completely burned. Do you know what happens when something enters the fire? It becomes *like* the fire." In my utter and complete ignorance, I calmly sat there wondering at his words. I could never have imagined the life that was to follow.

Swamiji wanted tilk. Tilk was his word for tea plus milk. It was a hot beverage of boiled milk with black tea, some sugar and spices. The exact recipe varied over the years.

Swamiji's master was a great yogi and saint from Bengal, well known in the Garhwal and Kumaun mountains as Babaji. Swamiji's book, *Living with the Himalayan Masters*, tells many wonderful stories about Swamiji's youth and his life as a young swami roaming the Himalayan mountain range.

Babaji raised Swamiji from the age of three. He was often brought to the cave monastery, where Babaji taught other swamis and yogis. They had limited access to food, milk, tea, sugar, and ate only one meal a day. Swamiji was a young boy, very active and growing well. He drank lots of milk; the others complained to Babaji that Bholia (Swamiji's childhood nickname), was drinking all the milk, and that there was none left for them. So Babaji told him not to drink so much milk.

Well, Bholia was very, very stubborn, and he thought, *Okay, I take a vow from this day not to drink milk.* As the days passed, he became thinner and thinner, until his master one day asked him what was wrong. Bholia told him that he wasn't drinking milk. So Babaji told him to drink milk, but Bholia said, "No, I have taken a vow not to drink milk, because you told me not to drink milk!" Then they came up with the idea of putting tea in the milk, so it would not be 'milk' any more; it was tilk. And that was how Swamiji started to drink milk again, as tilk, without breaking his vow.

I was set the task of making tilk. Being unprepared, I went down to the main kitchen of the hotel, boiled some milk and put a tea bag in it, thus creating tilk for the first time. I brought it to Swamiji. He then agreed to see the few appointments that were still waiting for him. He told me to burn incense in the room and to hide his cigarettes. Then, one by one, he quickly finished the appointments.

After Swamiji's lecture the next day, he wanted to leave early for the airport. I drove him to the airport, where we ate sandwiches and waited for the plane to depart. Again he asked me to come up to Honesdale. I told him I would come a month later, as I had a gig to play, and that I wanted to earn some money before coming there. He dropped the subject, and left for Pennsylvania.

After the conference was over and we were all back at Light of the Mountains, I told the others what had happened. They were excited and amazed. Some were skeptical, but John gave me his blessings. I was still buzzing with excitement when I went to work the next day.

At work, the company was going through some reorganization and cutbacks, and I received my pink slip. I called the director who wanted me to play in her musical. Strangely enough, as she explained it, she thought that there was a bassoon part in the musical, but as it turned out, there was none. Within a span of three days, my life had been rearranged, and I had no more excuses to stop me from going to Pennsylvania.

John gave me his blessings, and wrote a nice letter to Swamiji saying that he was transferring his spiritual charge of me to Swamiji. But John gave me one piece of advice, and that was, not to change my name. He told me that to change my name would be to shift my allegiance from him to Swami Rama. When I was initiated into the Sufi order, John gave me the spiritual name Chalice.

And so ended my life of a year and a half at Light of the Mountains; and so began my life of 16 years with Swami Rama. I packed up my bassoon and a few possessions that fit nicely into the back seat of my car, and headed up to Pennsylvania.

The Institute was very impressive and extremely well organized. The long entry driveway curved down to the main building, passing through an open field to the right, often dotted with bales of hay in the fall. To the left were woods as far as the eye could see. Altogether, the Institute was nestled on 400 acres of land surrounded by state game lands. It was an island nestled in a green hilly sea.

The Institute at one time had been a flourishing Catholic seminary, but as enrollment dwindled, they were forced to put the seminary up for sale. The imposing building, the overtly efficient infrastructure, and institutional way of living were somewhat intimidating to me. I was used to an artist's life, a free bird in the Blue Ridge Mountains, free to come and go as I pleased, close to the land and close to nature. Misgivings in mind, I resolved not to unpack my suitcase until I was sure I wanted to stay. After all, I didn't know who this Swami Rama was, and what he wanted of me.

Swamiji met me briefly in his office, and then arranged for someone to give me a tour of the campus. The main building had a number of seminar rooms, where lectures and workshops were conducted by the faculty on topics of holistic health, yoga, comparative psychology, and Eastern religion. Training programs in yoga psychology were also offered to physicians and therapists. There was a large auditorium downstairs where Swamiji usually lectured, that could seat up to 600 people.

The Institute offered different kinds of residential programs with people living on campus, working part or full time, and practicing yoga and meditation. These residents were housed in the main building; the men's wing was downstairs, and women's wing was upstairs. Dating was not allowed, unless the couple concerned was interested in getting married. Many of the people who participated in the residential programs were at a crossroad in their lives, some recently divorced, some recovering from illness, even a few genuine seekers. The Institute offered an invaluable service to these people, allowing them to live in a structured environment where they were safe and secure, and giving them an opportunity to become introspective and work with themselves and their habit patterns.

Everyone ate in the dining hall, where the food was a constant source of complaints and grumbling. The food was vegetarian, fresh, relatively low fat, holistic, and to some, tasteless. Personally, I was very happy with the food, at least most of the time.

A small building, across from the boiler room, had originally been a convent to house the Catholic nuns. When I came in 1980, it was being used for the Combined Therapy Program, a program combining diet and nutrition, yoga, meditation, biofeedback, and homeopathy, to treat various illnesses. Dr. Rudolph Ballentine was the director of the Combined Therapy Program, assisted by a staff of doctors, nurses, and trained therapists. The Combined Therapy Program, designed by

Swami Rama, was one of the first holistic inpatient treatment programs in America. Patients received personal and customized care according to their individual needs. The doctors consulted with Swamiji on many of the cases.

Swamiji was a master of intuitive diagnosis as well as homeopathy, and personally trained his staff of doctors and nurses.

Dr. Brian Bustard, a psychiatrist from Toronto, had come for a visit to Honesdale to meet Swami Rama. He was staying in the seminar wing of the building, and Swamiji called him to his office for an appointment. Swamiji told Brian that he had a hole in his heart. Brian did not believe him because he had been thoroughly examined and tested by doctors and was himself a doctor. There was no indication that he had a hole in his heart. But Swamiji insisted that he go to the local hospital in Honesdale and have the test done. Skeptical, Brian went for the test. Surprisingly enough, the test results came back showing that he did indeed have a very small hole in his heart.

There was also a nine-year-old boy, the son of the manager of East West Books in New York City, who was diagnosed with an aggressive form of skin cancer. It was very unusual to see this form of cancer in a child. The parents brought him to see Swamiji. Swamiji said that it was not cancer, even though the doctors and pathology laboratory had diagnosed it as cancer. The young boy had complete faith in Swamiji and told his parents not to worry, because if Swamiji said it was not cancer, then it was not cancer. When they returned to New York, they received a phone call from the pathology laboratory indicating that a mistake had been made and that the biopsy was not malignant.

There was also a homeopathic pharmacy in the building, run by Pat Klein, a registered pharmacist who made the remedies with the purest ingredients and in the traditional manner.

The Institute had a publishing house called 'Himalayan Publishers, the resource for holistic living.' They published several books on yoga psychology and holistic health. Swamiji himself was a prolific writer. They had recently acquired a Heidelberg printing press that was housed in town. When the press was running, the whole building used to shake. Samskriti was Swamiji's secretary, and her husband Gopala was the manager of the press. One of the old barns on the campus was being remodeled to house the printing press and related offices. They had a complete printing set-up from editing and typesetting, to art and design, printing, distribution, and shipping. The whole Institute was very impressive, highly organized and efficient.

The residents were expected to attend prayers twice a day, at 6:00 a.m. and 10:00 p.m. in the meditation hall. Attendance at prayers was mandatory, and three absences in a row, without any excuse, resulted in expulsion. In the early days, Swamiji was very strict about discipline. He expected the students to be serious about meditation, and if they were not, they had to leave.

Everyone placed a cushion on the carpeted floor to mark their place, and a chart was kept of everyone's spot. Swamiji taught us to meditate at the same time and place every day in order to firmly establish the habit of meditation. Swamiji had a cushion kept for him at the front of the meditation hall facing the students; the students faced east. The prayers were taught to the residents during their orientation phase, and were recited by the group in the meditation hall.

Bala, the head of the Residential Program usually led the prayers, playing the harmonium for accompaniment. The prayers were composed of Sanskrit verses from the *Upanishads* and Saundarya Lahari. All in all, it was very beautiful and meditative.

Early morning hatha classes were offered at 6:30. The classes ranged from joints and glands exercises, beginning hatha yoga I and II, to intermediate and advanced levels. The Institute had a large institutional kitchen. The cooks prepared food for at least 100 people per meal, and up to 600 people at large weekend seminars. The meal timings were fixed and the kitchen staff had strict rules about closing the kitchen on time and not saving food for stragglers. In the early years, the kitchen staff was very disciplined. They worked long hours, prepared the food in a wholesome environment and took their own meals only after everyone else had been fed. Sometimes, they even went without food if there was none left.

Next to the kitchen was the dish room, where all the residents were expected to wash their own dishes. Everyone had to sign up for a dish shift and for a housekeeping duty. Housekeeping duties ranged from watering plants, mopping floors, cleaning bathrooms, and doing laundry. The housekeeping department was run by Mira Delahunte. It was a thankless job, the sort of job that no one noticed as long as it ran like clockwork, but everyone complained about, if there was the slightest glitch.

There were many medical doctors, Ph.D.s and therapists in the Institute going through the residential programs. They lived on campus and followed the routine like all the others, which included doing a dish shift or cleaning the bathroom. Swamiji used to say, "Throw a stone and wherever it lands, it will hit a Ph.D." And that was what Swamiji wanted. His mission in the West was to train professionals—doctors, psychologists, and therapists—in yoga science and thus inject holistic health into the medical mainstream of America. In the last 20 years, holistic health, bio-feedback and stress management have become mainstream modalities, largely due to Swamiji's research and influence.

There were a few other buildings on the land. One of them was an old barn that had been converted into four apartments and was known as the Baby Barn. Whoever lived there ended up having a baby. There was also the Chateau, a small wooden house on the crest of Sound of Music Hill. Swamiji had lived in it for a short while and then handed it over to Dr. Clarke and his family.

The Sound of Music Hill was an expanse of rolling forest that resembled the opening scene in the movie 'The Sound of Music.' You could stand on the crest and look out onto waves of rolling green hills.

There was an old sheep barn that had been converted into the Eleanor N. Dana Research Laboratory. Mrs. Eleanor Dana of the Dana Foundation was a benefactress of the Institute. The Research Laboratory housed specialized equipment for conducting research on yogic practices, brain waves, breathing and heart function. Much of the research conducted there was published in the Himalayan Institute Research Bulletin.

Swamiji was very fond of building and constructing as well as landscaping; so there was always an ongoing project.

3.
From Honeymoon to Boot Camp

Swamiji had an apartment in the main building on the ground floor. There was an outer office, an inner office, dining room, small kitchen, conference room, bedroom and bathroom. He also had a house off-campus, in the area known as Seelyville, between the Institute and the town of Honesdale. Swamiji would work or reside in either place as he wished.

After I arrived, Swamiji called me to his office where I was introduced to Kevin, Mahima, and some of the regular people that attended on him and worked at the Institute. Swamiji always had two to three secretaries helping him at a time. I learned from them how to serve Swamiji's food, set the table, look after his guests, do the laundry and clean house. He also handed me a copy of the book, *Practical Vedanta of Swami Rama Tirtha* and said that Swami Rama Tirtha was the greatest Sufi of his time.

It was well known that there were three phases of being Swamiji's student: 1) you could do no wrong, 2) you could do no right, 3) you did not exist. This was a cycle that repeated itself over and over again in the life of a student. Since I was a newcomer and had been invited to come, I was in the first phase: I could do no wrong.

Swamiji included me in all the activities, invited me to all the meals, and treated me like a royal princess. He let me sit with him, be close to him, and watch what was going on. It all seemed like one big, long, party to me. Everybody seemed to be having fun, and they were all hustling and bustling about.

I had an intense desire to cook for Swamiji, so I was informed about the Bottom Fighting Incident. Just before I arrived at Honesdale, there were three women who used to look after Swamiji and cook and clean his apartment. Swamiji's kitchen was very small. It had a skinny refrigerator, and a narrow four-burner electric stove and oven. There was not much counter space or maneuvering space. The three women were in the kitchen, all trying to do something at the same time. One of them tried to push the other out of the way with her bottom, and she, in turn, pushed back with her bottom, and hence began the infamous Bottom Fight that became immortalized. Swamiji roared and kicked them out of his apartment. I was clearly told — no bottom fighting allowed!

Swamiji used to spend a lot of time in the dining room, or what he called his Crummy Kitchen. The TV was on one side, closets on the other, the tiny kitchen on one wall, and the conference room across from it. He had a wooden dining room table, and used to lie down on the carpeted floor with his head under the table to watch TV.

I was a women's libber. And Swamiji loved a challenge. He used to look at me and say, "Women should be beaten." And I would silently say to myself, *You and whose army?* He loved it, and rarely missed an opportunity to tell me that women should be beaten. To emphasize the point, he would sometimes give me an annoying whack on the side of the head. And I did get annoyed. My mother had drilled into me in childhood that I should never let a man hit me. So every time Swamiji said women should be beaten, or gave me a whack, the little tape recorder in my mind would go off and I would get annoyed. But one day it so happened that I saw the tape recorder go off and didn't react. After that Swamiji completely dropped the exercise.

Once he called me into his apartment. We were both sitting at the dining table; he was smoking and blew cigarette smoke in my face. I said, "How rude." He laughed and laughed. When Samskriti joined us, he told her I had called him rude. Samskriti was beside herself, rolling with laughter.

Samskriti became my secretary mentor. She was blond, slender, wore glasses, and was about nine months pregnant. She was also Secretary of the Board, and had quite a ferocious reputation. But she was always very kind to me and I had a lot of respect for her.

Swamiji used to refer to his students as his 'collection,' like the bridegroom's party at Shiva's wedding. Shiva had all sorts of characters in his entourage, ranging from the saintly and beautiful, to the ugly and macabre. He used to say in his lectures that our mind goes with us wherever we go, like a garbage can. So, amongst Swamiji's students could be found all types of people. We were all collectors' items.

Samskriti taught me how to handle the appointments, answer the mail, and do the filing. Amongst the files was a notorious file called the Goofy File. This was a collection of goofy letters that had been sent to Swamiji over the years. One of the more famous ones was a letter he received from a woman, describing an encounter she had with Swamiji, where he materialized in her room through the vents in her air conditioner, holding a cattle prod. The rest is up to your imagination.

Soon after I arrived at the Institute, Samskriti gave birth to a baby boy whom Swamiji named Nirvana, after the old sadhu that looked after him in his childhood.

Nirvanji was an old, illiterate swami in the monastery who was assigned to Swamiji as his tutor in his childhood. He could not read or write, but he knew every Upanishad by heart. He used to sit in one posture all day long and never got tired. He was an advanced siddha, a very gentle and powerful soul. He looked after Swamiji for the first 16 years of his life.

Nirvanji had a kutia (small thatched hut) in Rishikesh, next to what is now Sadhana Mandir, Swamiji's ashram. Swamiji would sometimes stay with Nirvanji in that kutia when Rishikesh was still a wild jungle, and elephants would cross the Ganges and scratch their backs against the hut, making the whole thing shake.

One night, Swamiji heard Nirvanji inside the kutia talking to someone, and the next day asked him who it was. Nirvanji said it was an old cobra inside his kutia; he kept asking it to leave, but the old fellow wouldn't go!

After Swamiji had been in America, he came back to Rishikesh much thinner than when he left. Nirvanji got ready, put on his mismatched sandals and said he would go with Swamiji to America to cook for him. Then Swamiji had to explain to him that you need a passport and visa; you can't just go like that.

Swamiji said that Nirvanji left his body in 1982 and was buried somewhere in the vicinity. I visited that kutia in 1985. It was a small wooden rectangular room, with a concrete floor, a small overhead shelf and some wooden pegs in the wall. There was a hole in the concrete floor where the cobra used to enter. The kutia has since been destroyed.

In contrast to the kutia of Rishikesh, Swamiji's apartment in Honesdale was opulent. As he was very fond of antiques and art pieces, his conference room was decorated with beautiful pieces from all over the world. There was a long wooden table in the center with carved ivory inlay of Indian elephants and kings. There was a large dark carved rosewood sofa from China. He had beautiful Persian rugs in the conference room, many unusual carvings, statues, antiques, lamps and tables. The conference room was quite a showpiece. Everyone called it the White Conference Room because of the white walls and carpet.

One wall was completely of glass, and two walls were lined with windows. All along the window sills were varieties of plants, especially cacti. Swamiji called the cactus the swami among plants, because it thrived best if left alone. One day I was trailing behind Swamiji as he inspected all the plants along the window sills, giving directions for watering and pruning the plants. There was a Christmas cactus that always had at least one blossom on it whenever Swamiji was there, no matter what season it was. He said he would ask her to bloom for him and she would. I casually asked Swamiji if plants had egos, and he replied, "Of course, how else can they stand upright?" Then I commented that at least they don't fight with each other, to which he replied, "How do you know?"

His bedroom was simple, just a mattress on the floor, and lots of closet space filled with Yukatas, underwear, sweaters, shoes, socks, jackets, some Nehru suits, silk kurtas/pajamas, and jogging and tennis suits. Swamiji had very good taste in clothes and wore only the best suits and designer shoes. But that was for the public. In the privacy of his own apartment, he wore his Yukata, or just his boxer shorts and T-shirt if he felt hot.

Himalayan International Institute of Yoga Science and
Philosophy of the USA, Honesdale, Pennsylvania

The bathroom was small and simple, nothing out
of the ordinary. Swamiji himself rarely took a bath or
shower, because he practiced the prana bath. His skin
was as soft and smooth as a baby's bottom, and he
never smelled bad, even though he rarely bathed. In
fact, there was always a very faint pleasant fragrance
around Swamiji, in spite of his heavy cigarette smoking.

His outer office was small, with a desk, a coffee
table made out of a slab of polished tree trunk, and a
large black reclining chair that he sometimes napped
in. The outer office was used mostly for appointments
and mantra initiations. His inner office was also small,
but had a large desk and bookshelves. Swamiji was
very artistic and kept art pieces like hanging carpets
and silk paintings wherever appropriate. In fact, he
was an excellent interior decorator and could make
things go together in ways you would never expect.
Yet, with all that glamour and expensive detail, he
chose to spend most of his time under the table in his
Crummy Kitchen.

There were a few signature items that were always present wherever Swamiji resided, anywhere in the world: a telephone, a TV/VCR, cigarettes, spittoon, and a dog. These things were always present.

Swamiji always had at least one dog with him; he said they were very protective and loyal. Once Swamiji told me that in his childhood he had a pet greyhound. She had a litter of puppies. He wanted to know what dog's milk tasted like, so he wriggled in with the other puppies to drink. After that she was very protective of him and loved him very much.

He often spoke of his dog, Jackie, a German shepherd he had in India. He used to tie Jackie to the leg of his cot at night. One night a thief broke in and Jackie chased the thief with the cot in tow.

But Swamiji's pets were not restricted to dogs. In his youth, he also had a pet bear named Bhola. The bear used to follow him around the mountains and sleep with him in the cave. The other swamis complained, because they had to cook rotis for the bear, and it ate too many.

Then there was the pet elephant. She used to follow him around in Rishikesh. They would pass by a small wooden stall and Swamiji bought candies for her to eat. Once when Swamiji was not there, she went to the stall on her own to get candies, but the shopkeeper wouldn't give her any. So she smashed his stall. Swamiji had to pay for the damages.

There was another small room on the other side of Swamiji's outer office where his personal attendant stayed. After a few days of my arrival, I moved down into that room and lived there for the next 13 years. It was a plain simple room that had a desk and chair, a sink and mirror, and of course, a telephone. When the reception desk closed at 10:00 p.m., the night phones were switched to my extension, and I became the night telephone operator. This was primarily because Swamiji received and made many phone calls at night. The incoming calls would go through my phone, and I would connect them to his office.

Swamiji's house in Seelyville sat atop a hill and commanded a very nice view of the township of Honesdale. On the ground floor, the house had a kitchen, and a large open room that was the combined living room/dining room. There was also a fireplace. The sliding glass doors opened onto a patio that looked out on the town below. There was a loft upstairs that Swamiji used for his bedroom. Of course, Swamiji spent most of the time on the sofa downstairs, next to the fireplace.

To the side of the house was a swimming pool where he could swim for exercise. Swamiji was an excellent swimmer. One or two of the male residents would stay at Swamiji's house in Seelyville to look after it and take care of the dogs. Swamiji had three Dobermans: Raja, Ruby, and Ringo. The most famous of these dogs was Raja. Unfortunately, I never met Raja because he had died by the time I moved to Honesdale.

> Swamiji told many stories about Raja and how intelligent and well trained he was. Raja would not eat unless Swamiji told him to eat. Sometimes he would put a dog biscuit on Raja's nose, and saliva would be dripping out of Raja's mouth, but he would not eat until Swamiji told him to eat. When Swamiji was in Glenview, Gopala used to take care of Raja. Swamiji used to lie on his stomach on the floor and have Gopala and others massage him. Then he would cry out "Raja! Raja!" and Raja would come and stand over Swamiji, straddling his body, growling at the boys, even though Gopala used to take care of him. In Justin O'Brien's book, *Walking with a Himalayan Master*, there are some amusing stories about Raja.

Raja died when Swamiji was in India one year.
Swamiji was with his master and had his head in his
lap, when Babaji told him that Raja had died. Swamiji
said, "You always take away the things I love." Babaji
said, "You blame me for everything."

When I came to the Institute in 1980, the Dobermans Ringo and Ruby were living with Swamiji in
Seelyville. I wasn't very fond of dogs; in fact, I was
afraid of them. That was perfect, because Swamiji
didn't allow anyone to be friendly with his dogs; he
said it spoiled them. They were watchdogs, not pets,
and anyone who tried to pet his dogs would be
reprimanded, or even debarred from his residence.
Ruby was very strong and muscular, and I found her
unblinking stare to be somewhat unnerving.

One day Ruby and Ringo encountered a skunk;
so Swamiji told me to go to his house in Seelyville and
give them a bath. I asked around and discovered that
there were two common methods for removing skunk
juice from a dog: One is bathing with milk, the other is
bathing with tomato juice. I chose tomato juice and
brought a couple of gallons up to the house. I was a
little scared of them and had only cold water from a
hose to wash them down with. They weren't very eager
for the experience. No doubt they felt they smelled just
fine. With great trepidation, I hosed them both down
and washed them with tomato juice. They didn't seem
to mind one bit.

Swamiji would go back and forth between his
house in Seelyville and his apartment on campus. He
had a large jeep and would either drive himself or have
someone else drive him. He liked to drive and the
necessity of having a road didn't seem to deter him,
for he was known to take off across fields leaving only

dust in his wake, or to drive through compost heaps splattered with garbage.

He often invited his guests up to his house to entertain them, or he worked on his books there. He would come to the campus to give lectures, keep appointments and take care of business.

A typical day in the life of Swamiji during that time would start around 5:00 a.m. He would call me, and I would go to his little kitchen and make him a cup of lemon tea. Then I would make a glass of orange juice and leave it on the dining table for him to drink later. At that time, Swamiji did not eat breakfast.

Swamiji slept on the floor in his Crummy Kitchen. We would spread a blanket on the carpet for him to sleep on, and keep another woolen blanket for him to cover up with. In the early mornings, I would tidy up and empty his ashtray and spittoon, trying to be unobtrusive. If the mood seemed conducive, I would sit quietly and wait for instructions or conversation. If not, I would tiptoe out.

By 8:45 a.m., the residents were buzzing around and the offices were open. Reception opened its doors, the doctors' offices opened and they started their rounds to see patients. Swamiji would be very busy during this time, talking to people or consulting with the doctors, or taking a round of the campus. I used to slip into his apartment when he was out, to quickly clean, vacuum, dust and water the countless plants in the conference room.

My duties included making Swamiji's appointments, answering phone calls, delivering phone messages, mail, and notes. Scheduling his appointments was always a precarious job. When the job was handed over to me, I was told to collect the names of people who wanted to talk to Swamiji and then show him the list of names. So I did that. And he said to schedule them all for the next morning at 15-minute intervals. And it was done. There were about 12 names on the list, and he went through most of the appointments. At the end he stopped, and told me to schedule the rest for the next day. Then he wanted to know if I was trying to kill him by scheduling so many appointments. So I asked him how many should I schedule, and he said all of them. The next day was a repeat performance; again he got mad and asked me if it was humanly possible to see so many appointments. Again I asked him whom he wanted to see, and whom not, and again he said everyone. Finally I asked Samskriti what to do, and she gave me some 'sage' advice: Only schedule those that had legitimate business, like mantra initiations, questions about administration, medical consultations and follow-up appointments; screen out the goofy ones. Experience taught me not to tell Swamiji of each and every request to see him. I learned to discriminate and schedule the ones that had legitimate business, or those that Swamiji asked for. It was a tricky business, and I was not always right. Somebody or other was always mad at me. For the most part, the ones that needed to see him did, or received the help they needed elsewhere.

Swamiji used to say that being a swami was like being a prostitute. People thought they could come to see a swami at any time of the night or day; a swami was public property.

When I first started doing secretarial work for Swamiji, he sat me down and told me that I would be blamed for everything. He told me that in order to understand him, I should see him on three levels — man, sage, and baby. He said that he was a yogi first, and a swami second.

Swamiji wanted to change my name but I said no. He called me his goofy Sufi. In the Sufi tradition, a spiritual name is given as a blessing and as a quality you aspire for in your spiritual development. When I said no, he said it would be a name only between the two of us and nobody else need know. So I said okay. He gave me the name Kamal, the Sanskrit word for lotus, the symbol of yoga. It represents one who lives in the world, yet remains above. The next thing I knew, he started telling everyone to call me Kamal and not Chalice, and to inform others of my new name.

I was very proud of my honesty and straight-forward nature. Swamiji put me to the test. There was a lady visiting from France who wanted to write a biography of Swamiji's life. She was a guest of the Institute, and Swamiji extended every courtesy and consideration to her. When the time came for her to leave, she asked if we had a car to drop her off at the New York airport. So I checked with Swamiji and he said okay. I informed the lady that a car would be arranged, and went back to Swamiji. Within five minutes, he told me to go back and tell her that no cars were available and not to use his name. I protested, saying that I had just told her that we would provide a car. Nevertheless, I went back to her and said that no cars were available, feeling very uncomfortable about it, and wondering if she thought I was insane. She looked rather puzzled, but said okay, and made her own arrangements. When she met Swamiji to say good-bye, he cancelled her arrangements and provided one of the Institute cars to take her to the airport. I learned that pride takes many forms, even attachment to an ideal.

Swamiji was very particular about his food. Lunch was his main meal of the day. The usual fare consisted of basmati rice, *moong dal,* a leafy green vegetable like spinach, some paneer (curdled milk similar to cottage cheese), green salad and fruit salad, perhaps a desert, and chappatis. Swamiji would make his own chappatis in his little kitchen. For supper he usually had spinach soup, whole wheat toast, and fruit salad with a paneer dressing.

As a young boy Swamiji used to disturb all the swamis in the cave. When they meditated he used to open their eyes, or throw rocks at them. If his master ignored him, he would deliberately break something, or do something naughty for attention. He once urinated into his master's water pot, and they had to go three miles to get clean water.

He did not want to cook for the swamis in the cave, but they made him cook. He quietly put rocks in the dal, or added red chilis. One day they caught him, and forced him to eat what he had prepared.

Swamiji never allowed us to serve him food cooked by any other person, unless we asked him first. Many Indian visitors would come and bring him delicious Indian sweets, but we could not serve it to him unless he knew who had prepared the food. There were a few people whose food he would always take, but most of the others he would not. I can only guess as to why he was so particular, but I know that at different times in his life, people had tried to poison him.

Swamiji told us another story about his childhood. He was born in a palace into a very wealthy family, but there was greed and jealousy among the relatives. One day, his aunt served him a glass of milk, and from nowhere a black cat jumped onto the table and knocked over the glass. His master came and scolded the aunt for trying to poison Swamiji, and told her to never do that again.

I loved the Indian sweets that people brought for Swamiji. The rule in the kitchen was that anything over three days old was thrown out. I used to count the days from the arrival of the sweets, hoping that some would be left over after the third day, for me to eat.

As a child, Swamiji was very fond of *jalebis*. In his early childhood he went with his master to the river to take a bath. On the way there was a jalebi stand. Swamiji wanted to have jalebis right then, right there, but his master told him to wait. Swamiji threw himself on the road and started kicking and screaming. He blocked the traffic and refused to get up. Finally, his master told him to put sand in his mouth; only then would he give him jalebis. He did as told. Then his master asked him if he wanted to eat. Swamiji said no, he wanted to wash his mouth. So they went to the river, took a bath, and on the way back his master gave him jalebis to eat.

For the first month that I was at the Institute, I enjoyed basking in the sunshine of Swamiji's approval. I could do no wrong and life was grand. People came and went, we ate good food, laughed, watched TV and movies on the VCR, and in between, did some work.

Swamiji loved being massaged. It was often a group effort with one person on one leg, another on the other leg, one on an arm, one on the other arm, feet, head, and one on his back. If there were more free hands, they would try to find a spot to massage. And Swamiji would mumble that it felt like ants were crawling over his body, and boasted that no one else could withstand so much massage. True, whenever we could, we would find something to press. It gave us the opportunity to do personal service to the guru, a practice that is prized in the Indian culture. He instructed me to massage one leg at a time, and not both legs together. Once, I was pressing both legs with both my hands, and received an electric shock that went up one arm and down the other. "That's why I told you not to press both legs together," he said.

Swamiji was an excellent host. When he was entertaining guests, he put out a royal spread and was himself charming and entertaining. He had a great sense of humor and could keep the whole room in stitches. He was extremely charismatic, and when he entered a room, all eyes instinctively flew to him. He was in command, literally, a king among men. Slowly I found myself catching this disease of adoring him. My women's lib flew out the window; I jumped when he said jump, and sat at his feet and scurried about like all the others. I possessively ironed his clothes, even his underwear, cleaned his apartment, and paid heed to his smallest request or concern.

I was saturated with love. I was in the presence of pure, unconditional, selfless love. For the Sufi, it was the divine Beloved in human form. Here was a master, a realized soul in a human body, here was the entrance to the Divine, and like all the others, I hurried to the door waiting for a crumb from that divine table. His presence was intoxicating; the air around him was charged with electricity, filled with anticipation, every atom of my being vibrated with recognition. I was addicted. And once I had surrendered, kicking and fighting every inch of the way, I was evicted.

Every summer the Institute held an International Congress on some aspect of holistic living, inviting speakers in the field from all over the world. The first Congress was held in Chicago in 1976 and there were more than 1,000 attendees. That was during the height of Swamiji's fame as an authority in the field of the mind-body relationship. In June of 1980, the Congress was again held in Chicago; I stayed back in Honesdale attending the telephone. Swamiji would call from time to time to check for messages. Soon after his return to Honesdale, he went to Japan for a couple of weeks. Swamiji had been involved with Sukyo Mahikari, a large organization in Japan that practiced healing with light. Swamiji had often visited their center in Japan.

It was after his return from Japan that Swamiji lowered the proverbial boom. One morning at 5:00, he called me into his Crummy Kitchen and gave me a thorough tongue-lashing. He covered everything from my personality to my beliefs, habits, clothes, religion; nothing was spared. It lasted for a painful 45 minutes. He told me to make a plan for my life and get out. Stunned, I went back to my room, rather numb from the whole experience. Up to that time, I was basking in the sunshine of his approval and could do no wrong. Suddenly I had been blasted, and didn't know what to do next. I fell back on my Sufi background, remembering stories of madzubs and dervishes and their strange ways, and remembered that if the master has given you many sweet fruits, why should you complain of one bitter one?

So I carried on with my duties as best as I could, and as unobtrusively as I could. I had enjoyed the first phase of a student's life of doing no wrong, and entered the second phase of a student's life of doing no right. What came after that was the hardest and longest — being ignored. I was now in boot camp. Up to that time, I was accustomed to freely come and go to Swamiji's apartment, and sit around and enjoy all the fun. Things changed. I was given a job in the business office and a shift at the reception desk. I still scheduled Swamiji's appointments, took phone calls and cleaned his apartment, but the honeymoon was over.

Swamiji commuted back and forth between the Institute and his house in Seelyville. I had to attend the night phone, and wait for the receptionist to come on duty at 8:45 in the morning, before I could leave my room. I used to wait and wait by the phone anticipating Swamiji's call. Nothing happened. If I left my room to go to the bathroom or to the dining room, he would immediately call me as soon as I got back, and demand to know where I was, and why I was not attending to the telephone. I yearned to be able to sit at his feet again, and be in his company, but he did not allow it. I could deliver the messages, do my work quietly, and leave. If I sat very still, and kept my mind still as well, then he would allow me to sit. But as soon as I fidgeted or my mind wandered, he said, "You go."

It was Swamiji's habit to sleep on the floor in his Crummy Kitchen, but occasionally he would change the location. He said that traditionally, swamis were not allowed to sleep in the same place for more than three nights in a row. One night he wanted to sleep in the big conference room, so we spread his blanket and got it ready for him. The conference room was full of plants, and in one corner was a very tall rubber plant whose top leaves used to brush the ceiling. The next morning he was still in the conference room talking to some people, and called us to look at the rubber tree. It had shrunk about six inches. We looked all around to see if it had been cut, or moved, but found no evidence to support that. Again, the next night, he slept in the conference room, and the following morning the plant was back to its normal size. Pandit Rajmani has an interesting account of this incident in his book, *At the Eleventh Hour.*

Guru Purnima comes in the month of July, and 1980 was my first year to observe this event. On the day of Guru Purnima, students gather to be with the guru and receive his blessings. Traditionally, the student offers a bundle of sticks to the guru representing the student's desire for the guru to burn his karma. At the Institute, Swamiji would have a big bonfire, give a short talk on the meaning of the word guru, have kirtan and distribute prasad to everyone.

So on the morning of Guru Purnima, I waited in my room feeling very happy that I would be the first one to see him on that auspicious day, and offer my pranams (respects). By 8:00 a.m. he still hadn't called, and I was anxiously waiting in my room. Panditji came and knocked on my door, asking if he could see Swamiji. I told him that he was not yet awake and the door was still locked. Somehow, Panditji convinced me to open the door, and let him in to see Swamiji. I felt sort of disappointed, because I had wanted to be the first to see him on that day. After a few minutes, Panditji came back, knocked on my door and asked where Swamiji was. I told him that he was in the room, but Panditji said that he was not there, and that he had searched the entire apartment. Then Panditji left, saying he would come back later.

After Panditji left, Swamiji called for me. I greeted him and made his lemon tea, and went about my business of tidying as usual. Then Panditji came in and told Swamiji that he had looked for him all over the apartment, but had not found him. Swamiji kept quiet, just took a long draught on his cigarette, and stared at the tip of his cigarette or off into space. He was very fond of doing that when he didn't want to answer any questions.

I still had an intense desire to cook for Swamiji, so from time to time he started teaching me how to cook. Himalayan Mountain Bread was a favorite dish of his. He made a pizza dough, and blended together moong dal, green peppers, onions, garlic, and tomato as a sauce along with the Indian spices of turmeric, cumin, coriander, and then spread it over the pizza dough. He would sprinkle almonds and raisins on top, and then sprinkle cheese on top of that. It was a meal in itself. He used to squat down in front of the oven, and look through the glass door and called it pizza-vision, instead of television.

Swamiji was a very good cook, and would issue instructions to be followed precisely. He said he would show me how to do it three times only; after that I would have to do it on my own. If I committed any mistake at any time, he would give me a whack on the side of the head and say, "You go." End of lesson. He taught me how to make chappati dough and it became my daily duty to make the dough in the morning and let it sit in his kitchen until lunchtime. Then Swamiji himself would make rotis (Indian flatbread) out of the dough. He was mostly fond of making one huge *parantha* in the iron skillet in those days. That was a flatbread folded in the shape of a triangle and fried with ghee (clarified butter) in the skillet. It was very tasty. He also taught me how to make split moong dal. He showed me three times, and then I was to do it on my own, in precisely the same way. The preparation of dal also became a daily duty. I would prepare the dal and chappati dough, and leave them in his kitchen. I was not allowed to eat, only prepare. And I had to do it exactly as he had shown me, every time. (During this time, the rest of his food was prepared by Shari Harris, the Combined Therapy cook. When Panditji's wife Meera came to the Institute, she started cooking the main meal for Swamiji.)

When I first arrived at the Institute, I was not very certain if I wanted to stay. The whole situation was very overwhelming; I did not know who this man called Swami Rama was. One day we were sitting at his dining table talking, and he abruptly asked me if I wanted to stay or go. I said I didn't know. Then he said, "Do you want to be raped?" I looked at him like he had just stepped off the planet Mars and said, "No." "Then stay!" he said. About three months later, I received a phone call after 10:00 p.m. from my mother. She was hysterical and sobbing on the phone. It took me about five minutes to get her to calm down and tell me what was wrong. A man had telephoned her and said he was a friend of mine and wanted to speak to me. She told him I had moved to Pennsylvania, and was no longer there. He asked for my contact information, and she gave him my phone number and address. He hung up, but then called right back and said, "Do you know where your daughter is?" And again she told him I was in Pennsylvania. Then he told her that he had kidnapped me, raped me, pumped me full of drugs, and was going to dump me in her front yard, and if she ever wanted to see me alive again, she should not call the police. Somehow she yelled at him and said, "You're lying!" and hung up the phone. Then she telephoned my brother-in-law to come over, telephoned the police, and then telephoned me. I calmed her down, and told her I was safe and sound, and that nothing had happened. Later the police came and told her, "He won't call again."

A few days after that happened, I mentioned the incident to Swamiji, and without batting an eyelid he said the exact same words, "He won't call again." That's all he would say about it, but a few years later, I asked him if he had prevented that karma from happening to me, and he said yes.

Mrs. Dana was a delightful Southern belle from the old school, elegant and refined, permeated by the gentility of the Old South. Mrs. Dana's deceased husband had been Chairman of the prestigious Dana Foundation, and Mrs. Dana was Chairperson of the Himalayan Institute. She spent a lot of time at the Institute under the doctors' supervision. She doted on Swamiji, and he lavished her with attention. When she came to visit, along with her white poodle Annette, she was given Suite 6, the special guest room on the ground floor, a few doors down from Swamiji's apartment.

Swamiji and Mrs. Dana had a little dance they did, where he would call her Jezebel and Hussy, and she would act appropriately scandalized. The doctors visited her daily. She had a private nurse to attend on her, and one of the women residents used to give her massages. She was entertained with tea parties, and the women residents would often visit her suite playing the harmonium and leading kirtan.

Mrs. Dana offered a matching grant of one million dollars to establish an endowment fund for the Institute. Swamiji worked hard, night and day, collecting pledges from the centers and individuals to raise one million dollars to match the grant. It was done, and the endowment fund was established to give the Institute financial security. Swamiji always said, "The Institute is in your country, for you people."

Swamiji could charm anyone, and get away with the most outrageous things. He had the advantage, because he could look at you and know your past, present and future. He knew what was in your heart and mind, even before you became aware of it yourself. As Dr. Arya (an eminent scholar and disciple of Swami Rama) once said, "When Swamiji sees the seed, he starts chopping down the tree."

Swamiji used to travel a lot on weekends to lecture at the different centers: New York, Glenview, Milwaukee, Indianapolis, and Minneapolis. I was always left at the Institute, to attend the telephone and catch up on sleep. But my favorite task was emptying the refrigerator. Any goodies leftover were fair game, and I couldn't wait to get at them. On one occasion, when Swamiji's car had pulled out of the driveway and out of sight for New York, I started to empty the refrigerator and placed all the leftovers, delicious Indian sweets, on the dining room table. I was positively salivating in anticipation when Swamiji coolly walked into the kitchen, sat down at the dining table, lit up a cigarette, looked at me with a twinkle in his eye, and said, "Driver forgot something." "Really?" I said, as I nonchalantly started to wipe down the counter, pretending that I had not been caught red-handed. After a few minutes, the driver walked in, and they both left. I learned a valuable lesson after that—to wait a little longer before raiding the refrigerator. The possibility of being caught made it much more fun.

Swamiji personally taught me how to make two Indian sweets: *sooji halwa*, and *burfi*. For sooji, we roasted Cream of Wheat dry cereal in a wok with a little ghee, added some cardamom powder and sugar, raisins and nuts, boiling water, and then cooked the mixture for a few minutes. It was quick and simple. The burfi was a different story. The American version of burfi was made from ricotta cheese, cream cheese, butter, sugar, cardamom powder, saffron and topped with chopped pistachio nuts. One day after lunch, Swamiji called me to make burfi. He put the ricotta cheese and cream cheese in the wok, and showed me how to stir it. He told me to stir exactly as he had shown me, and not to burn it. Since it was his custom to nap after lunch, he lay down on his blanket in his Crummy Kitchen, and went to sleep. I stood at the stove, and kept stirring in the figure '8' style he had shown me. Time passed. He was softly snoring, and I didn't want to make any noise, for fear of waking him. More time passed, my arm was aching, so I switched back and forth between the right and left hands. The cheese was becoming very solid, all the liquid had cooked out of it, and I started to wonder what to do next. Then, after three hours had passed, Swamiji woke up, came to the stove, added the final ingredients, and it was proclaimed burfi.

I used to count the days, waiting for the third day to pass, so that I could eat whatever was left of the burfi. On one such occasion, I ate whatever was left on the plate, feeling quite happy with myself. Then Swamiji called me into his office, where he was talking to Justin and Theresa O'Brien, and told me to bring them some burfi. Cornered, I simply stood there and said there wasn't any. Swamiji asked, "Why not?" I replied, "I ate it." He said, "Thank you," and they all laughed.

Every month there used to be a residents' meeting, where all the full-time residents would get together and talk about their problems. Mostly they would complain about this or that, such as the food and their housekeeping duties. But when Swamiji attended the meetings, they became public persecutions. These were times when Swamiji would take the opportunity to expose somebody's faults in front of the other residents. Everybody would cringe and hold their breath, hoping they weren't next on the list. Well, it's the job of the guru to cut the ego, and these meetings were always ripe opportunities. Swamiji said it was good for the residents to get together once a month, and let out their egos on each other. Gopala was always a good sport, and Swamiji would often call him up in front of the group, even at public lectures, and tell him to dance. And then, Gopala would go up in front of the audience, and do a little jig of sorts. He really wasn't half bad.

When H.H. Swami Rama first came to America, he had long hair and wore flowing Indian clothes. Ordinarily, the letters H.H. stood for His Holiness, but

Swamiji
lecturing in the
auditorium

Swamiji said they stood for Hindu Hippie. Swamiji really did not like being put on a pedestal or treated like a godman. Whenever Indian guests would come and visit, he would always tell them not to touch his feet. And he especially disliked receiving cut flowers.

The center in New York would often organize three-day weekend trips, for the people of New York to come over in a bus and spend the holiday at the Institute. Swamiji was always a gracious host, and lectured to them. On one particular weekend, he got out and played volleyball with them.

Swamiji enjoyed exercise, and encouraged people to participate in sports like volleyball, tennis, or to go out jogging and walking. He emphasized that although we are not the body, it is important to take care of the body, so it does not become an obstacle on the path of enlightenment.

During the summers, on special occasions like the fourth of July, the kitchen staff would organize a picnic out by the pond. On one occasion, there was home-made ice cream, and as Swamiji was about to taste his, he remarked to us, "The difference between you and me, is that you eat for yourself, and I eat for God."

One day when I was working in the business office, Swamiji walked in wearing his burgundy robe, looking a complete mess. His hair was all mussed up, he had cigarette ashes and tilk stains on his robe, and he was unshaven. He stood by my desk in the office, but didn't say anything; neither did I. Then he left, and came back about 20 minutes later. He stood by my desk again and didn't say anything; and neither did I. Only after he left, did I notice that he had changed his robe, brushed his hair and shaved. He must have heard my thoughts.

Swamiji was fond of building things and land-scaping. Every year, there was at least one construc-tion or landscaping project he would get involved in. And of course, there was Rocks and Roots. This was the annual event when Swamiji would make all the residents leave their offices and go out and clean up the grounds. There was organized mayhem every-where; everyone enjoyed it, because Swamiji would supervise and join them here and there, starting fires with the collected debris. It gave them an opportunity to work and interact with him on a personal level.

It was around October of 1980 when I started to feel that I needed mantra initiation. I had been at the Institute for five months, sold my bassoon and left music altogether, and unconsciously, if not con-sciously, committed myself to Swamiji. My Sufi teacher was 600 miles away, and although I still corresponded with him, I felt I needed a teacher close by, to study with. So I asked Swamiji if he would initiate me. He

said, "Why? You are already my student." I let it drop,
but felt like a boat cast adrift. Then one morning
Swamiji suddenly called Panditji, and told him to give
me mantra initiation. It was around this time that
Swamiji put Panditji in charge of mantra initiations
and spiritual discipline, and rarely gave any personal
initiations after that.

One morning, back in Swamiji's apartment, I was
making him a cup of lemon tea. He walked into the
kitchen after coming out of the conference room,
puffing on a cigarette. I smiled, and then turned back
to the pot of boiling water. He said, "What are you
smiling at?" I said nothing, and smiled again. He sat
down at the kitchen table and said, "Are you laughing
because Swami Rama is a poor man?" Then I laughed,
and put my hand on my chin. He said, "I forgot!" and
went back into the bathroom. He had come out with
half of his face lathered up with shaving cream, and
the other half clean-shaven.

It was in the month of October that a strange
incident occurred, whose significance none of us would
realize for another year. I used to wait in my room by
the telephone for Swamiji to call, before I would enter
his apartment to make the usual cup of morning tea.
Time ticked away and there was no phone call. Finally,
around 9:00 a.m., he called and I went into the
apartment, expecting to find him in his Crummy
Kitchen, but there was no Swamiji. So I went around
to the bedroom. He was still in the bed, under the quilt.
On the window sill, he kept a small wooden Japanese
lamp, and it had fallen over. He said the wind blew it
over, and told me to put it back. I didn't remember
there being any wind that night, and his window was
only cracked an inch or two to let in some fresh air. He
was acting kind of silly, so I left the lemon tea next to
the bed, and did the morning chores. A little while

later, he called again for lemon tea. I went back to the bedroom again, and he was still in bed and had not touched his tea. I made fresh tea and left it for him. Finally, he came out and was staggering around like he was drunk, and said that he was 'intoxicated.'

Soon it was time for Swamiji to go back to India. He customarily spent the summers in the U.S., and winters in India. In his absence, I was given many other jobs to perform. Over the years they included receptionist, bookkeeper, cook, typesetter, office clerk, and secretary to Dr. B. During the long winter months, when he was gone, he would often call in the middle of the night because of the time difference, and at those times I was happy that I had night phone duty.

4.

An Uncertain Future

The winter passed uneventfully, but 1981 was to be a very intense year. Swamiji came back from India in the spring, but was quite ill. He was suffering from diffuse internal bleeding. This was actually connected to the unusual incident that had occurred that morning in October 1980, when he didn't get out of bed.

On that fateful night, Swamiji was doing an advanced yogic practice that involved temporarily leaving the physical body. Although he had practiced the technique in the past, this time he did not take the necessary precautions before attempting the practice. He knew that any loud or unexpected sound during the practice would be devastating.

When the small wooden lamp on his window sill fell, it made a loud, clapping sound, which shocked him unexpectedly out of his body. His master quickly came and forced him back into his body, otherwise he would have been permanently severed from it. The effect of that sudden shock to his nervous system and its subtler aspects explains why he was reeling around that morning, as if intoxicated. He was very disoriented.

While he was away, Swamiji had traveled to Hong Kong and Japan to undergo a battery of tests. But the doctors were not able to diagnose the source of the problem, and simply said it was diffuse internal bleeding of undefined origin. He continued to suffer from this condition for many years. Once when we were feeling sorry for him, he said, "Who are you to pity me? Everything is grace of Divine Mother."

The future seemed very uncertain. Because Swamiji was very ill, he prepared to hand over the administrative duties of the Institute. He appointed Dr. Rudolph Ballentine as his successor and President of the Institute. Mrs. Dana became Chairperson Emeritus, and Dr. John Clarke became the Chairman. He also appointed Dr. Arya as the President of Sadhana Mandir Trust, Swamiji's ashram in Rishikesh.

At the same time, he dictated a document describing the vision he had for the Institute. He wanted to purchase more land around the Institute to create a medical city, one with a medical college and facilities to study alternative approaches to health and healing. He envisioned his medical city as having its own post office and bank, residences, and a school for the children. It was a vision ahead of its time and could not be accomplished in America for various reasons; it has since materialized in India, as the Himalayan Institute Hospital Trust.

Swamiji sold his house in Seelyville to the Institute. He said his master had scolded him for owning property and becoming a householder. He also gave his outer office to Dr. Clarke, and his inner office to Dr. Ballentine. He left the large apartment and moved into the special guest room, Suite 6, and also saw appointments there. Suite 6 was much smaller than his previous apartment, having only a bedroom, attached bathroom and a sitting room. However, construction of a brick cottage for Swamiji was well underway. It was situated off a ridge, in a private space away from the main building. A few weeks before his departure, the cottage was completed. The dogs Ringo and Ruby were brought from Seelyville to the main campus, where they were kept in the fenced-in yard of the old Chateau. Ringo passed away shortly after the move, but Ruby remained at the new cottage in the woods.

The International Congress that year was held at the New York Statler Hotel in Manhattan. It was my first time attending the Congress; I was very excited to see New York and stay in a fancy hotel. I shared a room close to Swamiji's suite with Sujata, another Honesdale resident who had served Swamiji in the Glenview center. We set up a makeshift kitchenette in our room with a couple of electric burners, a blender, and boxes of vegetables and other cooking supplies. We washed the dishes in the bathtub.

While Swamiji was backstage waiting to lecture, he told me to find Dr. Arya to ask him when Shankaracharya was born. I found Dr. Arya and asked him, but he could not remember. Then, Swamiji told me to go and ask Pandit Rajmani the same question. He also could not remember. During his lecture, Swamiji mentioned the correct birth date of Shankaracharya, which I do not remember now.

As Swamiji was walking offstage, he suddenly turned around, seized the microphone and said, "You are already hypnotized." Nobody understood why he had done that. But many years later, Illeana de Geyndt, a long-time student of Swamiji, explained it. She was at the Congress and was walking close behind Swamiji as he was walking away. She mentally asked him what he thought about hypnotism. He suddenly returned to the stage, picked up the mike and answered her unspoken question.

In the spectrum of unusual phenomena was an event that occurred one day in Honesdale while Swamiji was lecturing down in the auditorium. Almost everyone was attending his lecture, but a few of us were left in the main kitchen and office to work. In the kitchen, I noticed the clock on the wall. Its hands were moving in fast forward motion. The other cooks also observed it. Out of curiosity, I went into one of the unoccupied lecture halls upstairs, and observed the same thing. In the office the wall clocks were also in fast motion. All the wall clocks were in fast forward motion while Swamiji's talk was going on in the auditorium. After his lecture, the clocks went back to normal. I mentioned it to Swamiji afterwards, but he kept quiet. It was a peculiar occurrence that I have not seen before or since.

The summer of 1981 was also the big push to get the graduate school, the Program in Eastern Studies, established at the Institute. Eventually, the graduate school became accredited through affiliation with the University of Scranton, offering a two-year Master of Science degree.

The summer passed quickly; soon fall and Swamiji's inevitable departure for India were at hand. One afternoon, Swamiji confided to me that he was going back to India to return to the life of a sadhu, as in his youth.

> When Swamiji was Shankaracharya of Karvir-pitham, his name was Swami Sadashiva Bharati. Before that he was known as Patti Wala Baba, a young naga baba who used to eat the leaves off the trees and roam around the Himalayas, and as Ram Dandi when he roamed around Gangotri. He was also known as Bhole Baba or Bhole Prabhu, the gentle sage, because he used to sing and play the *veena* sitting under the trees in Rishikesh.

He said he was going to leave everything and would just sit and meditate under a tree, but he would not beg for his food. And if he died, he died. With all my sincerity, I told him that I would also go to India, get a job and bring him food every day under the tree, so he wouldn't have to beg. He looked at me with a half-smile, and so much love, that there were tears in his eyes. I also had tears in my eyes. Swamiji remarked, "Everybody wants to touch my feet, but nobody wants to touch my heart." When Swamiji left for India that year, the halls were lined with tearful residents, afraid that he would not return.

Before leaving, Swamiji had received word that his own master, Babaji, was going to leave his body. In December 1981, Babaji called his disciples together. Swamiji knew that at this meeting he and Babaji were going to decide who would live and who would drop his body. One of them would remain in the world, and the other would take mahasamadhi. When they met, Babaji asked Swamiji if there was anything he wanted. Swamiji remained silent. Babaji dropped his body and extended Swamiji's life.

5.
A Remarkable Patient

We were all very concerned about Swamiji's well-being so I wrote to him when he was in Nepal and received the following reply:

January 4th, 1982

"After my Gurudev left for his heavenly abode, I don't feel lonely but I do feel something like a self-created responsibility towards the monastery. But I am not fit to go there now and live forever. I am preparing myself for that. Maybe in four years time I will consider going back to the deep mountains.

"Now I am almost determined to have a small thatched ashram 45 kilometers from here, where there is a fascinating landscape facing the Himalayan snowy blanketed peaks. I have completely withdrawn myself from Indian and Nepali people. Only three or four people will be allowed to come and see me, and that's all....

"I have firmly decided that I will lead a completely isolated life and plunge into the deeper aspects of my being. I will pray for you all. There will be no more world with me....

"My master has given me a few more years, and I want to really utilize them in samadhi....

"My love for you people is immense and inexplicable, and you all have served me with great love. The Institute is yours and in your country. You know better how to manage it. Dr. B. and Dr. Clarke are able and will do their best to serve the Institute. I have no attachment toward the Institute.

"I have seen enough of the world and people from East and West; selfless service is not at all appreciated anywhere. I am not sad when I am saying this. I have tried to serve you all but somewhere I must have committed mistakes, because the human in me is exactly like the human in anyone. I have learned a lot. I have also turned my face from my country, and I have said goodbye to everyone in Delhi.

"I might come and see you for a month or so, but I will teach and the rest of the time I will remain in silence. But I can do this for only three or four more years. After that I will not move from the lap of the Himalayas.

"I hope the therapy program, graduate school and other programs are running properly. Through selfless service alone can one serve the Lord. There is no other way for modern man but to realize that the Omnipresent lives in all living creatures, and serving them is service to the Lord. The purpose of the Institute is to serve and motivate people towards self-training. I did my best, worked hard and was even humiliated many times. I have gone through immense problems in founding and building the Institute. But do not forget that it is yours, for you and in your country.

"While I dwelled in your country, if from these lips you have ever heard a taunt or harsh word, it was all out of love, and you should forgive me if anyone was hurt."

Swamiji returned to the Institute in the spring of 1982. His physical health was much better, though he continued to suffer from diffuse internal bleeding, off and on, for the rest of his life.

When he returned, he was also walking with a slight limp because of pain in his right hip. This was due to some nodes deep in the hip that were pressing against the nerves and causing a lot of pain, although Swamiji told us he only felt five percent of the pain we normally would feel. Apparently, these nodes had formed after some vitamin B injections he had received back in the 1970s, for treatment of a very serious head injury he sustained during a skiing accident. He had gone skiing in Colorado with some students, and had fallen out of the ski lift chair, down about 70 feet, landing on his head. His speech was affected, and it took him many months of music therapy to regain his speech. In the introduction to his book, *Indian Music*, he talks about how he rehabilitated himself through music.

He consulted Drs. Anand and Padma Talcherkar in Springfield, Illinois about doing a surgical procedure to remove the nodes. Swamiji agreed to the surgery but with conditions — no general anesthesia, and a time limit to perform the operation. He asked them how much time they needed, and they told him, half an hour. So he gave them 45 minutes to complete whatever they were going to do. Whenever the nurses came to take his vital signs, Swamiji enjoyed manipulating his pulse, temperature and blood pressure. After they had checked it once, he would tell them to do it again, and it would be different. He walked into the operating room; they gave him a local anesthetic on the hip. They made two incisions that were quite deep, and proceeded to remove the nodes. The time was up before they had completed the operation; so they asked for more time. But Swamiji told them to rip out the nodes. They had to finish the operation this way and put in the stitches. Swamiji walked out of the operating room.

The whole procedure was kept very quiet, because Swamiji did not want anyone to know about it. I arranged with Gus Gatto and Alan Regenauer to pick up Swamiji from Springfield and take him to Glenview. Gus Gatto was one of the pillars of the Glenview center. A pure bhakta and former wrestler, Gus was Swamiji's official bodyguard whenever he came to Honesdale.

Swamiji spent a little more than three months in the States in 1982. He had started to build an ashram in Nepal called Hansda Ashram and his mind was focused on that project. Of the few months he spent in the States, two of them were in Glenview with his 'Mama,' because she missed him and would soon be leaving her body.

Mama, Ann Aylward, was quite a personality. She had helped Swamiji establish the Himalayan Institute in its original headquarters at Glenview, Illinois. She was an elderly Irish woman from Chicago, who ran a restaurant and was Chairperson of the Institute in Glenview. I had the privilege of meeting this august personage only once when she came to Honesdale to attend the Congress. Many times, in Swamiji's lectures, he would say, "I have a mother, but she never married!" There was a special order of students at the Institute called the Bitchananda Order. This was an elite order, with limited enrollment of only highly qualified women. Mama was the original head of the order. When Mama passed away in the early 1980s, the Bitchananda Order was divided into two factions: the Bitchananda Order of the East, and the Bitchananda Order of the West. Brunette Eason became the head of the Western division, and Barbara Bova, who was studying homeopathy in India at that time, became head of the Eastern division. I was also an exceptionally qualified member of the order.

For a few years, Swamiji held 10-day retreats for the faculty on the campus. The faculty stayed in the old convent that was just behind the main building.

Theresa O'Brien used to cook for them and looked after them like a den mother. Their day was divided into sessions for practice, study, meditation, contemplation or walks. Swamiji met with them at certain times to teach. The rest of the time they were to observe silence.

One morning Swamiji called one of the male residents to mow the grass around the convent building. The resident protested because he knew the faculty was in silence and he didn't want to disturb them. But Swamiji told him to go ahead. The next day, at the same time, Swamiji again called the same person and told him to mow the grass around the convent. Again he protested, saying he had just mowed the grass the previous day. Swamiji told him to do it anyway. We can only wonder how the noise affected the silent retreat participants.

For the duration of the summer, Swamiji used the little cottage in the woods as his residence, and he would go back and forth between the main building and his cottage. By the end of the summer, he gave the cottage away to a resident, and they began construction of a log cabin, not far from the cottage, for Swamiji to live in the following year.

It was around this time that Himalayan Excursions tours came into existence. Dale Colton, the head of the Promotion Office at the Institute, was in charge of organizing these tours. Every fall or winter, one or two groups of about 30 each, would embark on spiritual and cultural tours of India and Nepal. These tours included time at the ashrams to practice meditation and some sight seeing as well.

6.

Cosmic Flushes

Before Swamiji left for India, he had strictly warned Alan Regenauer not to drive for three months, from January to March of 1983. Earlier in the year, Swamiji had transferred Alan from the Chicago East West Bookstore to manage the New York East West Bookstore. Alan drove back to Chicago to spend Christmas with his family, and planned to return to New York before January 1st. For some reason, his return was delayed by three days, and he was unable to leave until January 3rd. He was tragically killed in a car accident on the way back. It was later revealed that he suffered from a condition that makes people prone to falling asleep at the wheel. He died instantly. I sent a telegram to Swamiji in Nepal as soon as we received the news of Alan's death, and received the following letter in reply.

11th January 1983

"I feel so sad that those who claim to love me do not listen to me and hurt me. Alan did the same thing. I warned him a thousand times not to drive in January, February and March at any cost. But the call of death is perhaps more powerful. Now I feel that if my people do not listen to me, why should I get attached to them?"

Swamiji returned to Honesdale in the spring of 1983 and was happy to move into his new log cabin. He spent most of the spring transforming the barren tract of land on the crest into an exquisite Japanese garden. Larry and Maureen Warren had created a greenhouse on campus, which supplied most of the beautiful flowers that were planted in the Japanese garden. By the time Swamiji had completed his magic, there were flowerbeds everywhere, a rose garden, concrete pagoda lamps and other concrete block sculptures. A massive tree trunk, turned onto its side, became a lacquered sculpture. Swamiji also created two lotus ponds and a waterfall. It was marvelous.

And the amount of effort that had gone into creating this masterpiece was also marvelous! Daily, without fail, from 5:00 a.m. to 11:00 p.m., Swamiji was up at the cabin supervising the masonry work, landscaping and construction. To begin with, there were many Rocks and Roots days that spring to clear out unwanted weeds and rocks. One of the major offenders was poison ivy; the hill was covered with it. The blessings of the poison ivy plant were bestowed on many of the residents who had come to pull it out. Many people were covered with blisters, some worse than others. Nevertheless, the hill was cleared and the beautiful garden Swamiji had envisioned was beginning to reveal itself.

The land on which the cabin had been built was solid rock, the type of shale that is found everywhere in the hills of Pennsylvania. There were many huge rocks around. Swamiji decided that some of the boulders had to be moved; so he called the boys to help clear them out. There was one very large slab of shale he wanted to convert into a tabletop. Having seen that the four legs were solidly set into place, he enlisted Larry Warren and Bruce to lift it into place. Try as they

Swamiji landscaping at the log cabin

Looking down at the meditation hut at the Japanese garden

did to lift it, it proved to be way beyond their capacity. They looked at Swamiji apologetically, and said it was just too heavy to lift. Swamiji said it wasn't, and very softly told them to lift it on the count of three. They did as he instructed. This time they were able to effortlessly place the slab on top of the legs. Larry and Bruce just stared at each other in utter disbelief.

Swamiji always appreciated the hard work of his helpers, and usually invited them to stay for lunch at the cabin. Those days, I often found myself preparing lunch for 20 to 30 people who ate with Swamiji. One day, as a special treat, Swamiji made mountain bread for all of the workers. He directed the boys to dig a pit in the ground, and start a fire in it. Others were deployed to gather some maple tree leaves to make a coating for the bread. He made one large, round flat bread, coated with a thick layer of leaves. After the fire coals were sufficiently hot, but not too hot, Swamiji put the bread on top of the coals and buried it. After 15 to 20 minutes they dug it up, brushed off the ashes and the leaves, and gave everyone a piece of it to eat. It was delicious.

By the time the summer of 1983 rolled around, the Japanese garden was nearly completed. Swamiji called my mother up to Honesdale. He sent her a ticket, and immediately admitted her into the Combined Therapy Program for three weeks. He was very sweet to her while she was there, and afterwards he continued to telephone her regularly to ask how his 'sweetheart' was, calling her his pumpkin pie or zucchini pie depending on how much weight she had lost. My mother was duly impressed with Swamiji and once commented that he was the only real man she had ever met, a sentiment shared by many others.

Hansda Ashram in Nepal was well under way by now, and the Queen Mother of Nepal was on her way to the United States. Her itinerary included a visit to the Himalayan Institute. In anticipation of her visit, final plantings were rapidly completed in the Japanese garden. Now that the gardens had been set, the ponds built and the lawn cleared of poison ivy, rolls of sod were brought in and laid down to finish the total effect. Swamiji himself received the Queen Mother and her entourage, and gave them the grand tour.

Swamiji was also very close to the Prime Minister of India, Mrs. Indira Gandhi. When the Indian government learnt that Swamiji was building an ashram in Nepal, Indira Gandhi offered Swamiji $6,000,000 to build an Institute for Indian Culture and Civilization in New Delhi. Swamiji said he had created a competition between the two governments.

In contrast to the promises of the spring of 1983, the summer was laden with strange and disturbing events. It was a year of cosmic flushes, and several people who had been long-term residents left. There was a major shakedown, a trend which seemed to take place every 10 years, thereafter. There was drama everywhere. Swamiji was a public man, so he drew all kinds of people to him.

One day, a young man who had been enrolled in the graduate school, followed Swamiji while he was walking on campus. The boy picked up a stone and said he wanted to crack Swamiji's skull open and eat his brains. There was also a schizophrenic in Chicago who used to send threatening mail to Swamiji and even telephoned to say that he had placed a bomb in Swamiji's car. There were a couple of men from North Dakota who believed that the end of the world was coming; so they sent Swamiji a rifle through the mail, along with fifty-pound bags of beans and rice. Then there was the woman from Buffalo who had a scar on her arm, and told people that it was the place from which Swamiji had removed her brain. The list goes on and on.

The previous summer, another strange occurrence had taken place while Alan Regenauer was on campus. Because Swamiji wasn't feeling well, he decided to rest and be alone for a few days. Kevin and Mahima temporarily vacated their house so Swamiji could stay there and have some privacy. Only Alan Regenauer stayed there with Swamiji to attend to his needs. One night as Swamiji, Alan, and Kevin were talking, someone knocked on the front door. Alan answered the door and found a woman dressed in her bathrobe. He asked her what she wanted, and she said she just felt drawn to the house so she knocked. After she left, Swamiji asked Alan what he would have thought if he had seen her leaving his house in the middle of the night in her bathrobe.

As the summer of 1983 progressed, Swamiji again became very ill. He was bleeding internally and there were dark circles under his eyes. He became withdrawn. One afternoon when I went up to the cabin, I noticed a dent in the front screen door. He said he had fallen and hit it with his head. As he was changing his shirt for tennis, I noticed red marks on his arms and back. I asked him what they were, and he said the bushes had scratched him. It wasn't until some years later that I found out what had really happened. In a public lecture, Swamiji said that Babaji and Nirvanji had come to him in their subtle bodies and punished him 'for doing that which was not to be done.' They came to him and beat him with their canes, but he could not see them or fight back. They asked, "Do you think because we left our bodies, we can no longer come here and you can do whatever you want?" Swamiji said there was only one witness who had seen the cane marks on his body. I was that witness.

In India, Swamiji had the nickname, Stormy Baba, because everywhere he went there was a storm.

Once when Swamiji was doing an advanced practice, alone, deep in the jungles of the Himalayas, an extraordinarily beautiful girl wearing extra-ordinarily beautiful ornaments, came to him alone. He asked her who she was, how she had managed to come there all alone, and how her parents had allowed her to come alone? She replied that nobody could stop her, and that she just wanted to serve him. So he told her to pick up his kamandalu (water pot), which was charged with mantras. She said she was sorry, but she couldn't pick it up. Then, Swamiji took some water in his hands to do sankalpa and destroy her, but she ran away. She was a bhutani (ghost).

At another time, a village girl became pregnant, and accused Swamiji of being the father. He was arrested and detained in jail until the day of the trial. If he had been found guilty, they would have forced him to marry the girl. Finally, his master took pity on him and saved him. The girl became very emotional and said that Swamiji was not the father; she was in love with someone else.

There was a similar episode in which two Indian women wrote letters to Prime Minister Indira Gandhi, informing her that Swamiji was having affairs with them. Mrs. Gandhi called Swamiji to ask him for an explanation. Swamiji went to Delhi to show her the stamps in his passport, which clearly proved that he was not even in the country at the time these affairs were supposed to have taken place.

Apparently, things like this have been going on for many lifetimes.

Swamiji told me that seven lifetimes prior to this one, he had received a boon from Saraswati Ma (the

Indian goddess of wisdom), that he would be the most beautiful man on the face of the earth. Women were so attracted to him that they used to follow him down the street. It became such a problem for him that he had to drop his body.

The turbulent summer of 1983 at last came to an end, and Swamiji left for India, only to encounter more turmoil in Nepal. Hansda Ashram had been nicely constructed, and was very peaceful and comfortable, being in a remote location, northwest of Kathmandu. Down the hill from the ashram, Swamiji opened a free medical clinic and dispensary for the village people, constructed a school for the village children, and had pipelines installed to bring spring water down from the mountain to the villagers. Thus, in no time at all, he had become very popular among the local people. It was not to last. Nepal was a monarchy and jealousies arose.

7.

The Case of the Missing Cashmere

Back in Honesdale, one unsuspecting night, I received a phone call from Swamiji in Nepal, with the usual array of enquiries: How are you? How is everything at the Institute? Tell Dr. B. to call me, tell Shivnath to call me, or tell this one or that one to call me, or do this and that. But then there was this one small extra matter, attached to this particular phone call — *tell Charles Bates to return my cashmere suit.*

Swamiji was a big man, and from time to time, he distributed his clothes to other big men like Phil Nuernberger, Roshan Lal, Justin O'Brien or Charles Bates. Over the years, he had distributed many of his Yukatas, kurta/pajamas and Nehru suits amongst them. But not the cashmere suit. In fact, Swamiji had taken the cashmere suit overseas.

Charles had recently visited Hansda Ashram with a tour group, and Swamiji called me to say that while he was there, Charles had stolen his cashmere suit. I was to tell him not to do such things and to give it back. So I did. Whenever Swamiji called in the middle of the night, and wanted other people to call him back, I shamelessly woke them up. I called Charles and told him that Swamiji wanted his cashmere suit back. Naturally, Charles said he didn't take it and didn't have it. A likely story.

Swamiji called again and asked about his cashmere suit. I told him that Charles said he didn't have it, but Swamiji said, "No, he has it, and tell him to give it back. Tell him not to do like that. This is not good."

Then, I was to tell Phil Nuernberger and Shivnath to talk to Charles, to convince him to return the suit. I did, and they did, and still Charles insisted that he did not have the suit.

When Swamiji telephoned again for an update, I had to report to him that Charles still denied having taken the suit. And the dance went on, with people calling from here to there, and from there to here, and with everyone asking Charles why he had stolen Swamiji's cashmere suit.

Charles was steadfast in his denial, and I started to wonder if I should hire a lawyer, or if I would have to physically pry it out of his fingers. Dale, who had seen Swamiji's quarters in Hansda Ashram, looked at me slyly and suggested it was probably in Nepal in Swamiji's almirah (closet). Shivnath and Phil were the only ones convinced of Charles' innocence.

I had reached a point of complete helplessness in the situation, when the phone rang and it was Swamiji. He just casually asked how everything was going, but this time he did not mention the cashmere suit. So I asked him what he wanted me to do about the suit. Then he simply said that he had found it in his almirah. End of dance.

To say the least, Swamiji was inscrutable. To try to understand Swamiji was to attempt to measure the universe with a foot rule, as he was so fond of saying.

Meanwhile, in Nepal things were definitely heating up. There was talk of a coup and of the king taking over the ashram. Justin and Theresa O'Brien were in Nepal at the time, and Justin has given a firsthand account of that particular drama in the book, *Walking with a Himalayan Master*.

One of the Himalayan Excursion tours went over to Nepal that last spring at the ashram. Even on the last morning, Swamiji was found working in the garden, watering plants and pulling weeds. When everything was packed up and it was time to go, he simply walked away and never went back. The villagers lined up along the road and tearfully said good-bye to their great benefactor.

Swamiji spent the summer of 1984 in Manali, where he rented a house for a few months. He had a few students with him to help him write his commentary on the Bhagavad Gita, *Perennial Psychology of the Bhagavad Gita.* In the winter of 1984, he went to Mauritius. He did not come back to the States again until the spring of 1985.

Although life at the Institute went on as usual, it was difficult not having Swamiji's physical presence amongst us. In his absence, a meditation hut was built just below the Japanese garden and was eventually surrounded by a pond filled with goldfish. Also a children's school was constructed next to Swamiji's cabin.

With Swamiji away for such a long time, I attended weekend seminars, studied, and took hatha classes to become a certified hatha yoga instructor. After leading a beginning level hatha yoga class for a weekend seminar, one of the participants came up to me after class. He introduced himself as a preacher who had been in prison before he was reformed. He said that Swamiji had come to give a talk at his prison, and that Swamiji's talk had influenced him so deeply that he completely changed his ways. He added, "You never know what effect the words of a holy man can have."

8.

My First Visit to India

We gratefully welcomed Swamiji back to Hones-dale in the spring of 1985. One of the first things he said to me was that I was not well and needed an operation. But he wouldn't tell me what or when. It's true that I had lost weight, but I hadn't thought much of it. He told me not to eat salt, sugar, or fat. At the same time he told me to eat more and sleep more. Then he started one of his major campaigns of that summer — to marry me off.

Over the years, he had made feeble attempts to find a husband for me, much against my will. I had an intense desire to be in Swamiji's physical presence. I knew that if I were married I couldn't do that. So I dug my heels in and refused to marry anyone he brought before me.

If I became too moody, or wanted too much attention, he would just say the M word, and I would instantly be on my best behavior. "You should get married, so someone gives you attention all the time." These words always sent a cold chill up my spine.

But at times he really went to extremes. It was so bad, that any poor, unsuspecting male who walked through the front door became a possible match. It didn't even matter if he was already married. The only thing that seemed to matter was that he could breathe and walk. It annoyed me no end. I felt rejected and thought that Swamiji was trying to get rid of me. He even went so far as to arrange a job for me in Wisconsin. So I said, "Why? Am I going to die?"

That was exactly the point. I had reached the end of my allotted time on this earth. Marriage changes your individual karma to collective karma; it would alter my karma. Everyone kept lauding the benefits of marriage, trying to convince me that I should listen to Swamiji, because he wanted only the best for me. But I could not, and would not, cooperate.

In 1985, Swamiji had a lot of dental work done, and made frequent trips to his dentist in Minneapolis. He didn't visit the cabin much, but stayed in Suite 6 in the building. Countless hours were spent watching Hindi movies with the VCR. Swamiji himself didn't watch them. He just played them; whoever was in the room got to watch them. It was a Hindi movie marathon. But even though Swamiji didn't leave his room much, he knew everything that was going on in the Institute, and when people came to see him, he could repeat conversations people had in the front office or elsewhere.

Ruby had passed away, and we needed to get a new dog for Swamiji. After doing some research, we decided on an Italian mastiff. Dale went to pick up the dog, but it turned out to be so vicious that we had to return it. The next dog we decided on was an Irish wolfhound, a breed that was not vicious yet made good watchdogs. The Irish wolfhound is called the gentle giant, but they forgot to mention, mental midget. Swamiji named him Pinto. As a puppy, Pinto was already the size of a small dog. He soon outgrew the garden space and unconcernedly tramped through all the flowerbeds, driving Larry and Maureen crazy. But he had a very sweet nature, making everyone want to pet him. Hence, he soon became spoiled.

Swamiji never talked about my future. It was as if I did not have one. But early one morning, around 5:00 he called me into his apartment and said, "I have a plan for you. Finally you will be in India. Save your money, live off the interest and meditate."

In the fall of 1985, Swamiji arranged for me to go to India with the Himalayan Excursions group. It was my first trip to India, and I took to India like a duck to water. The group visited Delhi, Banares, Agra, Jaipur, Mussoorie, Rishikesh, and Dehradun. It was a real treat.

My first night in India was spent at the Hyatt Hotel in New Delhi. Lynn Gatwood from Chicago was my roommate, and we had some unusual experiences together in the room. The first night in the hotel, we both saw two small white lights floating around the room in the dark. When I asked Swamiji about it, he said these lights were two swamis from the monastery who had come to visit us. The next day Lynn's suitcase, which was lying on the ottoman, started to jump by itself. She had a red, soft-case suitcase, and it looked as if there was something inside the suitcase trying to punch its way out. We stood there looking at it, both scared and excited. We were laughing and squealing, and speculated that there might be a rat inside trying to get out. Cautiously we opened the suitcase, but there was nothing unusual to be found. Of course, nobody believed us, when we told them about the jumping suitcase. At least we both witnessed the same event.

When we arrived at the ashram in Rishikesh, I felt that I had finally come home. The ashram was located right on the banks of the Ganges, with a jungle on the other side of the river. In the morning, you could look out and see the sun come up over the foothills of the Himalayas.

Sadhana Mandir ashram in Rishikesh

The ashram was an oasis in a maze of noise and pollution. Rishikesh was originally a small village, but over time it had grown into one of the typically congested towns of India. The two most remarkable things about the ashram that initially struck me were the deep silence and peace that permeated the atmosphere, and the beautiful flower gardens everywhere you looked. You never had the feeling of being boxed in, even though it was not a very big ashram.

And Swamiji himself was different in Rishikesh. For the first time, I had a glimpse of the real Indian master in him. He was relaxed, dignified and majestic, in perfect harmony with his surroundings. Everyone revered him. It was the first time I had a sense of how awkward his life in America must have been for him at times — a life of schedules, administration, business, appointments, teaching students, problems, fund raising — a life of complete selfless service and being misunderstood.

In India, Swamiji was the master and he did not have to prove himself to anyone. His presence spoke for itself. He was in his element. In America he had to

Swamiji and Kamal standing on the ghat in front of the ashram

adopt foreign ways and customs. So he proved himself to scientists in scientific laboratories, and he spoon-fed us yoga science and Vedanta, shorn of all religious connotations. The Indian culture is ancient, and full of reverence for the great rishis and sages, who have come to the world to selflessly serve humanity. Swamiji himself was a citizen of the world, not confined to any particular country or religion.

When I met Swamiji for the second time in North Carolina in 1980, he had taken several minutes to examine the lines on the palms of my hands, but he never said anything. When I was in Rishikesh for the first time, I noticed that the lines had changed; a small line appeared that connected my lifeline to the line of destiny. I asked Swamiji what it meant, and he said it was my destiny to live.

After spending a couple of months in India, I returned to Honesdale. Swamiji remained in India for the winter, as was his custom. He was searching for land in India to build a new institute. He had no office or apartment in Delhi and used to operate out of the India International Centre. Soon the Institute purchased an apartment in Delhi, located in Sarva Priya Vihar, for Swamiji's use as a residence and a base for his work in India. Later another apartment was purchased in Malviya Nagar, to serve as the bookstore and guesthouse of the Institute. Swamiji's work in India had begun in earnest.

Many times, when Swamiji was in India and I was in Honesdale, I would find new cigarette butts or *beedie* (Indian cigarettes) stubs in his suite, in places where I was sure I had cleaned before. It was a reminder that he was ever present.

9.
Relentless Matchmaker

In January of 1986, Swamiji came to Honesdale and stayed for a month. One of the first things he did after arriving was to call the maintenance crew, Kevin and Larry, to tell them that there were rats in the basement. They seemed puzzled and said they weren't aware of any problem. When the Institute was built, the basement was constructed to be a nuclear fallout shelter. They went down to inspect, and sure enough, they found it was infested with rats. Swamiji was aware of what was going on, even through concrete walls.

He again stayed in Suite 6 and again held Hindi movie marathons, playing one movie after the other. One time he told me, "Nobody knows why I watch TV. It is so nothing disturbs my meditation."

It was during this time that Swamiji did something he had rarely done in the past—he started taking baths. Not just one bath, but a bath every night. After the bath, he would show us the dark dirty ring around the bathtub. He said it was dead cells coming off, and that he was rejuvenating his body.

Although Swamiji went back to India after a month, he returned to Honesdale for the summer as usual. Pinto, the Irish wolfhound was now the size of a small pony and was bent on destroying the Japanese garden. Swamiji gifted him to Dr. B., who had a large property with orchards, and could use a large dog. So we were again in the market for a new dog for Swamiji. Horst Rechelbacher, a student of Swamiji's and founder of Aveda Corporation, presented Swamiji with a purebred German shepherd, and Swamiji named her Princess.

Princess was very attached to Swamiji. Whenever she saw him, she would get so excited that she peed, no matter where she was. It became a problem for me, because I had to clean it up. When she saw him, she would squeal and squirm (just like the rest of us, although I didn't pee on myself), and would try to 'get into his system,' as Swamiji used to say. She would lie at his feet, and if allowed, put her head on his feet and just stay there. Of course, Swamiji forbade all of us to play with her, because he was training her to be a guard dog.

After Swamiji had showered Princess with love and affection, fed her dog biscuit treats, and thoroughly bonded with her, he started to discipline her. It looked suspiciously like the same technique he used to train his secretaries! Sometimes Swamiji would test her. He would tell her to stay, and would then have me call her. She would look from one to the other, not sure what she was supposed to do. The first time, she came to me when I called her. Swamiji scolded her and made her sit. The second time I called her, she didn't move. When Swamiji would go up to the cabin, he used to take rest on the sofa, and she would sleep on the floor next to him. She wouldn't leave until he told her to go.

When she was a little older, one of the male residents, Jean Pierre, started to train her to be a guard dog. She learned how to attack, roll over and crawl. But in front of Swamiji, she still peed on herself.

Swamiji had many Indian visitors, and one man who visited him at the cabin started to bend down to touch Swamiji's feet, as is the Indian custom. Princess positioned herself between Swamiji and the man, and wouldn't let him do it. Any time he tried to bow down, Princess would lick his bald head. Finally, he realized he had to do pranam to Princess first. Then, she looked at Swamiji to get his approval, and let him touch Swamiji's feet. She was a model secretary.

One day Swamiji went up to Toronto to attend a wedding, and a small group of us went along with him. On the way, we stopped at the Buffalo center, which was being run by Virat and Kiran. We were sitting around the room with Swamiji, when he asked us, "Which is higher, to love or to be loved?"

Almost everyone agreed that to love was higher, except for Virat, who felt that to *be* loved was higher, because you are not in control of that. When *you* love someone, your ego is still involved. Swamiji agreed, and said that to be loved by someone, is higher than loving someone. On a separate occasion, I asked Swamiji what was more important than love. He said, "The center of love."

In Swamiji's log cabin at the Institute, he had set aside one room as a meditation room that he kept locked. He did not allow anyone to use that room. However, one time he called Dr. Hanumanth Rao from Chicago to come to see him, and told him to spend one night in the meditation room of his cabin. The next morning, Dr. Rao showed me the window shade in the meditation room. It had ripped to form the shape of a Sri Yantra when he tried to close it.

A man came from Switzerland to visit Swamiji, and brought with him a small and very beautiful Sri Yantra that was engraved on a solid gold plate, about four inches square, with a tiny red ruby in the center. Swamiji used to show this yantra to different people. First he would make them wash their hands, and then allow them to hold it and look at it. While they were doing this, Swamiji would look intently at them. Most people could only hold it for a few seconds, and then handed it back to him. Finally, one day he told me to wash my hands and hold the yantra. So I did and gazed at it. There was a tingling sensation at the top of my head, and Swamiji was gazing at the top of my head. I held it as long as I could, and then turned to look at Swamiji, to see what he was doing. It felt as if I were standing there completely nude in a spotlight, with nowhere to hide. Then Swamiji took the yantra back and said nothing.

By this time, it seemed that Swamiji had dropped his matchmaking quest for me. Just as I was starting to feel safe, Pir Vilayat Khan came to Honesdale to speak at the International Congress. Swamiji met Pir in Suite 6, and they were having a casual conversation. Some of us were sitting on the floor, enjoying the interaction. I had met Pir twice before, on different occasions. Someone remarked to Pir that I had been a Sufi. Then Pir said, "Remember, you were a Sufi first."

Well, Pir dropped the ball, and Swamiji ran with it. Swamiji went on to say that he wished he were a Sufi, so he could get married. Then he told Pir that he should marry me, that he would never find a girl like me, and that he would marry us that very day in front of the fire if he agreed. Pir politely sat there speechless. I turned about thirty shades of deep purple, and looked daggers at Swamiji. Swamiji told me to go and make some fresh orange juice. While I was out of the room, I was told that he continued to extol my virtues to Pir. When I came back, he still had not exhausted the subject, and ended by telling Pir to take me with him.

I left the room and lurked around the hall waiting for Pir to leave. I had been assigned to look after Pir on his visit, but after that, I could not go in front of him; the poor man was dreadfully neglected. Afterwards, Swamiji simply said, "Pir must be thinking, *Why is he persecuting me?*"

Swamiji left for India in the fall, and the Himalayan Excursions tour followed with an itinerary for South India. Swamiji very kindly arranged for me to go with the group, and it was a very interesting experience for all of us. First, we stayed at the ashram in Rishikesh for a couple of weeks. There was a new member there, a Brahmachari. Brahmachari was a very short man from South India. We all liked to spend time with him, because he told us the stories and history behind all the temples we visited.

There was also an old swami who used to come to the ashram to teach Sanskrit to Brahmachari. According to Brahmachari, that swami and Swamiji used to communicate on the astral plane, even though they did not meet on the physical plane. No one was supposed to know about it, and that was why they never said anything to each other when they met. We all trusted Brahmachari, and thought he was close to Swamiji.

One day Swamiji called all of us together, and told us that the old swami taught Sanskrit to Brahmachari and nothing else, that was it. Of course, we all knew that he would say this publicly, because he didn't want us to know that they met on the astral plane.

The swami wanted to teach me some meditational techniques, and I went along with it, thinking that there was no difference between learning things from Pandit Rajmani or from this swami, as Swamiji usually sent me to Panditji for mantras. In my mind, it was like learning from another teacher in the tradition. I went back to America with the group and started corresponding with this swami through Brahmachari, who started giving me practices by mail.

Over the winter, the Institute had built an apartment above the White Conference Room so Swamiji would have a nicer place to stay. It was a big, spacious room, with a fireplace, an area for plants, a kitchenette, a bedroom with attached bathroom and two walk-in closets. It was quiet and secure, had a lovely view of the forest and made his stay with us much more comfortable. With my room located downstairs and outside the apartment, I felt like the guard dog at the base of the stairs.

10.
Kirtan Evenings

1987 was the summer for physical exercise. Swamiji had not been well through the winter and had developed sugar intolerance. We had to regularly monitor his blood sugar levels, and over the years he was diagnosed with mild diabetes that was treated with dietary control, exercise and oral medication.

To help control the problem, he started a more vigorous regimen of exercise. As a rule, when Swamiji was on campus he would play tennis almost every day throughout the summer. Now, he often played twice a day. In addition, he would go for long walks or jog in his room if it were raining. He also started to practice hatha yoga again. Once he demonstrated the head-stand and added that before you can stand on your head, you have to learn to stand on your own two feet.

At the tennis court, the residents and guests would gather around to watch the rather lopsided matches. There was never a shortage of ball girls, and sometimes there would be as many as five or six players in the game at one time, most of them playing opposite Swamiji. But the best part of the tennis games was the fun that came afterwards. Swamiji would sit on the lawn for a few minutes with the spectators and distribute toffees or cookies to the children. It gave the residents and guests an opportunity to see him and interact with him on a personal level. Swamiji was a

Swamiji socializing after the tennis game

magnet, a flame that drew the moths, and everyone was delighted to be around him.

This was also the glorious summer that Swamiji started to sing again. Though he was an accomplished musician, he told me he had given up music many years ago, under the orders of his master.

When Swamiji was on vacation from his studies at the university, he would often go to stay with his master at the cave monastery. However, there were other swamis living at the monastery who were also learning from his master.

As a young brahmachari, Swamiji had learned all the arts, including music and dance. He was an accomplished musician, played the veena and had learned classical Indian singing. His favorite style of singing was *Thumri*. He had a beautiful *tanpura* that was four feet in diameter. While he was at the cave, he would wake early in the morning to practice his *swaras,* as he strummed the tanpura.

The other swamis were accustomed to silence in the morning, and here was this young brahmachari practicing his swaras and disturbing their meditation. It was not just the singing that disturbed them, but the fact that he was singing Thumri, love songs about *bindis* and bangles, reminding them of the wives they had left behind! They went to Babaji and complained that Bholia was disturbing their meditation, singing about bindis and bangles, when they had come there to renounce, not to remember their wives!

Babaji did not take any action, until one day, a visitor came and remarked that Bholia was a very good singer. Babaji was a bit surprised to hear it and asked the visitor how he had come to know it.

"I heard him singing on All India Radio. Yes, and he also dances well."

"Really? How do you know?"

"I saw him dancing in the school play at the theatre."

Babaji thought about all this and decided that it was not good for Bholia's spiritual growth. Bholia had been accepting money for singing and was spending too much time practicing music and neglecting his meditation. He decided it was time to put a stop to all of this. So he called the other swamis together and told them to catch hold of Bholia the next morning so he could set him right.

They knew that this was not going to be easy, because Bholia was very strong and healthy. There were stories of how in his youth, he had wrestled with bears and tigers. But they were desperate to have peace and quiet in the mornings. They came up with a plan to trick him into submission and then called him. When Bholia came, they told him that he seemed to have grown since his last visit; they wanted to measure his height. They asked him to stand against a tree so they could make a mark. As soon as he did, they tied him to the tree with a rope.

Then, they took his beautiful tanpura and mercilessly broke it in front of him. After that, Babaji came and beat Bholia with his cane. Babaji took Bholia and held him in his lap. It was Babaji who was crying, not Bholia. Bholia asked, "Why did you beat me?"

Babaji explained that he wanted him to stop singing, because he had become distracted and was neglecting his meditation. He would not be able to fulfill the purpose of his life. Bholia replied that he could have just asked him to stop, and he would have done so. But Babaji didn't believe him. He said, "You don't listen to anybody."

Then Babaji told Bholia to take some water in the palm of his hand and do a sankalpa that he would not take up music again, until 1985.

It was not until 1987 that Swamiji earnestly revived his interest in music. Early in the mornings, without fail, he would practice his swaras. When I would take his morning tea to him, I would find him sitting on the sofa, already practicing his swaras and gazing up at the ceiling. He said it was easy to contact anyone on the other side; he would often call on the classical Indian maestros of yore to come and teach him. He said that if he made a mistake, they would give him a shock or a jerk. Swamiji had another assistant as well. When he would practice in the cabin, Princess would moan if his swaras were off the mark.

Swamiji also taught a few music classes to the residents. He explained that the swara should be formed the same way that the Sanskrit letter is written. That is, all the swaras should be sung according to the direction in which the letters of the *Devanagari* script are formed. If the letter curved from below to above, the swara should be formed by starting below the correct tone, and sliding up to it. Everyone caught his enthusiasm and wanted to learn Indian music. So he arranged for some teachers from India to come to teach

Swamiji leading kirtan in the auditorium at Honesdale

Indian music at the Institute. Because there was so much interest on the part of the residents, he started to hold kirtan sessions in the auditorium almost every night. This was a special treat for everyone.

As I had been a musician before I met Swamiji, he arranged a bamboo flute for me, so I could play along during the kirtan sessions. He said the flute represents the voice of God.

Those enchanted nights will be treasured in our hearts forever. All the residents, and some of the townspeople and families would come, and we would all sit on the floor of the auditorium, with Swamiji sitting on the floor in front of us. The lights were dimmed, and the air was laden with fragrance, even though no one had burnt incense. The curtains on the stage behind Swamiji seemed to gently sway along with the music, although there was no breeze. At times it seemed that the devas had also come to listen.

Swamiji began each session with *alaps,* singing in classical Indian style. Sitting silently as we listened, it was not long before we were transported into a meditative state. And then, with the utmost patience and compassion, he started to teach us how to sing kirtan. Here was this incredibly accomplished classical Indian musician trying to teach a group of Americans how to sing kirtan, when they didn't know the words, the language or the tune. But he never gave up on us, and in spite of ourselves, we slowly improved.

Everybody longed for the appointed hour of kirtan to come, so they could again sit in the master's presence and be transported. The young children also came, and vied with each other to sit in his lap or next to him. Swamiji himself enjoyed it more than anyone. We were very fortunate to have passed so many summer nights thus, at the feet of the master.

Swamiji was busy with many other things as well, especially matchmaking. He never tired of putting couples together. Those couples that found themselves on the marriage hot seat, often opted to have their wedding at the Institute. One such wedding took place behind the Baby Barn.

Samskriti, Gopala and their two sons lived in the Baby Barn. Samskriti used to work in the flowerbeds around the barn, and often saw a large brown snake moving slowly about in the grass. Many other residents had also seen this snake. It seemed to like people, because it was always coming up to them and had never tried to harm anyone. Sometimes it would hang out on the road, and someone would pick it up with a stick and put it back in the bushes out of danger.

This snake lived under a stone at the entrance to the Baby Barn. It used to curl up under the stone, next to a chipmunk. This odd couple, the snake and the chipmunk, shared their residence underneath the stone, in perfect harmony. Samskriti began to think of this snake as her pet.

On the day of the wedding, the big brown snake made an appearance at the gathering. When Swamiji

Swamiji with Princess and Raja at the Japanese garden

saw the snake, he called Panditji and told him he recognized this snake. It was an old soul that had been very lazy in its past life. Now it wanted to get out of its snake body, but could not. Swamiji told Panditji to go over to the snake and kill it, while reciting a particular Sanskrit shloka, and to tell it that Swamiji would give it a human body in its next birth.

Meanwhile, Princess had become a very well trained guard dog. Swamiji would often telephone the log cabin, and instruct us to hold the phone close to Princess so she could hear his voice. He would call her name, and she would cock her head this way and that, looking at the phone. Sometimes, we would let her off the leash at Swamiji's log cabin, and she would walk all by herself up to the main building to see him. So Princess wouldn't be lonely, Swamiji got a second dog, a big black Akita, and named him Raja.

Swamiji now stayed in his upstairs apartment most of the time, but sometimes used the log cabin as a place to entertain his guests. An older woman had been assigned the duty of staying in the cabin and looking after the dogs and the garden. One day, as Swamiji was expecting some guests, I telephoned to tell her to get the cabin ready. Someone picked up the phone, but all I could hear was heavy breathing. Then I heard the phone drop, after which there was silence. I became alarmed because I knew that she had a heart condition, and hurriedly drove up to the cabin to see what the matter was.

When I got there, I found her calmly watering the flowers in the garden. I asked her if she had heard the phone ring, and she said no. Then I asked her who answered the phone. She told me that only Princess was inside the cabin, and had probably answered the phone. That's why all I could hear was heavy breathing! And then Princess dropped the phone and dragged it over to the water bowl.

Swamiji said a student had to be tested in the beginning. If they were not married, he would tell them to get married. If they did not have children, he would tell them to have children. If they did not have an education, he would tell them to get a degree. Then, after 10 years, if they were still around, he would start to teach them.

Somehow, the matter of my correspondence with the swami I had met at the ashram in Rishikesh came up, and Swamiji asked to see the letters. I had corresponded twice with Brahmachari about the swami. Swamiji told me that the only thing that swami wanted from me was money, even though he had specifically told me that he did not want anything material from me. Swamiji looked at the letters and said it was all nonsense, and that he felt very sad. "Why did you go to him?" he asked.

I simply replied, "You are not teaching me."

That must have affected him. He called Panditji, and told him to write to Brahmachari, telling him not to allow that swami to come into the ashram again. The next year, Brahmachari suddenly left the ashram, without any explanation.

Experience is the best teacher. I learned that if Swamiji wanted to convey something to me, he would do it directly, and not through any convoluted psychic methodology. The other wonderful thing that I gained from that experience, was that from then on, Swamiji began to personally train me on the spiritual path. I never again had any reason to complain that he was not teaching me. He gave me some general guidelines to live by and instructions for meditation.

"Actual meditation begins after the successful attainment of two *kriyas:* the application of sushumna, and the purification of the samskaras present in the unconscious. There are three types of samskaras: samskaras from above, samskaras from within and samskaras created by the environment. Attachments, relationships, actions, thoughts, feelings and speech create samskaras. These have to be purified.

"Practice should be done at the same time and place every day, without any interruption, for a long period of time. Eat on time, sleep on time, meditate on time.

"Remember your mantra all the time. Mantra is not known by its meaning, but by its vibration, and each vibration has a form, a devi or a shakti.

"Practice not lying, not having harmful thoughts, and not speaking anything harmful toward anyone. Help anyone who comes in your path and asks for help.

"Food should be offered to the guru and to God before eating, even a glass of water. Never take food from anyone else's plate.

"Your body is a shrine, and *jiva* is the deva. Divinity comes first in life; everything else is secondary. Make sincere human efforts, then grace will come."

The fall came much too soon, and Swamiji left for India.

11.
Mastering Sleep

Over the course of the winter of 1987-88, I took up karate lessons, with a group of Himmies (residents) in town that were studying karate under Hidy Ochiai, an internationally acclaimed karate master, in the school of Washin-ryu Karate-do.

One day, after Swamiji had returned in the spring, I was serving him a cup of tilk. He took hold of my upper arm. By this time, I had been to a couple of karate classes, and saw the opportunity to demonstrate a simple self-defense technique, where you twist your arm, thereby breaking the grip of your opponent. So I twisted my arm, but nothing happened. Swamiji's hand was so big, that my little twist made no difference whatsoever.

He turned his big eyes on me and said, "You dare to use karate on me?"

I said, "I didn't do anything." Okay, you might consider this a big lie, but in my mind I had not used karate *on* him. I was simply in a playful mood and wanted to show off the technique.

He didn't let go of my arm, but again said, "You dare to use karate on me?"

Again I said, "I didn't do anything." I wasn't going to say that I had used karate on him, because I didn't use it *on* him.

Swamiji let go of my arm and stood up. I took two steps back. He said, "Say sorry!" I laughed. He took another step towards me. "Say sorry!" I laughed again, but stepped back.

He took my thumb, and with a simple twist, I found myself lying on the floor with Swamiji's foot on my throat. Again he said, "Say sorry!" I laughed. He pressed harder on my throat. I grabbed his foot with both of my hands, laughing to myself, because by this time I couldn't speak. "Say sorry!" He pressed harder, and I couldn't breathe, and it was starting to hurt. Then I thought to myself, *There is nothing higher than dying at the feet of the master, I will not say sorry.*

Swamiji took his foot off and said, "I never knew you were so obstinate, I could have killed you. I am never going to fight with you again."

Somewhat dizzy and disoriented, I got up, but never said sorry. That evening, when it was time for me to meditate, it was unusually clear and easy. I mentioned it to Swamiji the next day, and he said, "Yes, because I pressed your throat."

Swamiji was sent to Tibet to study Kung Fu with a famous master who was blind. With great difficulty he went to the cave monastery, where the Kung Fu master taught a few students. He came to the entrance of the cave. There was an attendant standing guard outside the cave. Swamiji bowed and greeted the attendant. The attendant gave him a blow and knocked him down. Swamiji got angry. Again he came to the attendant and bowed and greeted him. Again the attendant gave him a blow and knocked him down. Then Swamiji thought, mentally communicating with his master, "What is this? You sent me all the way here, and he's giving me blows." His master replied, "I already taught you this thing, you know how to defend yourself, so use it." Then Swamiji again went to the attendant and bowed, but when he tried to knock him down, Swamiji intercepted the blow and knocked down the attendant.

Then the attendant smiled and said, "You have passed the first test. Now you can enter the cave, where the master stays. He is an old blind man." There were some oil lamps burning inside, so Swamiji said, "I thought he was blind. Why the lamps?" The guard replied, "The light is for people like you, not him."

Then Swamiji came to the master who said, "I know you have passed the first test or you wouldn't be here. Now you have to pass my test." He held a small pebble in the palm of his hand, and told Swamiji to pick up the pebble from his palm. He was blind, so Swamiji thought it would be easy. He tried to pick up the pebble, but before he could pick it up, the old man closed his fist. He tried a second time, and again the old man closed his fist. Then Swamiji again communicated with his master, and said, "You sent me all the way here, and I cannot pass this test. What is all this?" And his master replied, "Separate your thinking mind from your body. Let your body pick up the pebble, but only witness it. He is watching your thoughts, and when he catches your intent to pick up the pebble, he closes his hand. I have already taught you this technique, so use it. Also, he is not able to hear our conversation, because his mind is focused on the pebble." Then Swamiji did as his master instructed, and easily picked up the pebble.

Then the Kung Fu master smiled and said, "Now you have passed my test. I know you have a very great master, or you could not have done it. And I know you are a worthy candidate. Now I will start teaching you."

Swamiji's master had told him that if he needed help, to contact him on the third try, and he would help him. That's why the first two times, Swamiji always tried on his own.

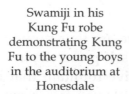

Swamiji in his Kung Fu robe demonstrating Kung Fu to the young boys in the auditorium at Honesdale

Swamiji had a silk Kung Fu robe in his closet, with a beautiful embroidered golden dragon on the back. He said that there are different schools of Kung Fu. Some use only the feet, some use only the hands, some use both feet and hands, and some use mantra.

When Swamiji first came to America, he visited Detroit. He wanted to go for a walk at night, but the hotel clerk told him not to go outside, as there were thugs and it was a bad part of town. Nevertheless, Swamiji went for a walk. Two thugs came up to him and tried to mug him. Swamiji quickly threw them down on the ground. One of them asked, "Can you teach me this?" Swamiji said he would teach them, if they promised to change their ways.

One day Swamiji wanted to demonstrate his martial arts to Phil Nuernberger in Honesdale. They

were standing in his Crummy Kitchen, and Swamiji
was holding a cup of tilk. He told Phil to hit him. Phil
protested saying he didn't want to hurt him. Swamiji
told him to go ahead and hit him. So Phil said okay,
and before he could even move, he was flat up against
the wall. Swamiji had not touched him and was still
holding his cup of tilk!

Swamiji taught us that there are four primitive
fountains: sleep, food, sex, and self-preservation. In
the monastery, the first primitive fountain that is
brought under control is sleep. Patanjali calls sleep a
modification of the mind, to be regulated and brought
under control. So one day, as I was giving Swamiji a
massage, I asked him to teach me how to master sleep.
He looked at me as if I were an insect crawling out
from under a rock, and said, "Master?!" Then, he
puffed on his cigarette and stared out into space.

In the chronicle of my life, the summer of 1988
will be known as the Sleep Episode; or more appropriately, the sleep deprivation episode. Somehow or
other, Swamiji engineered my life in such a way, that I
never had more than one and a half, to two and a half,
hours of sleep at a time. According to yoga science, it
is not possible for a human being to remain in the state
of deep sleep for more than three hours. Swamiji told
us that the rest of the time is spent 'tossing and turning
over the bed.' Swamiji said that he himself slept only
15 days out of the year.

Two or three of us would stay up with Swamiji in
his loft until about midnight. He always said his day
began at midnight. By that time, he had made all the
phone calls, and we had given him his massage. By
midnight Swamiji was usually bright-eyed and bushy-
tailed, ready for work. Of course, his work was on other
levels, and he would throw us out.

Then around 3:00 a.m., my phone would ring, and he would ask for a cup of tilk. So I would go upstairs to make the tilk, and would find him softly snoring away on his sofa. I used to sit quietly on the floor next to the sofa, and wait for him to get up. But nothing happened. A few minutes would pass, and then I would go back down to my room. After some time, the phone would ring again. He would ask, "Can you make a cup of tilk?" Again I would go upstairs and make the tilk. Then he would be awake, drink his tilk, and make some phone calls. Sometimes I would press his legs, and by then, it was time to start making breakfast.

Sometimes he would telephone me from his loft and say, "Can you call India?" He often called India in the middle of the night, because over there it was daytime, and he could reach people easier. So, in my mind I would think, *Okay, I can sit with Swamiji and use his phone because it has that nifty little redial button on it.* Then he would say, "Do it from your room!" and hang up.

Oh, the misery of it all. Those were the days of rotary phones. I had to dial about 10,000 numbers to get access to the international line, then the country code, city code and number, and more often than not, would get a recorded message, "All lines are busy at this time, please try your call later," in English or Hindi, if I got that far. Over and over and over again.

Sometimes I was so tired, I'd put my head down on the phone, and just rest my eyes for a minute. If I drifted off, the phone would suddenly ring, making me jump out of my skin, and it would be Swamiji saying, "Are you calling?" "Yes, Swamiji." Then, I would start all over again. I'm convinced that these were devices he conjured up to keep me awake.

As if this was not enough, there was a schizo-phrenic from Chicago who would go on binges, and telephone the Institute all night long. Or an emergency would happen at night, and someone would need to use the phone. If I tried to rest during the daytime, that was also interrupted by something or the other. If I sat in a chair, I'd fall asleep. I didn't dare drive a car, because I knew if I sat down, I'd fall asleep at the wheel.

And this was also another summer full of kirtan. We had kirtan two or three nights a week. There was lots of musical activity, with classes and kirtan and performances. Amjad Ali Khan came to Honesdale and gave a sarod performance. Whenever Pandit Jasraj came to the U.S., he would visit Swamiji and give a performance. It was truly delightful. All the musical giants of India used to bow to Swamiji and touch his feet. They respected his knowledge of music, as well as his saintliness.

There were a few of us residents who played instruments along with Swamiji at kirtan. There were one or two harmonium players, one or two tabla players, a violinist, Larry Warren on the western flute, while I played the bamboo flute. Larry and I sat next to each other at kirtan, as part of the accompanying musicians. We sat in the front row, directly in front of Swamiji. I remember as we were playing one night, I was wondering why Larry was hitting so many wrong notes. I opened my eyes and looked over at him. He had put down his flute, and was smiling, looking at me. My bottom hand had slipped off the flute, because I had fallen asleep. All the wrong notes were mine. I gave up and lay the flute in my lap, struggling to remain upright. I only hoped that the people behind me would think that all the swaying was because I was lost in the bhava of the kirtan. But the people in front used to exchange knowing glances and elbow each other, as I started to nod off, anticipating the nosedive to follow. And there sat Swamiji, right in front of me, watching it all.

Sometimes Swamiji would end the kirtan with a bhajan, and one of his favorites was a Kabir *bani*, 'Sochan Samaja Mana Priyare.' He would translate for us in English:

> "O mind, my friend, try to understand. If you are really a lover of God you can never sleep, not possible for you to sleep. If you are tired very much, you don't need pillows and mattresses, you just sleep; go to sleep. Kabir Das says, if you want to receive something, give everything that you have, then you will receive. Kabir says, O sadhu, listen. If you have once given (your) head and then you are saying that you don't have this, you don't have this, that's not devotion."

Needless to say, by the end of the summer, I had been thoroughly mastered by sleep, not its master. I crawled back under my rock, and never again used the word 'master,' when I asked Swamiji to teach me something.

There was a South Indian lady who lived in Scranton, and often came to meet Swamiji. She had a younger sister, suffering from leukemia from the age of 14, who was in America for treatment. They came to meet Swamiji and he gave both of them mantras. Swamiji told the older sister that he would give her younger sister an experience, and she would know it was true, because her younger sister would not remember him.

The younger sister became very ill, and was admitted to the hospital in Scranton. When people came to visit her, she would tell them about their past lives. She often saw invisible people, ancestors, in the room with her, and would tell her attendant to bring water for them. She was in a lot of pain, and used to beg the doctors to let her die.

She told her older sister that she had met God. So the sister asked her what He was like. "God is detached." She said she asked God if she was going to live or die. God said, "It depends upon you." She told God that she wanted to live and become a 'pioneering woman.' Later she told the doctors to take away the oxygen tent, and remove the tubes, because she was going to live, no matter what they did. Her older sister asked her if she remembered meeting Swami Rama, but she replied that she did not know him.

Swamiji said that when the oxygen supply is low, the sahasrara chakra opens. That was the experience he gave the younger sister, and it was valid. Afterwards she didn't recall anything of that episode, but she again remembered Swamiji. She recovered, and returned to Bangalore, where she did some social work and was written up in the local newspaper as a 'pioneering woman.'

As the summer came to a close, Swamiji left for India.

12.

Brahmacharya Vows

March of 1989 brought Swamiji back to Honesdale. This time, he told me to take brahmacharya vows.
He said he wanted to murder me, to kill my body of
samskaras. I was dismayed. I argued with Swamiji
about it for a week. He said that Shankaracharya was
right. Women are not interested in enlightenment, only
in finding a good man. Finally, he told me to take vows,
or the tradition would leave me behind. I agreed to
take vows. To formalize the agreement, he made me
submit a written letter of resignation from the Bitchananda Order. He said I could not be in two orders at
the same time; now I would be in the brahmacharya
order. I submitted my letter of resignation to Brunette
Eason, but she refused to accept it. Nevertheless, it was
official.

In April, Swamiji observed 10 days of silence
during *Nav Ratra.* Nav Ratra is a period of time in the
Hindu calendar, where devotees worship Divine
Mother in her nine aspects. The observance is usually
for nine days, but in some years it takes 10 days. That
year it was 10 days. During that time, Swamiji stayed
up in his loft, and did not see anyone, or make any
phone calls. I was the only one that was allowed into
his room, bringing his meals, mail and messages to
him. The room was often permeated by fragrance, even
though he didn't burn any incense. According to the
scriptures, many sages travel in their subtle bodies

through fragrance. Swamiji would read his messages, and sometimes write down a reply. Sometimes he used sign language, and would make a grunting sound. Eventually, I also started using sign language and made grunting sounds in return.

He had a small ghee lamp that he kept burning continuously. One day, when I was giving him a back massage, my hand was burned by the heat of his spine. On the ninth day, there was a heavy snowstorm. It was a very special opportunity for me to attend on him during this time. After it was over, he complained that he didn't understand my sign language or grunting noises! Later, he said he wanted to do a 40-day kundalini practice, where he would appear as dead; only the hair and nails would grow. He needed an attendant to make sure that he was not disturbed; however, he would not take any food or water. He said I could observe that practice also, but it never happened.

It was during this time that Swamiji began an *anushcharana* to Divine Mother for one and a half years for the benefit of the Himalayan Institute Hospital Trust (HIHT) that he was establishing in India. These were the days when he was always seen holding a mala, and doing japa. He even said his mala turned into a ring of fire.

During this time, Swamiji's *gurubhai* and Nirvanji frequently came to visit him in their subtle bodies. His gurubhai would hide his mala, and Nirvanji would bring it back. Many times, when Swamiji left his loft to lecture or play tennis, he could not find his mala when he returned. After a thorough search, we would find it some place where we had already looked earlier.

Every practice has certain prescribed limits, and the practice Swamiji was doing had a limit to the number of malas he could do in a day. But Swamiji always pushed his limits, and far exceeded the number of repetitions he was supposed to do. His gurubhai used to fight with him about it.

One afternoon, when I was giving Swamiji a massage, he was holding his mala in his hands, but it lifted up by the end, as if someone had taken hold of it. He said, "Stop," and I thought he was talking to me; then he started talking in Hindi to his gurubhai. They really used to fight, and Swamiji would have cuts, marks, and burns on his body as a result. Finally Swamiji complained to his master that his gurubhai wouldn't let him do his practice. His master then taught him how to protect himself. Later, his gurubhai asked Swamiji to teach him this technique.

There was always a competition between Swamiji and one particular gurubhai. They both knew the science of changing forms. One day, his gurubhai came in the form of a tiger, and tried to scare Swamiji, but Swamiji knew who it was, and threw a rock at him. Then, his gurubhai changed back to his own form, and was angry at Swamiji for hitting him with a rock.

Swamiji was always creating problems for the other swamis at the cave monastery. He was told that they were always protected during meditation, so he wanted to test this. He threw a cobra at one of the swamis while he was practicing, and the cobra burst into flames. Babaji was angry at Swamiji for doing that, and told him not to do it again.

When he was a young boy at one of the cave monasteries, there was a visiting swami whom nobody liked. Somebody pooped on the place in the cave, where he placed his bed and pillow. It happened three days in a row. Finally the swami left. Babaji called Swamiji and asked him if he had done this. Swamiji said, "Yes," and Babaji said, "Good."

Swamiji talked of two or three different cave monasteries. The ancestral cave monastery is in Tibet, and there is a 900-year old inscription on a rock, with the names of the sages of our tradition, which is 4,000-5,000 years old. He also spoke of a cave monastery in Manali, and one in Gangotri.

Swamiji said it is the sages that write the script for the universe. They are higher than the *avataras*. It is the sages that tell the avataras when to come down. Swamiji said he never dreamt, because his dream became a reality. One day of ours was only 1/100th of a second for him.

When I first met Swamiji, I asked him how old he was. He said, "How old is gold?" But in 1989, he told me he was 396 years old, and that he had been changing bodies for that period of time. Another time I asked him how we would recognize him, if he were in another body. He said there would be similarities in the face and mannerisms, and that the same physical scars would be transferred from one body to the other, as they were permanent karmas. He even showed me the scar on his abdomen, where the branch pierced him when he fell down the mountain, as recounted in *Living with the Himalayan Masters*. It was a very ragged scar close to where the appendix is. He was not born into the body we knew; he had taken on that body.

One day, when I was in his loft putting his laundry away, I did not see him anywhere. Then he casually came walking out of the bedroom, saying "Om." I asked him if he had gone somewhere, but he just smiled, "Himalayan mountain tricks." He would say that when he didn't want to explain something, like the time I gave him champi (an Indian head massage) while he sported a stubbly beard. At the end of the champi, he was clean shaven — without a razor.

Swamiji did not demonstrate siddhis very often. But one day, he told Ragani and me to tie a cloth around his eyes. We then drew something on a piece of paper in front of him. With his eyes blindfolded, he could draw the same thing, on another piece of paper. Another time, he was prancing around the kitchen downstairs with his mala in his hand, then it was suddenly laced through his belt, without him lifting his hands. Another little jig, and it was back in his hand. He also used to play with the volume on the TV, making it go up and down, without using the remote control. Sometimes he would cover his eyes, and describe to us the scenes taking place on the screen.

Once, when we were giving him a massage, his whole body shivered and he said, "Cold." I asked him, "What?" He told us he was taking a bath at Gangotri. He said he had many bodies, ten bodies: one in Honesdale, one in Gangotri, one above, and all ten looked alike. If he changed his body, they also changed. I asked him which one was the real one; he said they were all real. Then I asked him why does he need to have a body at all, and he replied, "How else can I meet you?"

One afternoon, he called me up to the loft, and I found him sitting on the sofa with his legs stretched out on the coffee table. He appeared to be very groggy, and asked me to put a cold wet cloth on the soles of his feet. As I did so, I noticed that his legs were changing color, first red, then white, back and forth, for some time. In lectures, and also in private, Swamiji had demonstrated how he could drain the blood from one side of his body into the other side, so that one side appeared white and the other side red. He said this demonstrated the Ardhanarishwar form of Shiva, half man, half woman.

Swamiji posing at
the Japanese
garden

Finally, I took brahmacharya vows in 1989. The first step of brahmacharya is discipline, detachment, and study. A brahmachari lives a disciplined life. Food, sex, sleep, and self-preservation are the four primitive urges that are disciplined and regulated. Food is regulated by how much you eat, when you eat, what you eat, slowly abstaining from those foods that are taken only for the sake of enjoyment. Sex is disciplined by abstinence. Sleep is slowly regulated by going to bed on time, and getting up on time, and not sleeping during the day. Slowly, less and less sleep is needed. Self-preservation is regulated by surrendering the self to the Self of all.

Discipline involves three levels: thought, speech and action. First you deal with action, then speech, and then thought. It is easier to discipline your gross actions than it is to discipline your thoughts. When a true state of desirelessness is reached, thought, speech and action will automatically fall into place. The four primitive urges are disciplined at all three levels.

Then there is the study of scriptures. The Bhagavad Gita, the Upanishads, and the *Brahma Sutras* are studied, in that order. A thorough understanding of one scripture with all its commentaries should be achieved before proceeding to the next.

Detachment is practiced in day-to-day life. You slowly learn to be detached from family and friends, realizing that love and attachment are two separate realities. Observing your internal condition, learning what your attachments are, is the practice of detachment.

There are three meanings of the word brahmacharya: celibacy, remaining in Brahman consciousness all the time, and channeling the shakti. The monastic meaning of the word brahmachari is he who knows how to channel the shakti. It refers to upward traveling, the final flight of kundalini. Control of the senses means to direct your energies towards spirituality. Swamiji did not want to impose any discipline on me, but said that discipline alone would help me.

He told me very pointedly, that I would be tested on the path; that two or three times someone would approach me for sex, and I was not to do it under any circumstance. He tested me on the dream level also. He told me I passed the test, but not 100 percent. When I asked him why not 100 percent, he said you should remember God all the time.

One time, Swamiji's master tested him and three other brahmacharis. Babaji gave them each a ring, and instructed them not to give it to anyone, but to return the rings to him at the appointed place and time. Babaji went ahead of them, and the four brahmacharis followed. They stayed one night in a village on the way. Babaji had already stopped there, and arranged for four prostitutes to go to each one of them, and steal the rings he had given them. That night, when the girl came to Swamiji's room, she started pressing his legs. Swamiji changed his form into that of a woman. The girl screamed and ran away.

The next day, when the four brahmacharis met Babaji, he asked them for the rings. Swamiji produced his ring, but the others could not. When Swamiji explained what had happened, Babaji laughed and asked him how he did that. But Swamiji told him, "It was you who taught me that."

Swamiji began teaching me step by step. He would often make a tape recording of his instructions. On one such tape, no matter where I stopped it, he said the same thing, over and over again. "Ganapati is not a god. Gana means self. Pati means master. Ganapati means master of the self." Later on, when I listened to the tape, those words were not on it!

In the fall, Swamiji left for India, but came back in the winter to hold a seminar. He did this a few times, giving seminars to raise money for the hospital in India. He gave seminars on the Path of Fire and Light, *Ishopanishad, Mundaka Upanishad, Mandukya Upanishad, Yoga Sutras,* and Saundarya Lahari. These lectures were video taped.

13.
Fund Raising
through the Islands

In January of 1990, I went to India with the tour group, for the laying of the foundation stone of the hospital by Shri N.D. Tiwari, Ex-Chief Minister of Uttar Pradesh. The group stayed for about a month, and then came back to the U.S.

It was very pleasant for me to do my practice in Rishikesh. One night in particular, I remember how all the sounds of nature were in harmony, from the Ganges to the wind, from the mosquitoes to the water pump; everything vibrated with Om.

In the summer of 1989, a young swami came to meet Swamiji at Honesdale. He had a long name, but Swamiji shortened it to Anand Swami. Anand Swami was staying in a rented house in New York State, not far from the Institute, where he was busy doing a *yagya* for Divine Mother.

The following summer, he performed another yagya for Divine Mother, in the same house. He was staying all alone in that house in the woods. One night, he heard the washing machine going on in the basement, and went down to investigate. Someone had put the laundry and soap powder in, water was filling up and it was churning, but it wasn't plugged in! He got scared, and ran away. Another day, someone rang the doorbell, and left a bunch of flowers outside the door. There was no one there. Swamiji admitted to me that he had done all that, to give Anand Swami some experiences.

Another time, Swamiji showed Anand Swami and Pandit Rajmani how he could absorb mercury through the skin, and excrete it through the urine. He said mercury removes all impurities, and the nicotine in cigarettes helps to remove the traces of mercury left behind. Perhaps, this is one of the reasons Swamiji smoked.

It was in the summer of 1990, that a small group of us went with Swamiji to Curacao for a seminar. The Sindhi community in Curacao was very generous and helpful in getting the hospital started in India. On the way to Curacao, we passed through Aruba. Everyone stayed as guests in different houses. There is nothing quite like Indian hospitality.

In Curacao we stayed in Ramesh and Vidya Daryanani's beach house. Swamiji would go from house to house, visiting the different families. He would send me in advance to prepare his food; so I went from house to house, making a mess of everyone's kitchen.

Swamiji's lectures were well received by the public. In one lecture he was talking about his famous diagram, the body-breath-mind-soul circle chart that he used to describe that relationship. There wasn't a blackboard, but a flipchart, a stand with large blank pieces of paper that he could write on with a magic marker. In Swamiji's enthusiasm for the subject, he accidentally tripped over the leg of the stand and almost knocked it over while trying to change the page. Dr. John Clarke, who was also a speaker, was sitting in the front row of the audience. In an effort to rescue Swamiji, Dr. Clarke leapt up out of his seat and vaulted onto the stage. Unfortunately, he clipped his foot and ended up on all fours on the stage in front of Swamiji.

Being somewhat surprised, Swamiji looked at Dr. Clarke, then at the audience, and said, "He's helping me."

Fortunately, I was sitting in the back of the audience. Seeing these two do their Marx Brothers routine, tickled me so much, I couldn't stop giggling. The seminar was a success.

That brings to mind another story I heard. Swamiji was lecturing in Germany. He was standing on a newly constructed wooden platform, when it suddenly collapsed. Everyone was shocked. There was only rubble and no one could see Swamiji anywhere. Slowly, he climbed out of the rubble, picked up the microphone, and said, "Lecture over."

Later in the summer, we also went to Jamaica. At the airport, we were all confused trying to read the signs, looking for our gate, when Swamiji quietly said, "It's gate No. 7," and proceeded. We all scrambled behind him, wondering how he knew which gate it was — 'Himalayan mountain tricks.'

In Jamaica, we stayed in the house of one of Anand Swami's devotees. From the rear porch, we could see the beautiful green-blue Caribbean sea and enjoyed the ocean breezes. Swamiji lectured to the Indian community in this house, and also visited a yoga center in Negril. At the yoga center, as Swamiji was speaking, a man in the audience starting asking very inflammatory questions about Christianity. The audience was getting annoyed. Finally, an intelligent man in the audience asked Swamiji to lead the group in a meditation. Swamiji readily agreed, and guided everyone to sit with their head, neck and trunk in a straight line, to gently close their eyes, breathe deeply, relax, mentally watch the flow of the breath, and so on. Then, during a moment of silence, Swamiji very quietly got up and left, leaving the audience with their eyes closed in meditation. I had kept one eye open to watch, and scrambled quietly to catch up with Swamiji. (This maneuver was so successful that I saw Swamiji use it at other places like Buffalo and Toronto.)

Swamiji traveled a lot that year, going from center to center, to raise money for the hospital. Fortunately, I got to accompany him to Glenview, Chicago, Buffalo, New Jersey and Toronto. Traveling with Swamiji was always fun, but also a lot of hard work. I used to pack his food, water, tilk, utensils and cigarettes into a shoulder bag, and then carry his carry-on bag, along with my purse and his briefcase. I remember huffing and puffing after him in the Pittsburgh airport, loaded down with baggage, and really dragging myself. He stopped, looked at me, and took one bag. He walked a few steps and turned to me and said, "This is heavy!" Then he went on to ask why I packed so much stuff, and finally said that if he ever saw that black bag again (the one with all the food), he would throw it off the plane. I took him seriously, and retired the black bag. I bought a new, smaller blue bag and smaller lightweight utensils and thermoses. In other words, I became much more efficient. I still packed the same food items, but it took up less space.

In 1990, Swamiji started Yoga International magazine, so that the public could have the benefit of reading about yoga from an authentic perspective, without any taint of yellow journalism, or using it as a platform for personal gain. The magazine has since become very successful.

Every year, Swamiji would teach Kevin and me something new. He reiterated that regularity and punctuality are very important in meditation. He said that during the time of meditation, we are fully protected; nothing bad could happen to us, and the tradition would look after our interests during that time. He was leading us from form to the formless. He taught us that mantra travels from guru to disciple. Even if you read the same mantra in a book, nothing is going to happen unless it comes from the guru. He also told us to keep a spiritual diary, and that all spiritual experiences need confirmation.

By the end of August, he left for India.

14.

Himalayan Mountain Tricks

Anand Swami came to see Swamiji in the winter
of 1990-91. Early one morning, Swamiji called him to
his room and gave him an ek mukhi rudraksha bead.
Rudraksha beads are seeds of a special tree that are
strung into japa malas. The ek mukhi is rare because it
has only one seam, or face. It is considered to be a
symbol of Shiva. Though it was snowing heavily,
Anand Swami insisted on taking Swamiji's car and
driving it to Scranton to visit some devotees. Everyone
told him not to go, but he would not listen. He had an
accident; the car flipped over, and his hand was pinned
under the roof, but was only slightly injured. Swamiji
said it was the ek mukhi that saved his life.

After the seminar Swamiji left with a small group
of students for a tour of Southeast Asia.

In the spring of 1991, Swamiji returned to Honesdale. I began to notice a few subtle things about
Swamiji. I am a tall person, and sometimes, when I
walked next to Swamiji, he was taller than me, sometimes the same height, and at other times shorter than
me. Interestingly enough, despite these changes, his
clothes always seemed to fit him. His personality also
seemed to change at times. When he was shorter, he
was usually very gentle and soft spoken. When he was
taller, he was very fiery and energetic. Even his feet
changed appearance, becoming paler or redder, larger
or smaller. I thought he was changing bodies, and

asked him about it. He said it was a siddhi, that the body would naturally get smaller or bigger, and change appearance in the course of a day. Once in a lecture, he made an interesting remark. He said the tradition is like a giant switchboard; there is always an operator to wear the mask of Swami Rama or Dr. Arya.

There were two in the tradition who knew the science of changing their forms, Swamiji and his gurubhai. Sometimes, when Swamiji would get up to wash his hands before taking his food, his gurubhai would assume his form and come and eat it. Then, when Swamiji would return and see his plate empty, he would ask, "Have I eaten?" His gurubhai especially liked kheer, and it was at times a problem. They used to do this to each other and create chaos.

Many times, Swamiji would leave his body and go to the monastery, while someone from the monastery would come and inhabit his body. This is how they were taught and learned many things. But for people like me, it was confusing. One day he would say one thing, and another day say something else. And when I said, you said this, he replied, "I never said that." Finally I understood, and just looked at him and said, "Somebody who looks like you said that." And he kept quiet.

One day, I had the pleasure of driving Swamiji to the eye doctor in Scranton for a new pair of reading glasses. I knew exactly how long it would take me to get there, because I used to follow the speed limits and the same path every time. It took me exactly 15 minutes to reach town from the Institute. We got in the car and drove to town, but it took only 10 minutes. The same thing happened on the way back. I thought about it, and realized that there was a whole section of the road that we didn't pass through. We had skipped five minutes of time and space!

"I am the son of a sage of the Himalayan mountain, I am a free spirit contented with Self pride." (in Swamiji's own handwriting)

Early one morning at 3:30, Swamiji telephoned me from the loft to come up. I came up and found him sitting perfectly awake and alert on the sofa, with the bright overhead light on. This was unusual, because I normally found him stretched out on the sofa with only a dim light on, and his hair all rumpled like a little baby. I asked him if he wanted a cup of tea, but he said no. I sat on the floor next to the sofa, and he politely asked me how I was. I said I was fine, and asked him how he was. His voice was very low and deep, not his usual voice. I looked at him closely, and told him his voice sounded different. He said it was just early morning voice. Then I remarked that I didn't know who I was talking to anymore. He looked at me and smiled. I asked him if he wanted tea or tilk, but he said no and told me to go.

Later that day, I asked Swamiji about the incident. He said it was Babaji, who had come and entered his physical body, and wanted to say hello to me. I asked Swamiji, if that were so, then where was he? And he said he was in his subtle body, sitting about four feet in front of Babaji. I asked him how it was possible. He said he was the kid of these sages, and they sometimes used his body. Sometimes they would stay for days, or weeks, other times only hours or moments. After a while, I could recognize about two or three different sages that used his body.

That summer, on Guru Purnima day, Swamiji was burning a ghee lamp on his coffee table in the loft. It was consuming ghee extra fast. He said it was burning in two places at once, Honesdale and Banares.

Swamiji also traveled around to lecture at the centers that summer, and I was privileged to travel with him to many of the places. In Chicago, as he was lecturing, he said it would be a hundred years before another person would come to America with as much knowledge of pranayama as he had.

We had a grand time in Curacao on the second visit. A smaller group went with him the second time for a seminar. Again, we stayed in Ramesh and Vidya's beach house. Swamiji stayed downstairs in their bedroom, and the rest of us stayed upstairs. That first night he gave the key of his room to Vidya, asking her to lock him up inside the room, and to come exactly at 5:00 the next morning to wake him up.

I was already down in the kitchen by that time making tilk. Vidya came at 5:00 a.m. and knocked on Swamiji's door. But at the same time, someone was knocking on the front door of the house. It was Swamiji. The front door was still locked, with bolts and chains from inside. His room was still locked from the outside. She was so surprised to find him standing outside the door. He said he had gone for a walk.

On one of those days, he went to Bhagwan and Rani's house for a meal. I went in advance to cook. I used to pack his change of clothes and toiletries, so he could take a shower and rest at the person's house. Rani gave him her bedroom to use. So, Swamiji told me to put all his things out in the bathroom, because he wanted to take a shower. I put his robe, underwear, razor, shaving cream, toothbrush, toothpaste, soap, and towel, everything, on the bathroom counter, so he could shower and shave. Shanta (Kay Gendron) was with us. Then he told me to take the key and lock him in from outside. And we left. I expected it would take a few minutes, wondering when to go and unlock the door and let him out. About a minute later, out comes Swamiji walking down the hall, all clean shaven and fresh with a new robe. So I thought, *That was quick.* Then I thought, *Wait a minute. How did he get out?* I quietly went back to the room. It was still locked from outside. I went into the bathroom. Everything was exactly as I had left it. He had not showered, shaved, or changed clothes. I minutely examined the razor for signs of usage. Nothing. Yet, he was clean-shaven and was wearing a fresh robe.

One morning in Ramesh and Vidya's beach house, I was waiting for Swamiji to call and kept doing my japa. I was watching the clock. But time wasn't moving. I became very restless and checked the other clocks. They all indicated that only five minutes had passed, yet I was doing mala after mala and knew that well over 20 minutes should have passed. I kept getting up and looking around, but the clock didn't move. Finally when Swamiji called, I mentioned it to him and he just laughed.

On another trip, we were at Newark airport. Swamiji had switched from cigarettes to beedies. I always used to pack and carry his food, and carried his beedies. Of course, Swamiji would always smoke whenever he wanted to, even in the non-smoking areas. There he was, standing and smoking a beedie in Newark airport, in a non-smoking zone. A young man, who worked for the airlines, came up to him and said, "Sir, you can't smoke here." Swamiji looked at him, blew smoke in his face, and said, "No English." After 1989, he used to wear his red robe all the time, even in public. There was a funny looking girl getting on the plane, who had rows of braids and odd things tied in her hair. She saw Swamiji and told him she liked his robe. He smiled, and said he liked her hair. I just watched.

In October of 1991, there was a devastating earthquake in northern India. Swamiji became actively involved in leading a movement to facilitate the distribution of aid to the needy victims. At one point he took a vow to fast unto death in front of the Prime Minister's residence in New Delhi, if their demands were not met. I was in Honesdale, and for those of us in the U.S., it was a very disturbing time because we did not know what was happening. We sent faxes from all over the world to the Prime Minister, in support of Swamiji's work. Finally, the demands were met.

15.
A Little Bird

In the spring of 1992, Swamiji again returned to Honesdale. Some time during the month of June, as I was serving Swamiji his lunch, I dropped the lid of a hot box on my toe. The sharp edge of the lid landed right on the root of the nail of my big toe. It was very painful. I wanted to make a quick trip into town after lunch, but with my toe injury I couldn't go. I was hobbling around and Swamiji asked me what happened. I told him I had hurt my toe. Then he kept asking me why. Finally, I said I must have been burning off some karma. He said yes, I would have been in a serious car accident, if I had gone to town at that particular time.

Because of Swamiji's blood sugar problem, he didn't take any sweets. Someone had made a special Indian sweet dish to celebrate her child's birthday, and wanted me to give it to Swamiji. Like a fool, I put it on his tray with his lunch, and brought it up to him. I showed him the sweet, and he said, "Are you trying to kill me?" Then he picked it up, and threw it across the room, splattering the bookshelf. Gayatri, Swamiji's tennis coach, was also sitting in the room. We didn't react, and I just walked over to clean up the mess. But that wasn't all. Then he picked up the entire tray and threw the whole meal on the floor. Gayatri had dal sprayed all over her hair. We started to clean up the mess. Swamiji turned his back on us, and looked at the TV. I went down and made another plate for him and brought it up. Finally, he ate something. He told me that if he celebrates one child's birthday, he would have to celebrate every child's birthday.

He went through a phase, where he kept increasing the volume on the TV set. Every day he set it higher and higher. It was very annoying, because I literally had to shout over the TV to give him his messages. Sometimes, he didn't hear me at all. Finally, I started to wonder if he had a hearing loss problem. As soon as I thought that, he looked at me with that 'you insect' expression, and turned the volume down. Many times, Swamiji did experiments that we simply couldn't understand, like how to make yourself impervious to loud noises.

We kept some drinking water in a small Austrian crystal carafe on Swamiji's coffee table, with the fragile drinking cup inverted over the mouth of the carafe. One day he was gazing at it intently. It started vibrating, where the lip of the cup touched the neck of the carafe, first slightly, and then with a loud continuous humming. I thought that a truck must have driven by, making the table vibrate, but there was none. He had a slight smile on his face. I was puzzled and I reached out to touch the carafe. He quickly said, "You go!" He was practicing a kriya where he could move objects with his gaze.

There were a few nights in a row, when Swamiji would experiment with different methods for opening up his nostrils. He would stick a rolled up tissue into his blocked nostril to irritate it and make it open. Then he would put a dab of Vick's Vaporub at the base of the bridge between the two nostrils. Or he would insert mustard oil up both nostrils on a Q-tip, or hold a pillow under his arm, or lie down on the opposite side. At the time, I thought he was having some nostril problem; I didn't realize he was teaching us simple techniques to open blocked nostrils.

Swamiji often went for a walk before breakfast. One morning, coming back from his walk, he started shouting for Gayatri and me to come quickly. There was a little downy woodpecker next to the building that had been hurt and couldn't fly. He told us to bring it up to his apartment. We picked it up with a towel, put it in a shoebox, and brought it upstairs. I put the shoebox under the table next to the wall. We brought some breadcrumbs and water for it. It just sat there quietly. When I checked on it later, it had started to move its head a little. We brought it some birdseed. There were some droppings in the box, so it seemed that the bird was eating.

It had a little rusty cap, and a white downy tummy. It was so small that it could fit in the palm of my hand. I thought to myself that woodpeckers eat insects; so I found a big fat cricket downstairs, and brought it up to give it to the bird. Swamiji strongly reprimanded me for bringing a goat to the slaughter. I asked him why was it okay to kill an insect flying in the room, but not okay to feed an insect to a bird? He said that it was okay to kill for protection, but not for food. It was the intention that counted. Many insects were killed as we walked on the ground, but it was not our intention to kill them.

He told me to go and pet the bird. But when I tried, it jumped out of the box and hid in a corner. Swamiji said it was no wonder, as I was talking of killing insects. He wouldn't let us feed the bird eggs either. But it did eat some corn and fruits.

Slowly the little bird started hopping around Swamiji's room. He let it go freely, wherever it wanted. We brought a cage for it, but the bird was so small that it could pass through the bars. We used to watch it hopping around the room. When it tried to fly, it usually fell on its face. But it slowly got stronger. Sometimes, it would jump onto the curtains and fly from curtain to curtain.

I noticed that one side of the little bird's head was bigger than the other side. I thought that maybe it had a head injury. Swamiji looked at me very intensely, and said, "That's the way she wears her hair." I couldn't understand why he insisted on calling the bird she, when we all knew it was a male. He even called the bird Kamal. We became confused, wondering if he was talking about me or the bird.

After a while, the bird started pecking the carpet, climbing curtains and hanging on screens, even pecking the woodwork. That night, I found it sleeping in the corner with its little head tucked under its wing. I picked it up; it was so light, it was just like picking up air with feathers. I put it in the cage. We all thought that it was doing fine, and would soon be able to go outside again.

Next day, I found it leaning against the wall, with its head down. I picked it up; it clung to my finger and looked at me. I put it in the cage. That afternoon, I brought some food for it, but when I opened the cage it was dead. Its body had become stiff, and its eyes were open, its tongue was sticking out, already hard from being dried out. Small bugs had started crawling over its body. I told Swamiji it had died. He said, "Are you sure?" I picked it up. I was sure. The little bird had flown away, and left its little body behind.

Swamiji looked away. He said, "Kamal died." The cold breath of truth passed over my heart, and I understood in an instant what had happened. I was holding my own death in my hands. I was moved to tears by that expression of selfless love. He told me to bury the bird. I wrapped it in a paper towel and buried it in the garden, where its elements would return to their sources. But now, the soul of that little bird was inseparably mingled with mine.

Swamiji said it was a lesson in love and attachment, and that the mystery of birth and death is known only to a fortunate few; that attachment causes misery, but love is eternal.

That summer I had a favorite shawl that I used to wear all the time. It was a plain cotton shawl. It was starting to look torn and tattered, but it was very comfortable. One day I couldn't find it. I looked everywhere. I even asked Swamiji if he had seen my shawl. He got up, took me to his closet, and handed me a large white woolen shawl to use. I thanked him, but it was too hot to wear wool in the summer. I missed my cotton shawl.

By chance I found my shawl in the closet stuffed behind some boxes. Next morning, when Swamiji called, I came in wearing that shawl. He asked me where I found it. I told him I found it behind some boxes. He said he had put it there. I was sitting there quietly, poking my finger through a hole in the shawl. He reached over, grabbed my shawl and ripped it. He said, "I hate that shawl!" I was so surprised to hear him say that he hated the shawl, that I started laughing. Once he told me he was embarrassed by the clothes I wore.

In August, Swamiji left for India. In October, he called me to come to India. I stayed in his flat in Delhi, and Swamiji stayed mostly in Rishikesh. The Delhi flat was nice, having one master bedroom, one sitting room, dining room, kitchen, two bathrooms, a servant's room, and a music room. My job was to answer the phone and work on a book. We were working on the rhymed version of Valmiki's Ramayana.

16.

Moscow Fever

The five months I spent in Delhi were very intense, very difficult, and very creative. Without noticing, we slipped into 1993. Working on the book was a true blessing. It was like seeing the entire Ramayana unfold before my eyes.

Swamiji used to come to Delhi about once a month. He would spend two to three days in Delhi, meet people, work on the book, and answer mail. But those few days with him rejuvenated me for the rest of the time that he was away.

There was a little myna bird that used to come and sit in the window whenever Swamiji was there. She used to sing her little heart out with the sweetest, most loving songs you can imagine. And she only did it when Swamiji was there, following him from window to window throughout the apartment. I used to tease Swamiji that she was in love with him. He would often say, "A little bird told me."

I remember one special afternoon with Swamiji in Delhi. It was after lunch and we had finished giving him his massage. There was a Bangla movie playing on TV. It had English subtitles: Swamiji asked me to read the subtitles to him, while he rested. It was the story of a young girl, whose family arranged her marriage according to an astrologer's prediction. The astrologer told the family to get her married to an old man on his deathbed. They were married, and the wedding procession carried them to the cremation ground. She was supposed to perform sati after her husband died, burning herself alive on her husband's funeral pyre. The *chandala* of the cremation ground befriended her and told her to run away. Finally, she and the chandala fell in love. But the old man didn't die. Eventually the river rose, and carried the girl and the old man out to sea, where they drowned; the astrologer's prediction was fulfilled.

I remember that afternoon, because of the intimacy of sitting with Swamiji, and reciting such beautiful poetry and prose. I was enthralled with the story, and Swamiji remained awake to watch the entire movie. It was an example of his love and compassion, for he knew that I sometimes felt lonely in Delhi.

The young man in charge of the office at that time was Vimal Dhasmana, a very sweet-natured boy; he became like my younger brother. He wanted to visit his parents in Rishikesh and left for a few days. After Vimal left, I felt so lonely, I literally started crying. When Vimal reached Rishikesh and met Swamiji, Swamiji scolded him and told him that I was crying in Delhi. He ordered Vimal to turn around and go back. Poor Vimal, no sooner had he stepped off the bus, than he had to get back on it.

When Vimal was back in Delhi, he told me that Swamiji scolded him for leaving me alone and told him that I was crying. I acted very indifferent about the whole thing, but I was secretly pleased that Vimal had returned, and was very touched by Swamiji's concern.

My practice in Delhi was intense, and Swamiji again warned me to live according to my brahmacharya vows. He said that during sadhana, the ovaries over-secrete.

I asked him, "On the path of brahmacharya, how do you deal with sexual energy without suppressing it?"

He said, "Meditate on the higher chakras." He told me to learn sublimation, not suppression.

I asked him, "Why is a human being incomplete?"

He said, "Because they should become God. Many follies make them incomplete." Swamiji said God is the sum total of everything.

By the end of March, I was back in Honesdale. Swamiji came in April. I was still having issues with brahmacharya. He said that when the time of miseries comes, God takes away your intelligence. For the first two weeks after he arrived, he called me into his apartment every day at 5:30 a.m. and hammered on me not to break the discipline. He even threatened to use his rod on me. He told me I had to remain celibate till the last breath of my life, and to 'go in the bathroom and cry.' I did. Finally, he told me to cry in the lap of Divine Mother. He said there are lifetimes, and there is a lease on life. His master had given me a lease on life, and I was not to misuse it.

In the month of May, Swami Veda was having serious heart problems. One day, Swamiji stayed in his room for 24 hours, and seemed to be simply resting. In the afternoon, he called me up to make him a cup of tilk. He started vigorously blowing his nose. Some big, funny looking boogers came out. He showed them to me, and asked if I had ever seen anything like that. I said, no. He said he was helping Swami Veda clear his arteries. Word came back from India that Swami Veda was stable.

One day, when Swamiji came upstairs after tennis, there was a piece of *kusha* grass on the table. He asked us who put it there. We didn't put it there, and didn't know where it came from. We had been

watching the Ramayana video series on VCR. The two
sons of Sita were called Luv and Kush. They are named
after the kusha grass. Kusha grass does not grow in
America. But there it was on his table. Later, he told
me that the sage Vashishtha had put it there.

One evening Samskriti and I had a brief but
interesting discussion with Swamiji on *vajroli* mudra.
Unfortunately, we were not worthy candidates for this
knowledge and started giggling, thus the conversation
ended. Swamiji said he had learnt all the yogic sciences
because he had to teach all types of people.

That year, Swamiji again taught Kevin and me a
new practice. He made a tape and told us to listen,
and if we had any questions, to come back again the
next night. As I was listening to the tape, he said, *After
you have completed xxx do yyy.* I went over the tape
again and again. Nowhere did he mention how to do
xxx. So when we went to him the next night, I asked,
"How do you do xxx?" He said, "What?" I said, "You
told us, after doing xxx to do yyy, but you didn't
explain how to do xxx." He looked at me. It wasn't on
Kevin's tape; it was only on my tape. Then he just said,
"No, no, no, you mean zzz." So I kept quiet.

When I was alone with Swamiji, I again asked him
about xxx. Then he gave me the practice. That part of
the tape, where he mentioned xxx, doesn't exist any
more. It's not there. It was only there for a brief time,
long enough for me to ask Swamiji the question.

We traveled around that summer, to the usual
places and also visited Leonard and Jenness Perlmutter
in Averill Park and Harshad Bhai in Connecticut. We
traveled in two cars. Normally, it took three hours to
make the trip to Connecticut. That night, it took us only
two hours, both cars traveling together. I figured
Swamiji was up to his "Himalayan mountain tricks"
again.

Somewhere around 1992, Swamiji announced his successors in a public lecture. There were two swamis from the cave monastery, who would be his successors. One would be his successor in the world, and another would be his successor in the monastery. These were the instructions from his master.

Later on, Swamiji received a small letter in the mail posted from India. Inside was a blank piece of paper. He showed it to me and Pandit Rajmani. He said that the swami who was supposed to be his successor in the world had sent it. There were tears on the piece of paper. The swami sent his tears, because he did not want to go back into the world. He thought that if he went back into the world, he would go backwards for so many lifetimes. Swamiji said that even fear of the world is bondage. In the summer of 1993, Swamiji appointed Pandit Rajmani as his successor at the Himalayan Institute in Honesdale.

In August, I accompanied Swamiji to Moscow. He was invited to lecture to the Russian Yoga Teachers Association. I found Moscow very interesting, having grown up during the Cold War. The people were very friendly. It was a mix between the U.S. and India. They had many aspects of Indian life, like stalls, road markings and cars, but they also had good roads, plumbing and electricity. The people wore clothes that were about 40 years behind the times. In the 1990s, the young people were going through a revolution, like the young American hippies of the 1960s. But the people seemed to be very poor.

Swamiji said he had been to Moscow 40 years earlier, and nothing had changed since then. He did parapsychological research at Moscow University around 1953. Sometimes, he used to mention his students in Russia. He must have had some students from back in the 1950s.

We stayed in a small apartment at the top of an apartment complex. It had one bathroom, two rooms and a kitchen. Fortunately, I packed some food with me, or we would have starved. Most Russians eat meat and there were only vegetables like potatoes, eggplant, cauliflower and onions available in the market. Swamiji did not eat eggplant, potatoes, or cauliflower. But we had to manage for three or four days. I also had to boil the water, because there was something called Black Fever, which could be contracted through the water.

Swamiji enjoyed the conference, and was very generous with his time for the Russian students. He was also well received. On the first day when Swamiji spoke to the group, there was a Russian translator on stage with him. Swamiji would say something, and then she would translate that into Russian for the audience. At the end of the lecture, she had some questions written on index cards that she had received from the audience. She came to a question that she quietly asked Swamiji, so that none of us could hear her. Then Swamiji boomed out to the audience that a man should not ejaculate every day, it was not good for health. There was pin drop silence in the audience. The young woman looked quite embarrassed. Swamiji turned to her and said in exasperation, "Well, you asked the question." The next day there was a young man doing the translations.

One afternoon in the apartment, he told me he was going to do something and not to be alarmed. He drank a lot of water, and then went to rest. The weather was very gloomy in Moscow. The TV shows were gloomy too and were broadcast only at certain hours.

Swamiji was resting for a long time and didn't get up. Finally, I peeked into his room. He was drenched from head to toe. All his clothes were wet.

He had a high fever, and was sort of incoherent. Fortunately, he had warned me in advance. I had wondered what would happen if he got sick in Moscow, with only me there. I gave him some Advil to bring down the fever. He slept.

I thought we would have to cancel his lecture that night, but he told me not to. When the time came, he got up and gave the lecture. When we got back to the apartment, the fever came back. He said he was doing a kundalini practice to burn the dampness out of his system, that was induced by the damp and rainy weather of Moscow. But I found out later, that there were a lot of sick people at HIHT who had high fevers during that time. Who knows? Maybe he took on somebody's Black Fever in Moscow. You could never be certain where Swamiji was concerned.

When the time came to go to the airport, he threw off the fever, and walked out of the door. By chance, we met someone at the Moscow airport who knew Swamiji, and he helped us get through the formalities quickly. Our flight landed an hour early in Delhi. In Delhi, Swamiji again had fever, and was quite sick for a few days. We left Delhi for Rishikesh.

Over the years, there had been some construction to expand the ashram. A large dining room and a new meditation hall had been added and Swamiji's new apartment was above the meditation hall. There were also a few extra buildings for guests to stay in, and a special block was built at the north end of the ashram for the visiting groups.

One time, when an Italian group came to stay in the ashram, they asked questions through a translator, and the translator would convey Swamiji's reply back to them. That got to be tiresome; so Swamiji started answering their questions before they had been translated into English.

During one of the tour group visits to Rishikesh, Swamiji sat outside giving a talk to the group. A flock of little brown sparrows showed up and sat on the electricity lines running along the ghat. There must have been around a hundred of the little fellows. Everybody noticed them and said they had come to hear Swamiji speak.

Swamiji used to call me mentally. I could hear him call my name and would get up and go to him. He used to do it in Honesdale also. The other people around me never heard anything, but he did call. Once, someone was sitting in the room with Swamiji. I heard him mentally call me, so I got up and went to the room, and asked, "Did you call me?" The person sitting there said, no, Swamiji didn't call you. But Swamiji said, yes he had called.

The ashram had a very special atmosphere, and it was always wonderful to wake up by the banks of the Ganges. There were many mango trees, shrubs, exotic plants and trees growing around the ashram. Many cobras and kraits also passed through, as well as the occasional mongoose and monitor lizard. Three small spotted owls used to live around the ashram. They would come out at night, and sit close to Swamiji's window, and chatter away. Swamiji said they were sages, not owls.

There are seven stars named after the seven rishis. I once asked Swamiji if the stars are actually rishis, or just stars. He said they were rishis, very bright beings in the heavens.

There were several guard dogs at the ashram, mountain dogs, and a couple of Collies that were given to Swamiji from Russia. They used to roam about the ashram freely at night, and kept thieves away. It was well known in the neighborhood that the ashram had large guard dogs on their property. They also kept the residents in their rooms at night, because most people were afraid of the dogs. Many people complained of the dogs barking at night, but that was a service provided free of charge, for them to practice withdrawal of the senses.

Visitors came to the ashram to relax, rest, and meditate. When groups came to visit, there would be some organized lectures; otherwise, people were left to their own devices and enjoyed the spiritual atmosphere. It was very quiet, and very healing.

Swamiji himself was a healer. He helped countless people. Over the years, I noticed that he always brought new people in to be close to him for a short period of time, and then they would move on with their lives. Inevitably, I always discovered later on, that those people had some problem or other. Maybe they were sick, or in a crisis, going through depression, illness, divorce, or looking for a husband; each one had a problem. He used to take on their physical problems, and they would be cured. So I asked him, "Don't the people keep making the same mistakes over and over again?" He said, "Let them. They get cured, I'm a healer."

Many times, when we massaged Swamiji's feet, we found small pieces of gravel embedded in his soles. He said it was from walking in Gangotri, or walking in the Himalayas. We would pick them out. Again, the next day there would be more. But if he was in Honesdale or Rishikesh, how could he be walking in Gangotri?

Sometimes, in Swamiji's apartment in Rishikesh, I could hear people talking, or a woman humming, but no one was there. He said they were celestial beings. I said I wished I could see them, but Swamiji asked, "What if they have elephant teeth and roar?"

Swamiji had one huge ek mukhi rudraksha. It was round, and as big as an orange. He said it had been with him before, and had then disappeared seven years earlier. It was a type of Shiva lingam, one of a kind. He showed it to a few people after making them wash their hands.

Back at Honesdale, there was another drama brewing. Some of the disgruntled Board and ex-Board members of the Institute got together with a plan to sell and divide the Institute amongst themselves. They undermined the fabric of the Institute, and created insecurity and division among the residents.

In December of 1993, Swamiji sent a letter to the Board of Directors at Honesdale, stating that he would not be coming back. That day in Rishikesh, when he wrote the letter, he was completely undisturbed. He was asked to speak at Vanaprastha Ashram across the river. When the time came, we got into his jeep and drove through the jungle on the other side of the river, to the ashram where he was graciously received and delivered his lecture.

17.
A Trip to Tarkeshwar

In January of 1994, a small group of us went with Swamiji to Toli and Tarkeshwar. Swamiji's bodyguard, his driver, Vijay Dhasmana, Hemant Dhasmana, Ritu Singh and I accompanied Swamiji.

Our first stopover was Toli. The village of Toli was the birthplace of the body Swamiji was then occupying. He showed us the house where his father left his body, the building he was born in, and gave us a tour. (I found it very odd, because he had previously told me about the palace he grew up in.) He said his father was a very learned man. He knew the science of *swars*. He could answer any question, by knowing the time the question was asked, the day of the week, checking the position of the planets, and checking the swars. He said that when his father would do puja, prasad used to appear by itself. His father died soon after Swamiji was born.

We spent the night in Toli. Swamiji said he had promised to do something for these people, so he started a polytechnic school (vocational school) for boys, to give them skills and help them find jobs in the area. At night, the men danced and sang kirtans and *bhajans*. The women always stayed indoors; they were rarely visible. I played the flute while Swamiji sang. It was very cold there. There was hardly enough electricity for two light bulbs in the whole village. Milk was not easy to come by. There was one tap outside that had running water. And there was an outhouse.

When Swamiji drove around the mountains, he would put on the sirens and flashing lights and tell everyone in advance that he was coming. The local people used to line up to receive him, beating their drums. Big crowds would meet him, and he would distribute money.

We pushed off for Tarkeshwar the next day. We traveled slowly, and made frequent stops. On the way, Swamiji related a story from his youth.

> He was a young swami walking alone through the mountains. He met an old woman dressed in black. She asked him to carry her. So he carried her on his back. She was very light. He called her Mother. He put her down at a hut, to bring her some water. When he came out, she was gone. Though he inquired of everyone around, no one had seen her. At that place, he established a small temple for the worship of Bhairavi Devi, who was actually the old woman in black, that he had carried. He showed us the temple from the road.

During the trip, he would stop at police stations and just take over. The policemen would come out and give us tea, and we would use their bathrooms. Finally, we made it to the village below Tarkeshwar. We were received by crowds and drums. We stopped at the base, and drank hot milk before trekking up. It took us about two hours to walk to the temple from there.

It was a thrill to be with Swamiji in that environment. We sat on the trail to rest, and he started singing a bhajan. I could smell the fragrance of Babaji, and Swamiji became silent. "Bholia, why are you sad? Don't cry." That's what his master would say to him, when he missed him very much.

Tarkeshwar temple

On the way we stopped, and Swamiji's bodyguard showed Ritu how to fire the rifle. Ritu was
thrilled; she was the daughter of a police officer and
aspired to become one.

Then we entered the Devdar forest. Tarkeshwar
is described in *Living with the Himalayan Masters*, in
the chapter on 'Protecting Arms.' The temple is 900
years old. They say a great sage lived there, and he
protected everyone. As you enter, there's a tall Devdar
tree shaped like a trishul. On one side it is shaped like
the sign of Shakti, on the other side like the sign of
Shiva. From any direction you look, you can see the
three branches. At the base of the tree is a temple bell.
It is a holy tree. There is another tree shaped like the
tongs that are used in kirtan, or to tend a fire; it's also
one of the signs of Shiva.

We reached Tarkeshwar, and were graciously
received by Swami Hari. Swamiji assigned work to
whoever was there, to clean up the grounds and pick
up the trash. In the afternoon, he took us for a walk,
up to the ridge where he used to sit as a young boy

Swamiji sitting on his rock at Tarkeshwar, looking out
at the mountains

and gaze at the snow-peaked Himalayas. We collected
pinecones to burn in the fire. He stopped, and threw
off his poncho to show us a Kung Fu kata, and gave an
open challenge for anyone to attack him. We were all
silent. I remembered my last experience fighting with
Swamiji.

There was a small needle-like thorn that grew in
that area. Swamiji's clothes were covered with it—his
poncho, jogging suit, socks, long johns, turtleneck,
everything. We spent the night pulling out the thorns.
He said it was punishment from his master for showing
off in his ashram.

We bathed and rested, and went to the temple at
4:00 p.m. Swamiji performed a puja and gave everyone
blessings. He taught me a prayer, "O Lord, let me fulfill
the destiny of my life. May God help me to attain the
final goal of life."

That evening I asked Swamiji, "What is the goal
of life?"

He said, "Emancipation."

I asked, "Emancipation from what?"

"Bondage."

"What bondage?"

"Bondage created by the mind."

"What bondage?"

"Good or bad, right or wrong. You have to unite the individual mind with the cosmic mind. That is the goal of life."

At night we built a fire pit, heated some stones, and made mountain bread. It was very tasty. There was no electricity or running water there. At night the sky was full of twinkling stars. We all retired early. It was very cold. There was a deep silence permeating the night.

Next morning, Swamiji was up early, singing bhajans with his electronic tanpura, and I played along on the flute. He said that he got confirmation from his master in the night, not to return to the U.S. What he didn't say, was that he had also received confirmation to leave his body.

Somewhere there is a cave at Tarkeshwar, where Swamiji used to stay. He said that it was inhabited by siddhas. Once a shepherd boy and his girlfriend arranged a romantic tryst in that cave. The siddhas transported them 12 miles away, where they were caught and exposed.

We left in the morning. On the way down the trail, he showed us a hole in the ground where the path meets the side of the mountain. He threw a pebble into it, and told us to listen for the sound of it hitting bottom. He handed me an empty acorn shell, and said the bears ate the acorns. He sent Hemant and Vijay across the mountain in the other direction, to meet us in the village. On the way, Hemant found what looked like a blade of grass encased in a piece of transparent styrofoam. Swamiji told him it was the remains of a meteorite that had hit the earth.

We came down to the village, and they were waiting for us with drums. We left for Toli, where there was a function for planning the opening of the polytechnic school. Swamiji met with the village leaders, and set things in motion. Then we headed for Rishikesh.

During those days, Swamiji used to commute to HIHT, and return to the ashram at night. In the daytime, I stayed in the ashram, looked after the phones, did my japa, and started working on Swamiji's new book, Sri Guru Granth Sahib, transcreated in English verse.

One morning, after Swamiji had read the newspapers and eaten breakfast, he got ready to go to the hospital site. Suddenly he stopped, turned around and went into the living room where he curled up on the mattress to take what looked like an urgent nap. After about 20 minutes he turned over to the other side. After another 20 minutes he got up, remarked that he had just contacted 600 students, and proceeded to the hospital site.

Sometimes, early in the morning, I would hear Swamiji talking to somebody, or laughing. But no one was there. He used to go for a walk in the evenings, when he returned from the hospital site. One night, as I was rubbing him down with a towel after the walk, there was glitter all over his back. I asked him what it was. He said it was phosphorus.

Swamiji described different ways of taking a bath. There was the prana bath, water bath, wet cloth bath, bath of ashes, and rubbing down with a dry cloth.

One night Barb Bova and I were with Swamiji, and he held out his arms for us to massage.

I asked, "How many arms do you have?"

He said, "Four, when I am *Vishnu.*"

I said, "And when do you have 10 arms?"

He said, "When I am *Durga,* 20 when I am *Ravana,* 40 when I destroy the world. And then I meditate."

I responded, "Why do you want to be Ravana?"

He said, "I am the only one who is both Ram and Ravana, Shiva and Vishnu, and destroys the world. I am the same Ram in everyone's heart, but nobody knows who I am. I am in the world, but remain far, far away."

One afternoon at the ashram, I received a phone call from Bhagwan Daryanani, who had been staying at the ashram in Tarkeshwar. Bhagwan reported that Swami Hari had fallen down the mountain and hurt his shoulder. Bhagwan then took him to see a local doctor. He wanted Swamiji to know about it, so I delivered the message. Swamiji said that he knew about the accident when it was happening, and that he wanted Swami Hari to finish his karmas. Bhagwan brought Swami Hari to Rishikesh so he could recuperate in the ashram. When I told Swami Hari what Swamiji had said, he laughed. Swami Hari then narrated the incident. It was at night, and some of the villagers were also with him. It was a path that Swami Hari frequently traveled, so he knew it very well. It was dark, and he felt someone push him off the path, but there was no one there.

When Swamiji was not at the ashram, I used to sleep in his apartment, next to the phone. One night, I heard all this thumping and running around in the bathroom. There was no electricity and it was dark, but I got up to investigate. I opened the door, and heard all this scurrying about. I thought it would be better to investigate by daylight and closed the door. In the morning, everything was quiet, and I went in. We used to keep a bucket of water next to the toilet. In the bucket was a very large rat. It was standing on the tip of its tail, with just its two nostrils above water as if it had been immobilized. I took the bucket outside and dumped it out. The rat quickly ran away. Later, when I was cleaning the bathroom, I noticed one of the bath mats was missing. I looked around and found it under the sink cabinet. It had been stuffed into the drain hole. There was no cover over the drain hole so the rat must have come in that way. But who put the mat there?

At one point, there were so many obstacles to the growth of the hospital created by the local authorities, that Swamiji undertook another vow to fast unto death in front of the District Magistrate's (DM) residence in Dehradun, if the problem was not resolved. Swamiji calmly told me that on the first day he would take hot lemon water with a little honey, on the second day only water, and on the third day he would drop his body. But he told me not to worry. He said that once the Kanpur people learned of his fast, the whole city would come to Dehradun and break down the DM's door.

Swamiji went in his car, and parked in front of the DM's residence. We followed in our car. There were lots of policemen regulating the crowd, and press people interviewing Swamiji inside his car. Some hours passed, but the DM would not come out of his house. Finally, some women representing the women's voting block, spoke to the DM, and he agreed to meet Swamiji. The fast was averted, and the issues were satisfactorily resolved.

At the hospital site, Swamiji had a private apartment with two bedrooms, two bathrooms, a kitchen, dining room, living room and office. His bedroom was very simple, equipped with the necessary telephones, TV/VCR and spittoon. I was not much involved in the daily life at the hospital site, but it was always punctuated with functions of one kind or another. Either a Governor, Chief Minister, Sant, Government Secretary, or political leader was coming to inaugurate a wing, piece of equipment, department, or school. Finally, the Prime Minister was to come and inaugurate the medical college, but had to cancel his appearance, due to the local agitation for the formation of a new hill state — Uttaranchal (now Uttarakhand).

When all this civil agitation was going on, one of the tour groups from Honesdale arrived at the ashram. They had been scheduled to go up to Gangotri, but the local police had called a curfew due to the political unrest. The tour group was confined to the Ganga Kinare Hotel, just up the road from the ashram, and could not proceed to Gangotri.

During their confinement, Swamiji was very gracious to them. He was very generous with his time. The group would walk from the hotel to the ashram. Swamiji gave talks and granted appointments to each participant individually, and saw them, one-by-one, upstairs on the balcony of his apartment.

I was inside Swamiji's apartment trying to help coordinate the appointments. From inside the room, I could see Swamiji through the window, sitting on the balcony with his back to me, facing the individual. Swamiji asked the usual general questions: "How are you? When did you come? What is your name? Are you married? Do you have any children? What can I do for you?"

Swamiji was very gentle and soft-spoken with each person. To my utter amazement, about a fourth of the women simply started crying. Either they couldn't speak at all, or they just broke down and started crying. And Swamiji just sat there, patiently, in silence, radiating his compassion. Then he would say something like, "God bless you; come back and see me tomorrow."

After the appointments were over, I asked Swamiji why all these women started crying in front of him. He simply replied, "They let out their emotions on me."

The hospital had purchased a helicopter for going up into the mountains, but Swamiji started using it to commute to the ashram since the roads were often blocked due to the local agitation. Later he shifted his residence to HIHT, and seldom came to the ashram.

Swamiji was very ill during this time. His skin had some kind of allergic reaction, all over. It was red, and itched and burned. He went to visit a local sulphur spring to bathe in the waters, but it did not help.

One night the helicopter at the hospital was set on fire and blown up. The culprits were never found. There were threats against Swamiji's life. The police assigned two officers to shadow him and follow him around. Everywhere there was turmoil. All the forces of nature were against him.

Occasionally, Swamiji came to the ashram for the night. One particular night, he said that he had to do a special practice, and that nobody should know he was there, and that he should not be disturbed. Then, he locked himself in his bedroom. I stayed in the front room with the telephone.

At midnight, someone started banging on the door downstairs. I came out onto the balcony, and asked what the matter was. The guard said that two policemen had come, saying that Swamiji had called them. I replied that Swamiji's not here. Then Prem (the manager) came and said the same thing. I told Prem that nobody should know that Swamiji was there; Swamiji didn't telephone because the phone was with me. Prem sent them away.

As it turned out, they were very shady characters, very seedy and not in full police uniform. The dogs went wild at the gate and wouldn't let them in. Swamiji had once told me that when he was doing a similar practice, many years ago, some nagas (beings from a different world) came and threatened to kill him.

Swamiji was always doing practices that his master forbade him to do. He was always stretching the boundaries, experimenting. In the process there were many disturbances in the environment, sometimes with his health as well. People would hallucinate, talk nonsense, and he would receive pinpricks from every quarter. Babaji repeatedly warned him, but Swamiji never listened.

18.
Mahasamadhi

I was living in the ashram as a brahmacharini, and had no income. Whatever money I had at the time, which was around $900, I gave to Swamiji. I had to return to Honesdale for some legal work. Usually, whenever I went anywhere, Swamiji asked me if I needed money, or just gave me some without asking. This time I had nothing and needed some money. Swamiji didn't ask me if I had any money, even though mentally I was telling him that I had none. He kept quiet; I also kept quiet. He arranged a car for me. I left for Delhi, and got on the plane for the U.S. without any money in my pocket. Everywhere I went, I was met by someone, so I never needed anything. On the way back, the plane was delayed due to a storm in Atlanta, and I missed my connection. The airline put me up at an Atlanta hotel in their presidential suite, the only available room. They also gave me money for food, and arranged transportation to and from the airport. Swamiji had taken care of everything.

Meanwhile, Swamiji was very ill with a chest infection, and the doctors were investigating. In one conversation, I said, "You don't complain, but it must be painful. What does it feel like?" He said, "What is pain or pleasure? Who am I to feel? It is a concept of the mind and it is the mind that feels. Pain is created by the mind. This whole world was created by the mind." I said, "Whose mind?" He said, "Cosmic mind." I said, "If we all think you will be well, would you be well?" He said, "Yes, if everybody thinks I should beat Kamal, I will beat her." He said it was our minds that created his illness. Swamiji told Prem that his body had to go, nothing lasts forever, and it wouldn't be long now. "You people have to grow."

Samskriti came to see Swamiji in Rishikesh because she heard he wasn't well. Samskriti was very lively and it was fun having her around. It was the time of Holi, the festival of colors, and we wanted to play Holi with Swamiji, but he said he didn't play Holi. There was a small group of girls in the ashram that day, so Swamiji told me to telephone that Baba (Swami Veda) in his kutia and tell him that there was a group of girls there that wanted to play Holi. I called Swami Veda and told him, and he replied that being a swami, he only wore one color and he didn't play Holi. But if the girls wanted to come over for sweets, they were most welcome.

Samskriti became our gang leader, and we all went over to Swami Veda's building. It was very quiet and peaceful, and no sign of the usual group of boys that stayed there and helped Swami Veda. We quietly went upstairs and saw Swami Veda sitting in his meditation pose with his eyes closed. We were feeling too timid to disturb him, but Samskriti, being intrepid, went inside with her colors. Swami Veda opened his eyes in mock surprise, quickly pulled out a bag of colors he had hidden behind him, and we all played Holi. On our way downstairs, we were ambushed by his group of boys who were hiding behind the doors, armed with water pistols and colors.

Sadly, in March of 1996, Swami Rama was finally diagnosed with cancer, though he must have known for a long time what he was doing. He had a biopsy done at PGI, Chandigarh. By the time the cancer was

Swamiji sitting under his tree in front of his apartment
on the HIHT campus

diagnosed, it had spread throughout his body, and no one could determine the primary source of cancer. We all knew that he could cure himself if he wanted to, and none of us believed that he would actually drop his body.

Swamiji appointed Swami Veda Bharati as the Spiritual Guide of the Institute in 1996. He also appointed the Presidential Body as his successor in the Himalayan Institute Hospital Trust. The Presidential Body consists of four members: Dr. Mohan Swami, Vijay Dhasmana, Dr. Chauhan, and Vikram Singh.

Dr. Barb Bova, Dr. Ganasan, Dr. Mohan Swami and I accompanied Swamiji to Malaysia in May, where we stayed as guests of Dr. Mohan Swami in Kuala Lumpur. Swamiji had another biopsy performed, and underwent radiation therapy. He went through all the normal procedures to treat the disease, and told the doctors to treat him as an ordinary patient. In Malaysia, he told me that his time had come, that his master had called him. When I asked him, "Why cancer?", he said he did it to himself.

Swamiji also told us that he did not want any statues made of him, or any shrines set up, or any memorials or institutions in his name. But he did say that he wanted the teachings preserved, if possible.

During our stay in Malaysia, Swamiji kept a small oil lamp burning continuously. He also used to play mythological movies, like the Ramayana and Maha-bharata video series, in his room. In the Mahabharata series, there was a song that Rukmini sang for Krishna, pleading with him to rescue her from her fate. Swamiji used to listen to that song over and over again, and wrote down the words. Here is a rough English translation of his notes:

"Hear my plea,
Hear my plea, O my Master!
O Lord of the heart,
Hari, who dwells within my heart,
Peacock feather-crowned one,

This is a yearning of many lifetimes,
All the stars in the sky are the witness.
Listen to my earnest request, O my Master!

For long I've been waiting for you to manifest,
O Lotus-eyed Lord, remover of obstacles.
The one who worships your eyes,
Surrenders to you.
Hear my plea, O my Lord.

What more can I say? You are Omniscient.
O Lord of my prosperity, body and mind,
Have compassion and please say —"

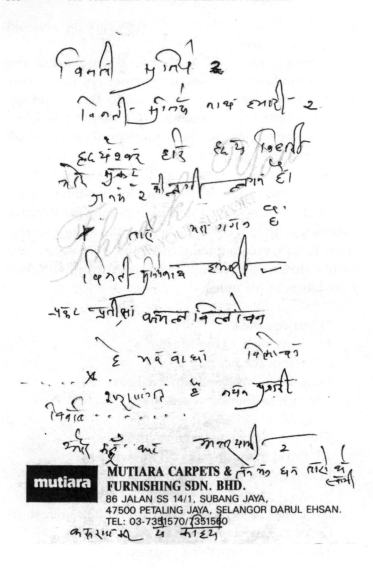

Swamiji's hand written notes of Rukmini's plea

When a person dies of cancer, it is a terrible thing to watch. The body is slowly consumed by the disease, and the organs slowly stop functioning. But when I look back at how Swami Rama handled the disease, I see no greater testimony to his mastery over the body and mind than this.

After the radiation treatment, we returned to the hospital site in India. Swamiji rallied and got a little better. He carried on with his favorite project of building the hospital, and never stopped working.

In addition to Allopathic treatment, he received Homeopathic treatment, Ayurvedic treatment, and Unani treatment. As I look back, I realize that he did all of that to protect us, so that later, no one could say that we did not treat his illness. Everything was thoroughly documented.

Back at the ashram in Rishikesh, I had made myself ill with grief, and was diagnosed with typhoid. Swamiji had me admitted to the hospital for a few days, where I recovered. He allowed me to spend the next five months at HIHT with him, before he left.

By August, the cancer was again spreading like wildfire. We took him to Delhi for a second round of radiation therapy, but there was no improvement. In spite of his pathetic physical condition, he used to take a daily round of the hospital to supervise on-going construction. Sometimes he would walk a little, and could also be seen in his trademark jeep, cruising down the road.

In October, Swamiji called Roshan Lal (one of his oldest and most devoted disciples), and me to talk to us. He told us that his time had come, that he was going to leave his body. He said that he wanted to be cremated in Haridwar. He told Roshan Lal to find a place for the cremation. He told Roshan Lal to light the funeral pyre, or if he could not, then Mahesh should do it, and if Mahesh could not, then Vijay Dhasmana should do it. I asked Swamiji whether a sannyasin could be cremated, because I was under the impression that they had to be buried in a samadhi or placed in the Ganges; but Swamiji assured me that sannyasins could indeed be cremated.

About three weeks before he left his body, he shifted from his apartment upstairs to the one downstairs, as it was too difficult for him to climb up and down the stairs. He stopped taking all painkillers. He did not sleep. He was conscious and alert all the time.

As the disease progressed, there were various complications. He didn't talk much. Towards the end, we used to communicate without speaking. For the last three days of his life, he dragged his corpse of a body around by sheer force of will. He stopped taking any food, just took sips of water. He stayed on the bed, propped up by pillows. It was only for the last three days, that he didn't go for a round of the hospital site, but stayed in his room. Now I understand that he never suffered, he was never confused about who he was, he never identified himself with the body. We were the ones that were confused.

By the time he left his body, he weighed less than one hundred pounds, and was literally skin and bone. For those who did not see him in that state, it is better to remember him as being hale and hearty. My role was to protect and nurture that body, so it was extremely difficult for me to watch it wither away.

The night he left his body, he got up and went to the bathroom and came back to his bed. He was having difficulty breathing, and motioned to us that he wanted to sit up. I sat on the bed next to him, with my right arm around his shoulders, and supported him against my chest. We were literally heart to heart. Then at 11:08 p.m., he left.

There was a jerk in his body, his teeth were clenched; he was in transition. A second jerk, and with the third jerk he left with the breath. (They say that the soul passes through three knots or granthis as it leaves the body.) I could physically feel his soul leave the body. It's difficult to describe, but there was a force that left, and with it some weight of the body was gone. The heart kept beating. Then slowly, very slowly, it stopped.

When he left, I let out a deep sigh and a few tears. Then I remained as I was, supporting the body for an hour, in silence. That was my farewell to the physical form. Then I went to my room and slept.

It is said in the tradition, that when a master leaves his body, it should be witnessed by at least five people, so that the tradition of consciously casting off the body continues. The names of those present, and how the master leaves the body are recorded in the monastery. When Swami Rama left his body, there were seven of us present: Dr. Barb Bova, Maithili, Vijay Dhasmana, Mahesh, Dr. Ganasan, Dr. Mohan Swami, and myself.

Swamiji left his body on a Wednesday, and it was cremated on Friday. People came from all over the world to pay their respects, and attend the cremation. The body was transported in an open truck, on the main road from the hospital to Haridwar. On the way, thousands of people lined the streets and offered flowers to the body as it passed by. Traditionally, women are not allowed to attend a cremation, but no force could stop us; all of the female devotees who wanted to, attended the cremation.

At Haridwar, Swamiji's body was covered with logs of sandalwood and the pyre was lit. His body was a sacrifice to Divine Mother, and the cremation was the final offering. He offered that body, to burn the karmas of his disciples. His compassion cannot be comprehended.

Once, back in 1987, he told us that the only vacuum in his life was that his master had left the body. He said that even though his master visited him daily, when you are in a human body, you want the warmth of another human body. If even Swamiji felt thus about his master, then what of us?

Swami Rama

Swami Rama was born in the Himalayas in 1925. He was initiated by his master into many yogic practices. In addition, Swamiji's master sent him to other yogis and adepts of the Himalayas to gain new perspectives and insights into the ancient teachings. At the young age of 24 he was installed as the Shankaracharya of Karvirpitham in South India. Swamiji relinquished this position to pursue intense sadhana in the caves of the Himalayas. Having successfully completed this sadhana, he was directed by his master to go to Japan and to the West in order to illustrate the scientific basis of the ancient yogic practices. At the Menninger Foundation in Topeka, Kansas, Swamiji convincingly demonstrated the capacity of the mind to control so-called involuntary physiological parameters such as heart rate, temperature and brain waves.

Swamiji's work in the United States continued for 23 years and in this period he established the Himalayan International Institute of Yoga Science and Philosophy of the U.S.A. Swamiji became well recognized in the U.S. as a yogi, teacher, philosopher, poet, humanist and philanthropist. His models of preventive medicine, holistic health and stress management have permeated the mainstream of western medicine.

In 1989 Swamiji returned to India where he established the Himalayan Institute Hospital Trust in the foothills of the Garhwal Himalayas. Swamiji left this physical plane in November, 1996, but the seeds he has sown continue to sprout, bloom, and bear fruit. His teachings embodied in the words 'Love, Serve, Remember' continue to inspire the many students whose good fortune it was to come in contact with such an accomplished, selfless, and loving master.

Glossary

AGNI SARA Yogic exercise for stoking the digestive fire

AJAPA JAPA Spontaneous, unbroken mantra repetition

ALAP North Indian melody set to a slow tempo

ANUSHCHARANA Rite of purification employing mantra japa

ASHRAM Dwelling place for spiritual aspirants

AVATARA Incarnation

BANI Spiritual music composition

DARSHAN Literally sight, viewing something holy

BEEDI Country cigarette

BENGALI BABA Baba: father; Bengali: from Bengal, a state in India

BHAGAVAD GITA One of the primary Hindu scriptures, part of the Mahabharata

BHAJANS Spiritual songs/hymns

BHAVA Feeling

BINDIS Ornamental mark on a woman's forehead

BRAHMA SUTRAS Sutras(aphorisms) related to Brahman, the Supreme Being

BRAHMACHARYA Literally walking in Brahman, first of the four stages of life, that of the student (sadhaka) whose senses are disciplined (celibate), male sadhaka: brahmachari, female sadhaka: brahmacharini

BRAHMAN The Supreme Being

BRAHMARANDRA A potential opening at the fontanelle, used by yogis to leave the body

BUDDHI Discrimination, one of the four functions of the mind

BURFI Indian confectionery

CHAKRAS Energy centers along the spinal column

CHANDALA Attendant at a cremation ground

DARSHAN Literally sight, used when viewing something holy

DEVA Shining celestial being, angel

DEVANAGARI Sanskrit script

DHIYO YONAH PRACHODAYAT Part of Gayatri mantra: May my mind be illumined

DHOTI Male garb, a cloth draped around the waist, covering the lower body

DURGA An aspect of the Divine Mother

GRANTHIS Knots impeding flow of prana

GRIHASTA One of the four stages of life, namely that of the householder

GURUBHAI Guru brother, disciples of same guru

HARIKATHAS Stories of God narrated/sung by spiritual minstrels

IDA Energy channel rising from the base of the spine to the left nostril

ISHOPANISHAD One of the principal Upanishads

JALEBI A pretzel-shaped Indian sweet

JAPA Repetition of a mantra

JIVA Living being

KARMA Literally action, often used for consequences of action

KIRTAN Spiritual chanting with audience participation

KRIYA Spiritual practice

KUNDALINI Coiled-up latent energy that is dormant at the base of spine

KURTA Indian shirt

KUSHA Type of grass used in religious rituals and for the meditation seat

LINGA Symbol of Shiva, one of the Hindu gods

MAHABHARATA Great Indian epic composed by sage Vyasa

MAHANTJI Head of an institution

MAHARSHI Great rishi or sage

MAHASAMADHI Voluntary act of dropping the body and being absorbed in the Supreme

MALA Rosary

MANAS Lower aspect of mind that imports and exports sensory stimuli

MANDUKYA UPANISHAD One of the principal Upanishads

MOONG DAL A soup-like lentil dish

MUDRA Yogic gesture or seal

MULADHARA Energy center at the base of the spine

MUNDAKA UPANISHAD One of the principal Upanishads

NADA Subtle, unstruck aspect of sound

NADI Subtle channel through which energy flows

NAV RATRA Nine night Hindu festival dedicated to the Divine Mother

OM Sacred primeval sound associated with creation of the cosmos, Mother of all mantras

PANDITJI Respectful form for pandit or scholar

PARANTHA Unleavened flat Indian bread

PINGALA Energy channel rising from the base of the spine to the right nostril

PRANA Subtle vital energy that flows through the subtle energy channels called nadis

PRANAYAMA Yogic science for expansion of prana based on breathing techniques

PRASAD Sanctified offering received in a temple or after a ritual

RAJA YOGA Literally royal yoga, the eight-limbed path of yoga which is systematic and scientific

RAJAS One of the three gunas (qualities) associated with action, passion and sensory stimulation

RAJASIC Imbued with rajas

RAMAYANA One of the great Indian epics that narrates the story of the Hindu god Rama

RAVANA A demon, one of the principal characters in the Ramayana who is slain by Rama

RISHI Seer to whom mantras are revealed, sage, usually a forest dweller

RUDRAKSHA Literally eye of Rudra (Shiva's fiery aspect), type of seed strung into rosaries for Shiva mantras

SADHANA Spiritual path

SADHU Saintly person, wandering holy man

SAHASRARA Thousand-petalled energy center at the crown of the head

SAMSKARAS Subtle memories and residue of past experiences stored in the unconscious mind in seed form

SANATANA DHARMA Eternal path of righteous conduct of Vedic origin

SANKALPA Act of determination, resolve

SANNYASI Renunciate, one in the fourth stage of life

SANSKRIT An ancient language that is the mother of most Indian languages

SANT Saint

SARI A dress worn by Indian women

SATTVA One of the three gunas, or qualities, associated with peace, tranquility and equanimity

SAUNDARYA LAHARI Literally Wave of Beauty, a poetic composition of Adi Shankara in praise of the Divine Mother

SHAKTI Female Energy

SHAKTI PATA Raising shakti by the touch of the guru

SHANAKARACHARYA The great 8th century philosopher-saint who reformed Hinduism. Also used as a title for the monks who head the spiritual institutions established by Shankara

SHASTRIJI Respectful form for Shastri or priest

SHAVASANA Corpse posture of yoga

SHIVA One of the gods of the Hindu trinity associated with destruction, Supreme Being

SHUKA NADI Astrological treatise ascribed to Sage Shuka

SIDDHASANA Posture of the siddha or accomplished one, a meditative yogic posture

SIDDHIS Yogic powers exhibited by Siddhas or the accomplished ones

SOOJI HALWA Indian dessert made from cream of wheat

SRI YANTRA Yantra or mystical energy diagram associated with Sri, the Divine Mother

SUSHUMNA Central nadi or energy channel rising from the base of the spine to the crown of the head

SWAMIJI Respectful form of swami or master, usually used for a renunciate monk

SWARAS Notes of music, melody

SWAR Ripples of pranic energy reflected in the breath

SWASTIKASANA Meditative yogic posture, the configuration of the legs and feet resembling a swastika

TANPURA Stringed musical instrument providing the background drone in Indian music

TANTRIC Related to the philosophy of tantra, the play and union of Shiva (male) and Shakti (female) energies

TAPAS Spiritual discipline associated with austerities and generation of spiritual fervor or heat

THUMRI North Indian romantic songs

UPANISHADS Philosophical doctrines that form part of the sacred Hindu texts called the Vedas

VAJROLI Yogic mudra controlling ejaculation

VEENA Stringed instrument used in Indian music

VISHNU One of the gods of the Hindu trinity associated with preservation of the universe

YAGYA Sacrificial ritual

YANTRA Mystical energy diagram used in tantric practices

YOGA SUTRAS Principal yoga text compiled by the sage Patanjali with 196 sutras or aphorisms

Himalayan Institute Hospital Trust

The Himalayan Institute Hospital Trust (HIHT) was conceived, designed, and orchestrated by Dr. Swami Rama, a yogi, scientist, researcher, writer, and humanitarian. The mission of HIHT is to develop integrated and cost-effective approaches to health care and development for the country as a whole, and for under-served populations worldwide.

Swamiji started this project in 1989 with an outpatient clinic of only two rooms. The hospital at HIHT currently has 750 beds and is serving approximately 10 million people of Garhwal, Kumaon and adjoining areas. The hospital includes a Reference Laboratory, Emergency Wing, Operation Theaters, Blood Bank, Eye Bank, Dialysis Unit, I.C.U., C.C.U., Cath Lab., and a state-of-the-art Radiology Department. The newly established Cancer Research Institute is providing radiation therapy in addition to chemotherapy and surgical oncology.

The Rural Development Institute is providing healthcare, education, income generation opportunities, water and sanitation programs, adolescent awareness programs and other quality of life improvement programs in the villages of Uttarakhand and adjoining rural areas.

The Himalayan Institute of Medical Sciences has now become HIHT University, a deemed university, recognized by the University Grants Commission. The University runs undergraduate (M.B.B.S.) and postgraduate courses (M.D./ M.S. and Diploma) in 15 disciplines. The medical faculty is also conducting paramedical degree courses in Medical Laboratory Technology, Radiology & Imaging Technology, and Physiotherapy.

The Himalayan College of Nursing offers a four-year B.Sc. program and a 3-year GNM diploma program. The uniqueness of these nursing programs is that the nursing students are provided hands-on training in the community and with the rural population.

In keeping with Swamiji's mission of integration, ,the hospital runs outpatient Ayurveda and Homeopathy clinics and the Ayurveda Center provides a residential Pancha-karma therapy program for detoxification, rejuvenation and treatment of chronic ailments. The Combined Therapy Program, pioneered by Swami Rama, has been a unique model of holistic health care for more than thirty years. The Combined Therapy Program combines biofeedback, hatha yoga, aerobic exercise, nutrition, breathing, relaxation skills, meditation and other self-awareness techniques.

For information contact:

Himalayan Institute Hospital Trust
Swami Ram Nagar
P.O. Doiwala, Distt. Dehradun 248140
Uttarakhand, India
91-135-247-1200
pb@hihtindia.org
www.hihtindia.org

Swami Rama Society, Inc.

The Swami Rama Society is a registered, nonprofit, tax-exempt organization committed to Swami Rama's vision of bridging the gap between Western science and Eastern wisdom through the integration of body, mind, and spirit. The Society was established to provide financial assistance and technical support to institutions and individuals who are ready to implement this vision in the U.S.A. and abroad.

For information contact:

Swami Rama Society, Inc.
2410 N. Farwell Avenue
Milwaukee, WI 53211 U.S.A.
414-273-1621
info@swamiramasociety.org
www.swamiramasociety.org

The Essence of Spiritual Life
A Companion Guide for the Seeker
Swami Rama
ISBN 978-81-90100-49-6; $12.95, pb, 136 pg

Sacred Journey
Living Purposefully and Dying Gracefully
Swami Rama
ISBN 978-81-88157-00-6, $12.95, pb, 136 pg

Let the Bud of Life Bloom
A Guide to Raising Happy and Healthy Children
Swami Rama
ISBN 978-81-88157-04-4; $12.95, pb, 100 pg

OM the Eternal Witness
Secrets of the Mandukya Upanishad
Swami Rama
ISBN 978-81-88157-43-3, $14.95, pb, 202 pg

Distributed in U.S.A. by Lotus Press, PO Box 325, Twin Lakes, WI 53181 U.S.A., www.lotuspress.com, 800-824-6396.
Distributed in India by Swami Rama Centre, HIHT, Swami Ram Nagar, P.O. Doiwala, Distt. Dehradun 248140, Uttarakhand, src@hihtindia.org, 0135-241-2068.